MEMOIRS OF AN OLD PARLIAMENTARIAN

VOLUME I

A Caricature of Mr. O'Connor drawn by "Spy"
on 25th February 1888

Frontispiece Vol. I.

MEMOIRS OF AN OLD PARLIAMENTARIAN

by

THE RIGHT HONOURABLE
T. P. O'CONNOR, M.P.

VOLUME I

ERNEST BENN LIMITED
BOUVERIE HOUSE, FLEET STREET, E.C.4

FIRST PUBLISHED IN

1929

PRINTED

IN

GREAT BRITAIN

CONTENTS

ILLUSTRATIONS

CHAPTER I

A journalist in a garret—Two lost jobs—A casual in Fleet Street—My Penny Dreadful—Translating Wagner—On the rocks and jilted—A night of despair—Mr. Beeton of the Cookery Book—My Life of Disraeli—Old journalists' haunts—My taproom speeches—The Press Gallery—Born with a family.

THIS is not an autobiography; but, before dealing with the personalities and incidents of my Parliamentary life, I think I ought to give some sketch of their chronicler, in myself.

In March 1880 I lived in a garret in Barnard's Inn. But even a garret in Barnard's Inn was promotion from experiences in frowsy lodging-houses, and to that extent marked a certain advance on what had been my disastrous fortunes for some years. I had managed to secure a situation on the *Daily Telegraph* within a few weeks after my arrival in London. I started my London life with four pounds in my pocket—the amount left of my salary in advance for my three weeks' vacation.

France declares War, July 15, 1870

I found myself in London at the very beginning of the Franco-German War, and it was just the moment, in some respects, for me. I had been an eager student of French and German during my University career, and the first job I got in London was to read through the French, German, and Austrian papers, where one could now and then supplement the very brief messages which came from the correspondents of the paper, most of whom broke down during the war. The glory of war correspondence belonged to Mr. Archibald Forbes and the *Daily News*. I had once the task of writing an article of two or three columns from the sketch of a man who had just taken twenty-four days, or something like that, to get from Paris, just about to have its siege complete.

A little incident in connection with that article gave me great encouragement. Not valuing my work as highly as I could have done, I had instructed the foreman printer to put it in minion leaded (small type for small things); but when I was about half-way through my article, Mr. Levy (as the late Lord Burnham then was), expressed his delight with what I had done, and suggested that it should be re-set, so that the article would appear in bourgeois—a more important type. It will reveal my fresh, guileless notions as a child of a poor country that I raised the objection that this change would cost some money—it might have been a sovereign or two, in a paper earning anything up to a quarter of a million a year! "Damn the expense!" said the future Lord Burnham. But then I had just begun taking a morning breakfast of coffee with two slices of unbuttered bread in a Drury Lane coffee-house, and looked at the economics of life from a modest angle.

The proprietors of the paper did not realize that I was not a young inexperienced journalist, who had all his business to learn; as a matter of fact, I had had three years' training on a Dublin daily paper; but the little success I had had with this article about the escape from Paris almost ruined me. I got restless, and thought I ought to have had more money and a higher position. I became a bit sulky, and allowed Mr. Levy to see my change of temper; so that a quiet hostility arose which came to a climax when asking an increase from three pounds a week (my original salary) to five pounds, I was given only four. In time there was an open estrangement between my employer and myself. Whether he first gave me notice or I gave it to him must remain an unanswered question. The result was, however, without doubt. I found myself once again on the stones of Fleet Street without a penny and without a job, and I had, living with me, two sisters and a brother whom I had to support.

Stanley discovers Livingstone, October 28, 1871

This unemployment did not last more than a day. I found admission at once to the then head of the *New York Herald* office in Fleet Street, and was immediately engaged at five pounds a week. I had some interesting experiences there—especially that of finding myself in charge of the office when the letters began to arrive which described Stanley's discovery of Livingstone. Here my timidity about money nearly lost me my job; for, instead of cabling those tremendously interesting despatches—cabling might have run into hundreds of pounds, and such a sum frightened me—I sent them by mail.

I remained with the *Herald* for a year and a half, and then, after the manner of rapid despatch which was—and I daresay is—the rule in an American newspaper office, I got a month's notice. No reason was given, except the necessity of making some reductions in the expenses of the office; and thus I was once more on the stony-hearted pavement of Fleet Street. I had then, as I have had all my life, a certain lack of push, initiative, and self-confidence. Another journalist would somehow or other, perhaps, have been able to thrust himself into some job, but I didn't; and for the terribly long period of nearly seven years I remained, except for a few months, without any regular job or certain income. There is nothing in which the profession of journalism has made greater advances than in the facilities to-day for a young journalist of any ability to find ready employment.

I will not stop to describe all the miseries through which I passed in these seven years. I daresay I could have got employment on the *Daily Telegraph* again if I had sought it with that proper apology for my foolishness during the previous period; but that insane Irish pride which, among many other weaknesses, I had inherited from my race, stood in the way. The *Daily Telegraph*, I believe, to this day regrets the loss of such service as I could have given them—and as I have given them at a later period of my life. I have often speculated whether it would have been better if I had remained with the *Daily Telegraph*. I should by this time, I daresay, have been somewhat of a newspaper fogey, my individuality swallowed up in the great anonymous machine of a great daily; but what I would have escaped!

Fleet Street, 1873–1880

Anyhow, I did not try the *Daily Telegraph*, and for seven long years I had all the experiences that ever befell the old authors in Grub Street. I had often to go without food, and I still remember the envious eye with which I passed the shops with sausages and mashed potatoes. I got some odd jobs now and then, some of them how ridiculous! Once I wrote weekly imaginative accounts of the great prize-fights of old. I filled the ring with the names of the great sportsmen of the period, beginning, of course, with George IV., to whom I was not tender. I had to draw the line at a description of the rounds; these were done for me by a fellow-Irishman—a doctor—who was an excellent amateur boxer. The paper got a good circulation—mainly through these picturesque prize-fights. I never saw, and never would see, a prize-fight. Next I tried my hand at a penny dreadful, and a correspondent of mine who remembers the wretched thing assures me that the climax of each instalment was seductive and thrilling. What I most remember is that the thirty-five pounds I got for it were very welcome. I also remember that the heroine was the young lady with whom I was then in love. Sir Wilfrid Lawson objected to the tone of some of these columns, and asked a question about them in the House. It was with difficulty I kept my countenance when he took me into his confidence. Among my worthier work I helped John P. Jackson, then an agent of Wagner, and on the staff of the *New York Herald*, to translate Wagner's operas.

I tried various means of providing against recurrent hunger; once I bought a dozen jars of Liebig's Extract. And in the midst of these horrors, and in the single room I occupied in an Islington lodging-house, I found myself on a Saturday evening with just three-halfpence in my pocket, and in my hands a letter which began with a cold "Dear Sir", and was the breaking-off of an engagement to a woman whom I had regarded as the centre and the only hope of the world for me.

That night can never be obliterated from my memory. I felt close to suicide, and had the obsession that it was not safe for me to remain in my room alone with the razor there—a very blunt and much worn razor, but good enough to put an end to a life, desperate now under agonizing sorrow. I went out; tramped all the way from Islington to Camberwell New Road—distances of that kind meant nothing to me at that time, for I was very slight and very active. I sought the companionship of another Irishman, a journalist like myself. When I knocked at his door, a pale-faced woman looked out, frightened, through the window. It was my friend's wife sitting there in hideous anxiety, for her husband had not come home. He had treated himself to that not uncommon luxury among Irishmen of the period, a little bit of a spree; and this poor woman, an Englishwoman not fully acquainted with Irish peculiarities, was keeping this lonely and anxious vigil. So we two sat opposite each other, equally miserable, until our common hope returned. He did ultimately come home—at four o'clock in the morning. I stayed with him till I saw him off to Liverpool on an engagement the next evening, and went home to my desolate lodgings with a lent half-crown.

Such, then, were a few of my experiences during these terrible seven years. At last a break came with my appointment to the position of sub-editor in a morning edition of the *Echo*, which had just been acquired by Baron Grant. The hours were long, from something like six at night to two or three in the morning; and ultimately I had to resign, and again was without a job, or the hope of one.

Disraeli's Maiden Speech, December 7, 1837

I resolved to try for the position of publisher's reader, and went to the late S. O. Beeton, husband of the woman who wrote the famous cookery book, and asked him for such work. He dissuaded me from the occupation, and made the counter-proposition that I should write a book. Now, I had begun as a shorthand writer and general reporter in Dublin. I have often thought that it is something of a handicap to begin in the lower ranks of the profession; at least, it was so in those days, and a reporter who would try for anything editorial was somewhat like the ballet girl who would demand the place of a *prima donna*. I shared the prejudice against myself; and when anyone proposed to me to write a book I felt as unnerved as though I had been offered the command of the Channel Fleet. It is part of the "inferiority complex"—which, though not recognized by others, is part of the inner temperament, and one of the potent disqualifications of an Irishman. But Mr. Beeton put the proposition in a way that made an immediate appeal. There had, he said, been a number of dramatic scenes in the history of the House of Commons, but nobody had ever yet tried to embody them in a single book. I at once suggested as one of these historic scenes the maiden speech of Disraeli, which, though everybody had heard something of it, had passed into a tradition the reality of which had almost come to be doubted.

I went to the Reading Room of the British Museum, little realizing that I was about to start on a path that was to lift me from hunger and poverty and obscurity to a place in my profession. The first revelation that came to me of the treasure-house into which I was to break was in another biography, an able one which had not caught much attention, by a Mr. Macknight, then the editor of a great paper—the *Northern Whig* of Belfast. In his pages I found frequent references to a paper called the *Bucks Gazette*. With eagerness and suspense I sought this journal in the Newspaper Room of the Museum; and there I tracked down, in its somewhat mouldy pages, accounts of the first election contest of Disraeli. Little knowing the importance of the man on whom it was pouring forth, week after week, every form of ridicule, vituperation, and many a stroke of personality, the paper built up a perfect portrait of the young Disraeli. There he stood before your eyes, with his grotesque dress, his lawn sleeves, his cane, his innumerable gold chains about a flowery waistcoat; his impudence, his self-confidence, his readiness of speech, his mordant wit.

Gladstone's Windows broken, February 24, 1878

I realized at once the value of the gold-mine on which I had thus unexpectedly fallen; and there and then I suggested to Mr. Beeton that, instead of writing a book about Parliamentary scenes in general—it was to be called *Scenes in the House*—I should write a biography of Disraeli. The time was opportune for such a book, for Disraeli was then Prime Minister, and he was engaged in the greatest duel of his life—that with Gladstone over his Eastern policy. It is, perhaps, difficult to realize the fervour and depth of the political passion of that epoch in our history. I was then, as I have been ever since, filled with a passionate desire to rescue the Christians of the East from the yoke of Turkey. I went to a meeting in Hyde Park which Bradlaugh had called, and at which he presided, and I was one of the pro-Gladstone crowd who were dispersed by the genteel mob organized by a Lieutenant Armit, and armed with switches formidable enough to scatter rapidly the unarmed Gladstone crowd. That very night the windows of the house in Harley Street in which Mr. Gladstone at that moment lived were broken; to which I may add the curious fact that among the crowd who came with stones in their pockets to join in the window-breaking were two young Irish people; one was Parnell, and the other was one of his sisters—Anna, the fiercest among them, and the one most like him in appearance and in character. That early prejudice of Parnell against Mr. Gladstone will be recalled in a later phase of this narrative. To me at this period, while Disraeli represented all that was evil, in his mind and character as well as in politics, Mr. Gladstone took on the proportions of the noblest of human figures. Disraeli was Beelzebub against an angel of light.

In the accounts I read of Disraeli in the *Bucks Gazette*, and in my study of Disraeli's first great book, *Vivian Grey*, I thought I had found the inner secret of this enigmatic figure; and, starting from that thesis, I wrote scathing page after page in the exposure of what I regarded as the unprincipled adventurer who at that moment was leading the British people into criminal paths, and was doing so under the impulse of a cold, dishonourable, selfish nature.

I spent three years over the book, sometimes working furiously, sometimes forgetting it for weeks. I had to spend a great deal of time collecting my material; reading practically every big debate in volume after volume of Hansard—for in most of the important debates Disraeli figured largely, especially after 1845. I may say in passing that the speaker whom I found most useful in giving me an idea of the issues of a debate was J. A. Roebuck; the one least fruitful was Gladstone. He was too involved, too prolix, and too metaphysical for such hurried reading as I could give. It was this experience—apart from the violent hostility to which my approach to worship for Gladstone had been transformed in the strain of the conflict between his Ministry and the Party which I was soon, and unexpectedly, to join—that elicited from me in an article (for which I think I was never paid) the prophecy that in future ages Gladstone would be one of the most unread of our great orators—a prophecy I think since realized.

Disraeli, 1804–1881

I worked under terrible personal difficulties. First, I was still without permanent employment; and, secondly, the alternation of a little money and of none at all produced the usual results with anybody except a Scotsman—it was either a feast or a famine. When the feast came after the famine, I let myself go. A decent old English lady with whom I lodged for many years used to say that, after I had received a five-pound note on a Saturday, I borrowed from her on the following Tuesday. S. O. Beeton helped a bit by advancing me on account of future profits an occasional five-pound note; but these advances were infrequent, depending on his good will and sometimes on the state of his own finances. It would have been more satisfactory to me if there had been a regular weekly salary. The very manuscript paper became a substantial item of expense. I was helped by a chemist—a friend of mine, with an Irish associate—who used to turn over to me the innumerable pages of advertisements for quack medicines which he received. They were usually printed only on one side, and I wrote my manuscript on the blank side. Occasionally I got some assistance from men poorer even than myself. There were three of them—all good fellows—who ended prematurely and tragically. One Sunday I went out leaving them behind with plenty of work to do; they were all drunk when I returned.

At last I got to the point when I seemed to have but two alternatives: either I would finish the book or the book would finish me. I then made the great resolve that it had to be finished in two or three months, or be abandoned. During these few months I worked as few writers have ever had to work. I started fairly early in the morning; I went on till four o'clock in the following morning; and then I got up again, usually at eight, and started once more. This brought my nervous system to an approach to collapse. I remember still, when I was dictating the last few sentences—my peroration, in fact—that I found myself reduced almost to tears.

The book, according to the original idea, was to be published in monthly parts and to run into two substantial volumes. In the middle of this Mr. Beeton died, after only one volume had been made ready. I had then to go to another publisher; and the first condition was that the book should be reduced to one volume; and so, in a way, I had to begin all over again.

"*Lord Beaconsfield: A Biography,*" 1879

But it was at last published; and then came my tardy reward. In a sense, and in a humble way, I could declare that I woke and found myself famous. The violent passions of the time, to which I have already referred, secured for the book an enthusiastic reception from the Liberal Press; the *Spectator* gave me a long and laudatory review; the *Standard* gave me a review nearly as long but fiercely hostile. The book came just before the great General Election of 1880, when the long duel of years between Disraeli and Gladstone was at last to be submitted to the judgment of the nation. My tremendous indictment of Disraeli was full of such explosive material against him that it became the *vade mecum*, so to speak, of all the Liberal candidates; and my name rose from the obscurity and hopelessness of Grub Street to signify one of the literary forces of the time. People who know little of my career, except in its later development, are still under the impression that my life was an unbroken and triumphant procession from boyhood onwards. As a matter of fact, it was not till I had written my biography of Disraeli that I realized I was much above the humble shorthand writer with, perhaps, some small ability as a descriptive reporter.

One other chapter of my training as a speaker and a politician I ought not to omit. So long as I was out of regular employment, my difficulty was how to spend the evenings. It may surprise even journalists of the modern type that in my early days in Fleet Street the reporter had no club, nor any other rendezvous except the public-house. There was the Gaiety Bar, where the male element was interspersed with the ladies of the chorus of the Gaiety Theatre; there was the Cheshire Cheese, where women rarely appeared, and where journalists stood at the counter daily, solidly drinking; and there was the Ludgate Hill Bar, where, again, the mere drinking was somewhat relieved by a number of attractive girls who were attending behind the bar. One of them, an especially beautiful girl, who was the object of every journalist's devotion, made a good marriage in the end—in fact, several of them married rather well; but there again the smiles of the fair were only part of the more serious entertainment of swallowing in succession a number of whiskies or brandies.

Looking back on that terrible time, I can re-create the tragic phases in the lives of so many literary men: the habits exacted their toll, and I do not think I exaggerate when I say that fifty years was about the average expectation of life with the journalists of my early days. I began life with a hatred of drink—my father was a strict teetotaller—and, with a stomach always hostile to drink, I used to wonder at the folly of men who insisted on pouring it down into their insides, with the certain result with them, as with me, of substituting very uncomfortable for fairly comfortable feelings. But it is a law of our social habits that it is much easier to get a drink at the expense of one's friends than a meal. I often took a drink because the cravings of an empty stomach welcomed anything; drink was better than hunger. It was my experiences in this way that gave me the indulgent view I have always taken of the vice of drinking—as, indeed, of all other human weaknesses—and that made me convinced that the last and wisest judgment on the subject was that of Liebig, the celebrated German chemist: that drink was as much the child of misery as misery was the child of drink.

There were some places where mere drinking was accompanied by other forms of entertainment; and the chief of these were the public-houses in which they had nightly debates. The most important of these resorts in those days were Cogers' Hall—an ancient institution still existing—and the Green Dragon. Best of them all I remember the Green Dragon. It would require the pen of Balzac to draw portraits of the strange, hopeless, fallen creatures I used to meet almost nightly at these oratorical jousts.

Gladstone's Reform Bill, 1866

There were several good speakers among them, but they were nearly all men who, by their misfortune or their own weakness, had fallen from high prospects. One of them was a barrister, a fine-looking man with a splendid presence and very fine oratorical powers: he was reputed to be a near relation of a great figure who was then in the Ministry or was about to be a Cabinet Minister. Our barrister was a typical Englishman. There was an equally typical Scotsman, who had written several books, and spoke with all the logic characteristic of his race; but his features showed the unmistakable sign of his dissolute habits. There was an Irishman, of course: his name was Finlen, and for an hour he had played a notable part. When Gladstone was proposing a reduction of the franchise—denounced with fury especially by the followers of Disraeli, who were to pass a still more reduced franchise the very next year—a deputation was given admission to Gladstone at his house in Carlton House Terrace. Finlen was one of the chief spokesmen of this deputation. Unfortunately for him and for Gladstone, the papers a few days afterwards contained a report of the proceedings against this fiery agitator on the part of his wife, and of his being compelled to come to the relief of her and her children. At once there was an uproar, and a comic paper gave a picture in which Gladstone was represented as lifting from the dust-heap the form of Finlen.

He was a small, rather good-looking man. I believe he had a case in his defence, and that an unsatisfactory wife bore at least a part of the responsibility for his wrecked home. Anyhow, he was a brilliant debater—indeed, the chief pillar of the debates—and he was a pleasant fellow. I remember still the effect it had on me when, seeing him looking unusually well and unusually steady, I asked him for the explanation. He then told me that he had got a job at his trade, which was that of French-polisher—his hand bore the mark of his work. He seemed quite happy. Ultimately he disappeared to America, and I never heard of him again.

The importance of these nights to me was that I got a hard training in speaking. The subject on which I spoke most often was Home Rule, then beginning to be taken seriously. On that subject I had to stand up to all kinds of people. One of my opponents was an old college chum who came from the North of Ireland, and, though a Liberal, was a violent opponent of Home Rule. My countrymen in London began to hear of me, and I got innumerable invitations to address meetings—especially in public-houses, where I was regarded by the proprietors as a useful addition to their power of attracting customers.

Home Rule Speeches before 1880

I spoke, I think, in nearly every taproom in the East End, especially where the landlord was an Irishman. I remember a strange experience when I found myself announced as a speaker at a meeting in a public-house in Harrow Alley, which was off Petticoat Lane. I found the landlord—a very good-humoured Irishman—surprised that I had turned up; he confessed that his announcement of my presence was just a little trade device. In compensation, he put before my companion and myself a good glass of whisky, and when he had brought me to a genial state of mind he suddenly announced that the meeting was awaiting me. I went into the next room to find one of the strangest gatherings I have ever addressed. It consisted entirely of East End Jews, and there was not even a single Irish face in the audience.

I still remember a Jewish boy who sat on a barrel in front of me. Never did I see a face, before or since, which represented to me so completely the detachment of an Oriental from all things Occidental. I argued and harangued and appealed, but the impassive face remained the same—quite good-natured, but as remote from me and my speech and Ireland and England as though he were a Chinese listening to an address one word of which he did not understand. But there was among my audience another Jew of a different type, a middle-aged man, very well groomed, and with a dazzling diamond in his shirt-front. He was most attentive, but his real interest came when I denounced the Arms Prohibition Act then existing in Ireland. "Do you mean to say", said this bejewelled Jew, "that you can't carry a revolver in Ireland?" I said "No". He turned away with indignation, and I am sure he became a confirmed Home Ruler from that time.

I dwell on these adventures, first to give some idea of the kind of man the voters in Galway approached when, just as I had turned thirty-two years of age, I sat in my squalid chambers in Barnard's Inn; secondly, to enforce the proposition that, in spite of my youth, I had already some of the professional training of a man who was destined for political life. Again and again, in the course of my writings, I have insisted, as the result of my experience, that the gift of speaking requires constant, almost uninterrupted, practice. The more frequently a speaker speaks, the better, as a rule, he speaks. That applies even to the greatest masters of oratory. I watched Gladstone in the House of Commons practically every night for nearly twenty years, and I had to watch him as a journalist, ever ready to pounce for material to enliven my nightly sketches on Parliament. I can say confidently that there was scarcely a sketch I wrote during this long period in which he did not supply me with much, sometimes all, of my copy.

Gladstone from 1880 *to* 1898

With this prolonged experience I am going to make the curious statement that Gladstone steadily improved as a session went on; he was at his best when the session was coming to an end. He had usually spoken every night, and often several times a night during the session, with the result that his manner reached an easiness, a self-confidence, a readiness, which brought out all his mighty resources of oratory and of elocution. Ultimately he got to the point at which there was such perfect harmony between his mind and body that every part of his person contributed its own share to the irresistible general effect. His voice would spontaneously and easily go through the whole gamut, from a whisper to a loud appeal, which was not, however, a shout; for Gladstone hardly ever shouted; no great English orator often does. His gestures with his hands were always appropriate; in the end you could see his feet gesturing, so to speak—taking up now one position and now another, as though he were going through the figures of a dance.

It will be seen, then, that this strange, and it might be thought almost disreputable, training as a speaker which I received during my years in the abyss was in some respects useful for my future destination as a Member of the House of Commons.

There are two more factors which I must mention as part of my early training. I was never a regular member of the Press Gallery, my engagements there being slight and irregular ones. I represented a weekly paper, but the Press Gallery at the time was so close a corporation that admission to it was not easy, and as representative of a weekly paper I was allowed to be there only one night a week. I did for a while get a more regular position as shorthand reporter. I remember that I took down a speech of Lord Hartington with fair rapidity, but my endeavour to read my notes was hopeless. While I was thus put to work for which I was not fitted, I did not get the particular job my fitness for which I was to show, until many years later—and that was as a descriptive chronicler of the proceedings of the House. That was work I did for between twenty and thirty years afterwards, and, I believe, always to the satisfaction of my employers. But I did not press my claim for this particular job, largely owing to that self-distrust which was then part of my character, as I have already said, and especially my distrust of my power of writing on anything. Thus this is one of the many examples of the damage I did to my own prospects, helping to prolong my agony as one of the unemployed, and casting such a dark shadow over some of my early years. Nevertheless, I had seen enough of the House of Commons from the Press Gallery, even in these fitful appearances, to give me a certain familiarity with its procedure and its methods, all of which helped me when I became myself a Member of the House.

Reporting in Dublin, 1867

The second factor which I must add to those I have already mentioned was that I had been regarded as the hope of my family. I have written, more than once, that every Irishman is born with a family, especially if he be the eldest son and gives any promise of a more prosperous future than that of his hard-driven parents. I began my care of my family when I was a young reporter in Dublin, bringing my two sisters and my younger brother to live with me, and supporting them and myself on a salary which I do not think ever exceeded two pounds a week. How often do I now look back on those years as among the happiest of my life! When I came to London and got a job, I did the same thing: the two sisters and my brother lived with me; they only left me when my dismissal from the *New York Herald* left me without the means of supporting them.

I must mention one incident when, for the first time—I think it was on account of my biography of Beaconsfield—I found myself with a cheque for £100 in my pocket. I thought the moment had come to do something really handsome for my people, and as some compensation for the neglect of them to which I had been reduced by my own needy condition. I knew also my own natural extravagance, and I had a conviction that if I kept the money I would spend it, and pretty rapidly; so I took £95 out of the £100 and sent them home. Perhaps this was the more of a sacrifice because at that very moment I had only one pair of boots, and they were dress boots, very thin in the soles of course, and rather porous. To add to the poignancy of this little incident, I may say that it was those boots I

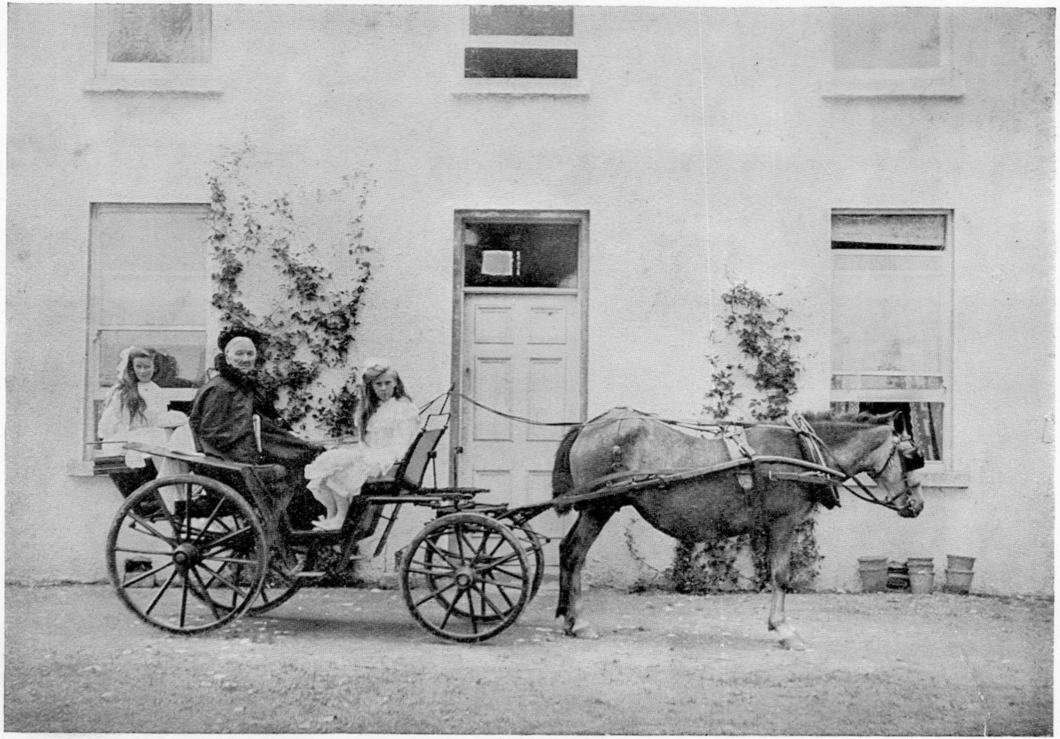

Mr. O'Connor's Mother and her Grandchildren

To face page 18

was wearing when, ascending rather a steep hill on the way to attend the funeral of the wife of my dear friend Justin M'Carthy, who had just died, I found I was too late, and saw the mourning coach returning from the cemetery with its silent and broken-hearted occupants, the husband and the two children of the poor dead.

CHAPTER II

Summons to the Hustings—My strange schoolfellow—A Libertine's gusts of piety—Mystery of a missing M.P.—My first days in England—Isaac Butt, a study in contradictions—My fight for election—A slender majority—Member for Galway.

Invitation from Galway, 1880

SITTING in my garret in Barnard's Inn, there came unexpectedly to me an invitation to stand for Parliament, and for the old city of Galway. Here, again, strange accidents played their part. If I were a novelist I could make a weird, almost incredible, story of the man and the events which brought about this invitation. My predecessor in the seat and I had one of those close and romantic friendships which sometimes arise between boys brought up in the same school. I shall be mistaken for a lady novelist, with a sheik as her hero, when I try to describe this strange personality. I sat next to him at school, in the college near Athlone—there was an ironical contrast between the name of the college and this figure—the College of the Immaculate Conception. The boys wore a band around their caps in what were supposed to be the colours of the Blessed Virgin, and our great feast day was December 8, the Feast of the Immaculate Conception. My poor friend became the most immoral man—sexually—I have ever known.

He came of an ancient but crazy stock. Part of his family lived in an old house in Galway that had a legendary and romantic history. The Warden of the town is supposed, after the classic model, to have executed from the window of this house his own son, for the boy was so popular that an executioner could not be found. He had murdered a Spaniard—there was a good deal of trade in the old days in wine between Galway and Spain—but the murderer was handsome, popular, gallant, and a devouring love had been the cause of his crime.

This old schoolfellow of mine might have been that romantic figure resurrected from the dead past. He had a strikingly handsome face, with features and colouring as delicate as those of a baby girl; a tiny nose, a cupid mouth; the colour was so high that people always suspected in him consumptive tendencies, and in this they proved to be right. The eyes gave some indication of the feverish temperament underneath this almost feminine beauty. They were blue, they were very deep-set, they were surmounted by a large, somewhat protruding forehead; they had a penetrating and almost cynical look.

And to add to the contradictions of this strange character, this girl-face was accompanied by the muscles of a prize-fighter, nerves of steel, and a cold and desperate courage. He was consumed by violent passions, and the curious thing to complete the strange make-up was that he had not a particle of sentiment. He would disappear for weeks together, and nobody could trace him. I once ran all the way from the Strand to Islington in the hope of tracking him down to the squalid and infamous resort where he was living with an appalling creature, whose profession proclaimed itself from her painted and bloated face. Her brazen look of defiant youth was gradually transformed by this terrible man to something like despair, and she became soon a broken wreck.

Portrait of an Irish Rake

I hope I may be allowed to add a few more strokes to this attempt at a portrait of an Irish personality peculiar,

I think, to his country. When I saw him for the first time after my arrival in Galway from our old boarding school, I was struck—indeed, I was a bit abashed—by the change in his expression. His boyish, open, jolly face had altered its expression to deadly seriousness and remoteness. I found the key to this extraordinary transformation in the fact that he had got under the influence of a young man who was being trained in the Jesuit College of the town for the priesthood, himself as remarkable and perhaps as typically Irish as his friend. This neophyte had obtained such a mastery over my schoolfellow that he had transformed the reckless rake into an equally fervent Catholic, who went to Mass every morning and to the Sacrament every Sunday, scourged himself with his own hand until he had sores over his whole body, and for months watched not only the Jesuit's every word, but his every look: when a woman passed him he turned away his eyes.

This terrible strain would go on for months at a time, and then would come the breakdown. The glimpse of a barmaid with a V-shaped blouse would be sufficient to light again the fire of his fiery sensuality; and that same night, and for weeks after, he would disappear—it will be easily understood where—and would be lost to everybody. The strange contradiction of character, on which I must insist, was that all this life of so-called pleasure was to him quite joyless. Fundamentally, he hated women; he made to me the terrible remark that he had always hated women, and had begun by hating his own mother. He adored his father—a very fine old fellow, who had risen from a workman to be the owner of a prosperous mill and a large fortune, according to the standards of his town. I should add that, in spite of these terrible vices, this friend was generous to a fault, spent his money as recklessly on others as on himself; and, finally, had very considerable talents and immense influence over men as well as women.

By a freak of fortune—just after his father had died and left him a fair sum of money—he was drawn into contest for the Galway constituency; he became the election agent of another Galway man who will appear in these pages—Frank Hugh O'Donnell. O'Donnell was elected, but was thrown out on quite a frivolous pretence by a partisan judge—the judges in Ireland at that time, where politics came in, were shameless partisans—and the constituency insisted that they should pay back the injustice by electing the man who stood nearest to O'Donnell. And thus, very much to his surprise, also to his dissatisfaction, my friend found himself a Member of Parliament.

There have been many curious figures in the House of Commons, and many tragedies of which the public know little, but assuredly never was there a stranger Member than this old friend of mine. He was a doctor by profession; and had started with some success a practice in Dublin; this he had to give up. He had just the little bit of money left by his father, and he proceeded immediately to spend it. And then he met an Englishwoman who had a small fortune. She fell in love with him—women were constantly in love with him—and they were married. Then came the few years that alone brought a little happiness into his life. With her money he bought a practice in Camden Town; his wife was a woman of exquisite taste, and she furnished the house beautifully. He began to have a good practice, and became a steady, married professional man.

Searching for a missing M.P.

Then this devoted wife got ill; took many months to die. He nursed her tenderly, for, so far as it was in him, he loved her. But the long illness broke down the amendment of his ways, and, with that fatality that always pursues these men of irregular passions, he went off on one of his sprees, and chose as the moment for this disastrous break the short interval between the announcement of the Dissolution and the General Election. I may render to this generation that the election of 1880 was announced in a peculiar way. Sir Stafford Northcote was then the leader of the House of Commons. Just after the Parliament had assembled Sir Stafford rose to answer an ordinary question, and then dumbfounded the assembly by adding, with the astounding preface "as I am on my legs", that a dissolution would take place in a few weeks. It was these few weeks that produced the tragedy of my old schoolfellow's life. Men given to "sprees" always choose the worst moment for them. While every constituency was panting for the presence of its candidate, my poor friend went off on his spree in haste, but alone, it need scarcely be said. As usual, he left no trace; and the newspapers were not so ubiquitous or so inquisitive as they are nowadays. So far as his constituents, his friends, his family were concerned, he had disappeared as completely as if he were dead. Letters, telegrams, messages of all kinds were sent by his distracted friends, concerned about the constituency, where he had a seat for life. No answer came. And thus it was that his constituents came to me. It was a curious and unwelcome paradox that I should be asked to mount to the House of Commons on the political grave of my closest and lifelong friend.

Why did they come to me—living in a garret, with no money and no record of political service? It all went back to my Life of Beaconsfield, which had raised my head above water and made me known a little in Ireland. There were other reasons. I had graduated in the Queen's College in Galway, and had acquired some distinction in my studies; but, what was more important for my future—though in itself very unimportant—we had a debating society connected with the College. Its meetings were usually held in private, but occasionally it held public discussions, to which the people of the town were admitted.

Though I was terribly shy, and did not know whether I stood on my head or my feet, I made a little speech at one of these public meetings. It was during the American Civil War, and I used to recall the fact, when I was speaking in later years, that this maiden speech of mine was in defence of the South. Knowing nothing about the merits of the struggle, I think I was mainly influenced by the discourse of one of those curious Irish "returned empties" that get back to Ireland—poor as when they go except in travellers' tales. This man—George Marshall I think was his name—had a great flowing beard, a belligerent look and manner. One of his tales was that, in his eagerness to discover a new star, he held his eye to a telescope for three years without interruption.

He was a fierce anti-clerical, and gave blood-curdling tales of how he had made war on the monks of Mexico. He was known as the Texan Ranger, and I fancy that he lived on his relatives, for he never did a stroke of work. He had proclaimed everywhere the chivalry of the South, and the fact that the Southern States demanded what might be called Home Rule established an analogy between their demand and that of Ireland. To a young Irish Home Ruler like myself, this was enough to justify their claim.

My second speech excited more attention; I quoted freely from Thackeray's indictment of the Georges, mentioning, among other horrors, the statement that George II. cared only for his fat German mistresses. This had the effect of driving out one of the audience with a loud protest; but then, he was a Presbyterian clergyman.

Finally I was chosen to be one of the four chief debaters in a set public debate. I forget the subject, but I prepared my speech with some care; it was, if I remember rightly, well arranged. When I sat down I had established my reputation locally, and Frank Hugh O'Donnell, who was, after all, something of a rival, proclaimed me the orator of the Literary Society. To add to all these things, I had an aunt in Galway whom everybody respected, and I had spent a good deal of my boyhood, apart from my college years, in the town, and in a way might be regarded as a Galway boy.

The Close of a Tragedy

I ought to finish up my story of the unconscious creator of my Parliamentary career by saying that, just before they left office, the Tory Government, whose Eastern policy both he and Isaac Butt, the Home Rule leader, had supported, very much to my disgust, threw him a small job. It was that of surgeon to a hospital in Demerara. When I came back a Member of Parliament I found him in my rooms almost a wreck and on the brink of delirium tremens. He went to Demerara with his broken constitution and his broken heart, broken by his own incredible folly and weaknesses. He lived only a year and a half. He had time, however, to enter into a fierce quarrel with the Roman Catholic authorities of the district, and he declared to his young second wife, whom he had married just before he left for Demerara, that if one of them came to his dying bed he would have the strength to rise and take him by the throat.

He was buried in the Protestant churchyard, without the rites of the Church to which for many years he had given such fanatical devotion. He was about thirty-five years of age when he died.

Such, then, I was when I entered the House of Commons for the first time. I had just turned my thirty-second birthday; I am told I looked even younger than I was, and might have passed for twenty-two. I had gone already through a very full life of hard work and hard times. I got the credit of having learned from these personal experiences a certain cynical outlook on life. It was not true. I remained at bottom of a confiding disposition, was no judge of character, and could easily be taken in by men and perhaps even more easily by women. The leading lesson my life had taught me was one of infinite, and perhaps even blind, compassion. I felt that there were few bitter experiences which life had still to teach me.

I was told by my friends who knew me in these dark years that my face gave an impression of constant melancholy, if not despair. In the fiery furnace of these bitter experiences of mine there was scarcely a type of human misfortune and even of human decadence with which I was not familiar. I could move easily and without any sense of superiority through crowds of fallen men and of fallen women; and most of them were of English and not of Irish birth. I never can trace in my opinions or feelings any anti-English bias, though I started with a heap of ignorant misjudgments which in these years had been burned out. I still remember the time when I regarded any Englishman as gluttonous, cold, selfish.

When a boy at home, I had never eaten meat at more than two meals in a week; when I now saw the two good meals of meat which most of those around me who could afford them ate every day, it confirmed in me the opinion of most untravelled Irishmen of that period, that Englishmen were a race of pagan gormandizers.

Once I was invited by an excellent English priest to go to the service of Benediction at his church, and afterwards to take supper with him. The very way he pronounced the word supper—which was something like "suppah"—offended my taste, and when at ten at night I found myself for the first time in my life in the presence of a supper on the table laden with a great hot joint of roast beef and a bushel of laughing mealy potatoes, I looked upon the priest—a most excellent fellow—as a very unworthy type of his cloth.

I was not taken at first with the face of the Englishman. I thought it expressionless and rather animal, though the multitude of fair-haired women, in such contrast to the usual darkness of the Irish, made me think of Englishwomen as a race of beautiful young goddesses. Curiously enough, amid these unfavourable impressions, I must add that I took a more favourable view than that of most people, outside the land of Cockayne, of the London accent, for to me the Cockney accent sounded melodious. I sometimes walked through the streets for the mere pleasure of hearing the Cockney speech.

First Impressions of England, 1870

One of my first impressions of London, on landing very early in the morning at Euston and going into a very humble coffee-shop for my breakfast, was the way in which my temporary companions spoke, although they wore such shabby clothes and made so poor an appearance. I listened to them with surprise and even with admiration. In my own country at that time accent revealed class. The upper classes, mainly educated in English schools and Universities, spoke, as a rule, with an English accent; and the English accent from the lips of these poor outcasts who were taking their scanty breakfast, as I was myself, seemed to class them with those who had been the aristocrats in my own country.

The presence of any sentiment in the English character, of anything soft amid what I regarded as its circumambient hardness, came to me with almost a shock of surprise. One night, when I was taking supper with an English friend and colleague—one of the finest fellows I ever knew—one of my fellow-guests gave a description of the keenness of his own emotions when, after a long journey abroad, he met his mother, and how tears choked him as he took her in his arms. I could scarcely believe my ears, and was frank enough to say to my host privately that I had not thought there was any such family affection among English people.

I set forth these almost childish impressions frankly, for they help to explain that gross misunderstanding of each other's character which kept the English and the Irish people so long apart.

To complete the portrait of myself, I must say that I was quite ignorant not merely of whatever poor gifts nature had bestowed upon me, but of the great resources of energy and of inherent strength both of my body and my mind. In the life without much purpose, except that of finding a meal, which I had led for many years, I assumed, as did others, that laziness, indifference, and an absence of all enthusiasm lay inherent in my nature. Under the inspiration of the great fight into which I was about to enter, I developed powers of action which were as much a surprise to me as to my fellows. As will presently be seen, I went quite fresh and untouched through the terrific all-night sittings; I spoke at innumerable meetings in almost every town in England, Scotland, and Wales; I addressed monster meetings in great halls, sometimes in more than one town on the same night. I travelled often from one of these meetings by night train to London and resumed, with apparently undiminished vigour, my work at my desk or at the House of Commons.

Even the tremendous fatigue of a General Election left me fresh at the end; but, all the same, nature did take its revenge. The hours of night work on the *Daily Telegraph* and the hours in the House of Commons and at public meetings brought on one of the most aggravating of human maladies, and I became a lifelong dyspeptic. There were always two or three hours immediately after meals when I was almost good for nothing; and, like all dyspeptics, I was subject to fits of profound depression.

But my activities in Parliament lifted me above these physical ailments by the inspiration of a great cause, a great battle-ground, and a consuming enthusiasm.

Parnell begins Obstruction, 1877

Parnell had just started the creation of that party which was later on to become omnipotent in Irish, and now and then English, politics. At this point in his career he was far from the great position to which he was to attain. The thick-and-thin supporters he had been able to gather around him from the old party were no more than about seven, and of these Joseph Biggar was the only one of much consequence. He had, it is true, among his general supporters two remarkable men in Frank Hugh O'Donnell, whom I have already mentioned, and John O'Connor Power; but both these men disliked Parnell and were extremely jealous of him. O'Donnell never got rid of the impression that it was he who made Parnell; and O'Connor Power had served years in the Irish cause, including several months of imprisonment, before Parnell had learned the alphabet of Irish Nationalism.

Under such circumstances, Parnell was on the look out for any young men that he thought might add to the strength of his supporters. I had met him several times during the later 'seventies, and from my place in the Press Gallery I had seen some of his earlier performances. I remember him still at that stage. It was a curious and almost incredible sight. The policy of obstruction which Biggar had begun, and Parnell improved and intensified, consisted at that time mainly in stubborn fights against time. Then as now, and indeed at practically all seasons, time is the very life-blood of a Ministry, and he who was able to waste that blood brought the Ministry to insurmountable difficulties. Every one of the ordinary methods was tried to wear down Parnell, even the device of leaving him alone to address an empty House. How little they understood that man of iron, with no nerves—at that time, at least—and with a disregard that amounted to positive contempt for all Englishmen, and especially the Englishmen who were opponents of his cause!

With no special powers of speech, except in moments of great passion and great emergency, Parnell was usually a dreary and a costive speaker. Yet you could see him there, standing up in the empty House, talking hour after hour quite indifferent to the fact that there was nobody listening and nobody to listen; and the tall, thin figure, the impassive face, the inscrutable eyes, gave to this spectacle an almost uncanny look. An observation he made to me about the absence of any hearers while he droned out his dreary speeches hour after hour to the empty benches was very characteristic of the man. He said he rather liked an empty House; it gave him more time to think. Nobody ever cared less for the opinions of other people than Parnell.

I cannot say that my first impressions of Parnell were winning; I accepted the usual judgment upon him that he was absolutely cold-blooded, and everything about him lent countenance to that judgment. He was cold in look, cold in manner, cold in speech. I remember one conversation with him which left a peculiarly unpleasant impression.

Isaac Butt, 1813–1879

Isaac Butt, the nominal leader of the Irish Party of the day, and really the founder of the modern Home Rule movement, was the most lovable and one of the most impossible of men. Of strong passions, of spendthrift habits, a stout, broad-chested man, with almost every weakness, and, in spite of a large income, constantly penniless, he had behind him in his earlier days a political life as a strong Irish Tory. Even when he was little more than a boy he had been put forward as a worthy combatant to face the great Daniel O'Connell in a debate on Home Rule—or Repeal of the Union, as it was then called—in the Municipal Corporation of Dublin.

He had gradually changed his views, had written extremely able pamphlets on the then terrible depopulation of Ireland through the Land Laws, and the consequent migration; had jumped into great popularity as the chief counsel in defending the hopeless causes of the Fenian leaders who were being sent to penal servitude at almost every assizes; and then, when the materials were otherwise ready for a new political departure and he launched his scheme of Home Rule, he found Ireland eager to receive the message, and, apart from his commanding popularity, was by sheer force of circumstances and by national acclamation, made the leader of the Party.

People forgot, with his winning personality before

them, his splendid powers of exposition, and his palpable honesty in his new views, all the scandals of his chequered past: his appearances before London magistrates for alleged attempts to bilk his cabmen, the solemn Commission that had been appointed to discuss the charge against him of having been bribed by an Indian Maharajah to plead his cause in the House of Commons, the stories of his innumerable debts. In fact, just at the time when he was being forced to the leadership of this mighty new movement, he had spent twelve months in Kilmainham gaol, according to the custom with hopeless debtors in those days. There were also reports that he would sometimes be interrupted at public meetings by a woman claiming him as the father of her illegitimate child, and now and then even such a child made open demand on Butt for the recognition of his paternity. As an instance of his equanimity and his remains of the piety that came from a parson father, people used to tell a story of his applying in gaol for a loan of the Governor's Bible, as the print was larger than that of his own, and could therefore be more easily read in his hours of retirement in his dimly lit cell.

When he first stood for Parliament as Home Rule leader, means had often to be devised to save him from pursuing bailiffs, who were anxious to send him once more to gaol for his unpaid debts.

A Clash and its Close

Butt found in Parnell a very recalcitrant follower. The policy of obstruction could never make an appeal to an old Parliamentarian with a gentle disposition and a winning smile, and there came once or twice open collisions between the ancient and dying leader and this stern young recruit. The struggle was closed by the death of Butt. I had always loved Butt, though I knew very little of him by personal intercourse; and when we discussed his then recent death, Parnell made my blood run cold as he described, in characteristically unemotional words, how the old man had died. There was no trace of the smallest approach to sympathy with this tragic end, in poverty and humiliation and despair, of the great, lovable figure that had created our movement.

One other early interview with Parnell at this period I remember. I was with him on the Terrace of the House of Commons. Somehow or other he realized that he had kept me after the usual time for an evening meal; and then he showed another side of his character, a certain courtly politeness that reminded one of the fact that he came of an historic Irish family of high social position, for he insisted that the waiters—against, I believe, the rules of the House—should bring me my dinner to the Terrace. It was not his hour for a meal, and he looked on.

I had not yet become quite convinced that in the clash between Butt's policy of conciliation, of the slow building up of a constitutional and effective Parliamentary party, and the more violent methods of Parnell, the merits were all on one side. I realized then that such weapons as Parnell and Biggar employed would be countered with some new form of resistance, which a House of Commons practically united against Parnell—for Liberals at that time were for the most part as much avowed enemies of Home Rule as the Tories—could easily devise. That is what ultimately happened. But what I did not foresee was that, in order to crush Parnell's methods, Parliament had to destroy the old House of Commons and substitute a new House of Commons, the difference between which and the House of Commons I entered in 1880 is not yet realized by any but those who belonged to the earlier epoch.

This view of Parnell's activities was pretty common, even among those inclined to support him. O'Connor Power misunderstood and underrated him, and, apart from an older man's jealousy at the rapid rise of this young upstart, he had a profound contempt for Parnell's political intelligence. He used to repeat as an example of incorrigible stupidity that Parnell had told him of a plan of his to go down to the House of Commons some night, address it in a green uniform, *à la* Robert Emmet or Lord Edward Fitzgerald, and so provoke a scene which would entail his expulsion from the House. O'Connor Power refused, at least once, to attend a meeting of Parnell's. At this period and for years afterwards, he was in a state of angry revolt against both Parnell and the Parnell policy. Justin M'Carthy made a speech in the early days of obstruction, in which, speaking again as an old constitutional Parliamentarian, he compared Parnell's and Biggar's activities to a childish prank such as turning off the gas.

When, therefore, candidature for Galway was proposed to me, I felt rather lukewarm. I had learned by heart the history of every Irish politician who was honest, with its recurring and tragic story of broken hearts and broken fortunes, and I felt that in going into that terrible life I might well be taking the road to ruin.

I felt that the more because at the time I had no settled position in my own profession. I had no money, I had no means of earning my bread except as a journalist, and I anticipated, not without good reason, that by joining the Parnell party I would become an object of such universal unpopularity in England as to make it difficult, if not impossible, for any journal to employ my pen.

Parnell in America, January 1, 1880

There was no Parliamentary salary in those days; nor, curiously enough, was there, as there was later, any public fund from which to draw support for the penniless members of the Party. By a curious contradiction, our national treasury was bulging with tens of thousands of pounds which had been gathered by Parnell on a mission to America. The Fenians who had helped Parnell to get the money had imposed a condition that none of it should be devoted to purely Parliamentary purposes. While, as will be seen, a band of brilliant young men were fighting the battle of Ireland on the floor of the House of Commons, and holding up Parliaments and Ministries, many of them were left with scarcely a penny in their pockets; some of them had often to borrow the price of their meals.

A characteristic story of Joseph Biggar, who had some £30,000 from a successful provision business in Belfast, was that he gave a loan of £10 to a brilliant member of the Party who had a dangerous cold and wanted the money to go to Brighton to recover. As soon as this poor fellow came back, Biggar promptly asked for a return of the £10, giving as his reason that this would encourage him to repeat the loan if it were asked again.

Now, I had made up my mind that, so far as I could, I would never be dependent on politics for my living. I had a horror of the subserviency it might create, and I knew that it would always be an uncertain source of income. This was my state of mind when, at last, in reply to innumerable letters and telegrams, I consented to accept the candidature for Galway. There was, however, an initial and insuperable difficulty. I would have to provide something between £100 and £200 to pay the sheriff's fee before I would be allowed to be nominated as a candidate. Where was I to get this money? There was only one place to which I could apply; and again my *Life of Lord Beaconsfield* played its part.

A Scotsman who had more than even an ordinary proportion of the hard-fistedness of his race had published a popular edition of my Beaconsfield book; it had sold enormously, and he must have had some hundreds of pounds of my money in his till. But when I asked for £100 on account of these profits, he pointed to the terms of my contract—the old contract for authors until they had become known and strong—that no money was to be paid to me until seven months after the date of publication; and only four months had elapsed! For three days I besieged this grim publisher. He spoke of the sum as something too gigantic for his resources; gave me a bill; I could not discount it. Meantime the hours were passing, until at last it came to be a set day and a set hour. On that day either I caught the 8.45 train from Euston and went straight to Galway, or I was out of the contest.

My publisher invited me to lunch to discuss the question; never did I see a man eat a lunch more deliberately, with big pauses between each mouthful, and solemn and disturbing silences. However, just as the clock was pointing to the closing hour of the banks, he made the proposal to me that he would give me a cheque for £95, allowing him £5 as commission for payment before the proper date. And with that cheque for £95 in my pocket and a few pounds more from another publisher—I was editing at the time a book on Ireland for Messrs. Blackie—I reached Euston at 8.45 and shortly after noon the next day I was in Galway and beginning my candidature.

The political conditions of Ireland at that moment are

well exemplified in the facts of my contest. The first remarkable fact is that this town with less than a thousand voters had two representatives in the Imperial Parliament. For these two seats there were three candidates. One of them, Mr. J. Orrell Lever, was a grotesque and almost incredible candidate for an Irish seat. He was a Lancashire man, I should say of very uncertain fortunes, and was quite illiterate—the favourite jibe against him was to repeat his chief slogan, which was in these words: "If you h'elevate me I will h'elevate you". He had been elected before and was something even of a popular favourite; his chief appeal was to a secular conviction and an obstinate passion of the people of Galway. They knew they had a beautiful and magnificent bay, and I believe, under proper and well-financed organization, one that might be made a splendid port of call between the far West of Ireland and the United States. The condition of the harbour, and its transformation to prosperity from its almost incredible poverty, was its first and last political purpose. Not seeing any immediate prospect of the advent of the realization of this golden dream of poor Galway, and realizing that Mr. Lever was either a dreamer or an impostor, I left the question of the future steam packet severely alone. But I remember the horror with which my supporters and myself listened to one of the students of the Queen's College, who came to my support, deliver a thoroughly logical address to prove that Galway could never be an Atlantic port. We were tempted almost to drag the poor young speaker down.

The Galway Contest of 1880

In the days of a Derby-Disraeli Government, when the counter-policy of the Tory Party to Home Rule and Land

Reform was a series of subsidies to Ireland, Mr. Lever had obtained a subsidy for the conveyance of the mails from Galway, and he had succeeded in getting a large number of people, mostly Irishmen, to subscribe to his shares. Misfortune dogged the enterprise from the first step. A ship went on a rock; the company disappeared. I myself sat by the bedside of a poor Irishman who was dying of starvation in London; his money had gone into the Galway Shipping Company. After the failure of the shipping line, Mr. Lever suggested that Galway should be made a great cotton-spinning centre, and I remember a solemn procession of Lancashire looms, which were drawn through the town and deposited in an empty building. There they remained till they rusted to extinction. But the vision of Galway as a shipping centre could not be laid. I see even as I write that some vessels have been induced to call there on their way to America.

I do not remember Mr. Lever ever making a speech, nor my other opponent, Alderman Tarpey, a true representative, and a very decent one, of the bourgeoisie of Ireland—liberal in opinions, fairly well-to-do as a hotel-keeper, a man of impeccable piety, and already with some distinction as an Alderman and ex-Lord Mayor of Dublin. On the other hand, there were crowded and enthusiastic audiences wherever I went. I talked myself into the House of Commons; but, young and inexperienced as I was, I did not realize that underneath and behind the scenes was an active campaign against me, and all kinds of stories were told of my life in London, one of which, more flattering to my charm than to my morality, I must repeat: that I got my income, such as it was, not from one, but from two ladies whose avocations may be guessed from their being reported as living in St. John's Wood. I could not have been returned but for the fact that, joined on to the town itself, where the voters were all shopkeepers and all against a penniless and unknown man like me, there was a small district, called Barna, entirely occupied by small farmers. It was a lovely little seaside town, where often as a boy I had walked with my father.

In Barna they were all carried away by the new Land gospel which Parnell and Michael Davitt had just begun to preach. They voted for me to a man. I may here insert a little fact which is not unilluminating with regard to the manner in which election contests were then fought. The voters in Barna had to come into town to the Court House to record their votes. I need not say that a walk of four miles was nothing to these sturdy peasants, but it was a tradition that on this particular day they should all be drawn in cars, and the cars that day formed a good slice of my election expenses. I was a young politician at the time, and I was sincerely touched when one of my committee shook me warmly by the hand and, looking into my face with an expression of warm affection, assured me that he could not have done more for me if I had been his own brother. He was, I found afterwards, one of the men who supplied cars to take the voters from Barna. The expense amounted to a large sum.

I took rather a subtle revenge by inducing Henry James, when Attorney-General, to put in his Election Bill a clause which enjoined the creation of a special polling booth in this particular district, and the subsequent candidates for Galway were saved this big item of expenditure for cars on the polling day.

The result of the counting was a surprise to everybody. Mr. Lever topped the poll by seventeen of a majority over me, but I had a majority of five over Alderman Tarpey. These five voters thus stamped my destiny as an Irish politician for the rest of my days.

I had a flattering but disturbing experience immediately after the poll was declared. My followers insisted on chairing me from the Court House to my hotel. I never was more frightened or more uncomfortable in my life.

One of those who voted for me was my own father.

CHAPTER III

The new member—My shyness of the House—Electing Parnell leader—First glimpse of Captain O'Shea—How I wrote my Parliamentary sketch—Portrait of Gladstone—Lord Randolph and the "Fourth Party"—Bradlaugh removed from the House.

I RETURNED to London Member for Galway, and my shyness and self-distrust will be demonstrated by the fact that I stood in the Lobby afraid or ashamed to enter the House, after nearly every other elected member had entered.

First Days in the House, 1880

My awe of the House was immense. A few days after this I was present at a debate; a rather wild type of Irishman named Lysaght Finigan, who by this time was a veteran of a few months, made me jump when he called out "Hear, hear". It seemed to me an act of shameless daring. And yet the first appearances of a new House of Commons are by no means awe-inspiring. The immediate task is to swear the members in, and this is done in a haphazard and almost riotous form. Members, in their eagerness to have the job over, hustle, rush, and form long queues, all amid a scene of merriment quite characteristic of the House of Commons. There is no mistake more generally made, especially by foreigners, with regard to the general demeanour of the House of Commons than to think of it as an always sober, staid, and reticent assembly. It could better be compared to the sea on an uncertain day, quiet and sunny at one moment, the very next vociferous and stormy; for in the House good-humour constantly lies in the wake of the fiercest passions. I have ventured to compare it to a boarding-school of boys, when it did not resemble even more a boarding-school of girls.

It is a wonderful demonstration of crowd psychology; its emotions rush from breast to breast with lightning rapidity; a small joke, which in private would scarcely raise a smile, leads to a hurricane of laughter. The great masters of the House of Commons are those who realize this mutability and this infectiousness of crowd psychology, and know how to play, as Gladstone could do so consummately, on its varying moods, from grave to gay, from passion to good nature. To all Parliamentarians who are striving to make their way, I would give the counsel never to forget that the House has a lighter and essentially good-humoured side. I will give as I go on many historic instances of this special temper of the House of Commons.

Before I finally came to grips with my position in the House of Commons, two important things had happened. First, there was the election of Parnell to the leadership of the Party. This was unexpected and, to a large extent, accidental. I found myself in a hotel in Dublin on the night before the meeting of the Irish Party, which was to be held at the Dublin Mansion House, to decide this question of leadership as well as several other important questions. Parnell's name had not been seriously mentioned as a candidate for the leadership, though he had fought during the election almost like a maniac of activity and ferocity. He was in the midst of a terrific campaign for funds in America when the unexpected dissolution came, and he had gathered for the first time since O'Connell's death a tremendous fund for the national cause. At less than twenty-four hours' notice he was on his way back to Ireland; he allowed himself to be nominated for seat after seat; he made war on some of the members of the old Party who hitherto had been regarded as more or less orthodox in the faith; yet it was more than doubtful if he commanded the majority of the new Party. To many of them he was hateful; a number of them disliked his policy, which, as will be presently seen, was revolutionary in essence; his halting speech could make no large appeal to a country where eloquence had nearly always been the chief title of a politician to fame and power; he was more or less regarded as an honest but a fanatical and blind monomaniac. I remember a talk with James O'Connor, an old Irish politician, immediately after Parnell had been defeated in his first election. James O'Connor was instancing the large number of votes which the Nationalists had polled—especially, as O'Connor added, when one realized what a hopeless candidate they had to represent them. Parnell was the hopeless candidate.

Mr. Shaw succeeds Mr. Butt, 1879

Besides, there was ample reason for accepting that compromise to which politicians are always disposed to resort. It was not many months since the death of Isaac Butt; Mr. William Shaw had been appointed as his successor, and from many points of view it seemed an admirable arrangement. It was rather to the advantage of Mr. Shaw that he was a Protestant. One of the most profound mistakes made, with regard to Irish politics and politicians, by Englishmen of all parties, was that religious bigotry or even religious sympathy played a serious part in its choice of policies or politicians. Isaac Butt, the first leader, was a Protestant and the son of a Protestant clergyman; William Shaw was not only a Protestant, but had been a Nonconformist clergyman; and Parnell was a Protestant, and a pretty strong one too. When we were travelling to Galway on the mission of forcing upon the constituency a hated candidate, Captain O'Shea, in order to close his mouth as to the relations between Parnell and his wife—not a very appropriate occasion for the discussion of religious views—Parnell said to me emphatically: "I will die in the religion in which I was brought up", which was that of the Church of Ireland, kindred in faith to the Anglican Church. I was rather surprised, for on previous occasions he had expressed strong agnostic views—adultery has some strange results.

William Shaw, then, was apparently quite certain of re-election. It was in that expectation that I started to walk to the Mansion House. My companions, if I remember rightly, were the late Mr. John Barry and Mr. Timothy Healy, though he was not yet a Member of Parliament. I think I was the first who suggested that we should propose Parnell. Healy, with his eager temperament and his then blind worship of Parnell, and John Barry, who had belonged to the extremists' section of Irish Nationalism for many years—he had been, in fact, a member of the Supreme Council, the secret body that governed the Fenians of the time—were, of course, at once enthusiastic. We met Parnell on the way to the City Hall. He did not give us any encouragement, seemed rather taken aback by the proposal, and rather favoured the nomination of Justin M'Carthy as a compromise between Shaw and himself. This was the state of things when we entered the City Hall; nothing was yet decided, and the supporters of Parnell were rather timorous as to the result of their nominating the chief they wanted.

We had an eager debate, in which, partly owing to that severe training as an impromptu speaker to which I have already alluded, and in the midst of men as yet too inexperienced and, therefore, too shy to speak, I was allowed to make one of the first and most pronounced speeches in

Parnell's favour. The men around him were nearly all unknown to me, and I to them. One of them I disliked on the spot—I came to admire and love him very soon after—because he wore a green tie, and I had always a horror—partly, I dare say, from my London training—of any of these public manifestations of political opinion. I wore a red tie usually, just as Sir Charles Dilke did in his early days, not as an expression of political opinion, but because I thought it suited my complexion; but I gave it up when Mr. Ramsay MacDonald in the Lobby one day half-laughingly welcomed my wearing of the tie as a symptom of sound Labour opinion.

Two members especially attracted my notice at this eventful meeting: one was a very tall, vivid old man, with a face more leonine than I have ever seen. He wore a long white beard; he had high cheek-bones, a narrow face, eyes that even in old age seemed to blaze; he will reappear in these pages. His name was The O'Gorman Mahon, and he carried with him the magic of a great past. Here amongst these youngsters new to politics and even to life was a man who had stood by the side of Daniel O'Connell in the great fight for Catholic Emancipation up to 1829, when the cause was won. He had figured in a thousand stories of challenges and duels—not mock-heroic duels, but duels with loaded pistols. He had since done strange things as an impromptu Admiral or General in the revolutionary politics of South America, and now, in the glorious and still virile sunset of his life, had come back after an absence of more than a quarter of a century to his own country and to its new fights.

Parnell elected Leader, May 17, 1880.

Beside him, for he was his colleague in the representation of County Clare, sat a man of a very different type.

Poor old O'Gorman Mahon, from that day to the day of his death, wore the same suit of a shabby tweed with the rather glaring colours of a Scotch plaid. But this other man stood out from all his colleagues as the one well-dressed man in the place. He was a real dandy, though a tasteful one. His face and expression were in harmony with his clothes; he had a round, placid countenance, with the mutton-chop whiskers then almost universal; he wore what used to be called a Prince Albert coat; his face was a little puffy and a little pale, and his expression was somewhat impassive. He gave me at once the impression of a man who had "lived", and had just come direct from the enjoyments of a club in St. James's. As a matter of fact, he was an ex-Hussar officer. His name, I learned, was Captain O'Shea. How little any of us, least of all Parnell himself, then realized, or could have realized, what a tremendous part he was to play in the future of Parnell and of Ireland! It is worth noting that O'Shea was one of those who supported Parnell for the leadership. It is ironical that Parnell gave this as one of his defences of O'Shea when, later on, he was thrusting him on the people of Galway.

The vote came at last; it was a surprise to most people. Parnell was elected, and by a fair majority—23 votes to 18. The chair had been temporarily occupied by Mr. Edmund Dwyer Gray, a great power in the Irish movement as proprietor of the chief Nationalist organ of the party, the *Freeman's Journal*. He, by the way, was up to that time a very strong opponent of Parnell. He belonged to the Whig tradition, was a man of clear and somewhat cynical judgment, had been a devoted follower of Isaac Butt, and held the then not uncommon view of Parnell that he was a somewhat shallow and untrustworthy fanatic.

After the election there came an adjournment for luncheon. Immediately afterwards, slowly, reluctantly, and with an abashed look, Parnell took the chairmanship of the meeting, and his great career as a leader began thus modestly.

I return to myself. These meetings in Dublin had at once rushed me to the front in my Party, and, on the reputation of a few not unsuccessful speeches I made in the House of Commons soon afterwards, I became one of the Party spokesmen. Afterwards I was hated, distrusted, covered with a Niagara of vituperation from the organs of every kind of opinion—Liberal as fiercely as Tory—sometimes I was shouted down; but I had made my footing.

This was all very gratifying, though I think I may say not unduly so. What advance I have made in political and Parliamentary life was always valued more by my friends than by myself. But still, there was this paradox of destiny within a few weeks—a nameless and penniless journalist playing a prominent part in one of the great Parliamentary conflicts of the age.

The question, however, still remained: how was I to make my living? This ate into my heart, and my friends who had known me in my pre-Parliamentary days noticed the deep depression which hung over my spirits, and made absent-minded and silent one who is not a silent man when in normal spirits. It was my realization of all the perils and disrepute and hunger which lay before a man who had nothing but journalism to live upon, and who had already foreseen the banging of the doors of every journal in his face. This immediate and most difficult problem received a rapid and unexpected solution, and one that by a stroke of luck was to overcome the immediate difficulty for me.

Morley edits "Pall Mall Gazette", May 1880

An old Scottish friend and colleague of mine gave up suddenly his position as the descriptive writer of Parliamentary proceedings for the *Scotsman*. He recommended me as his successor, and I was appointed, but I held the job for only a week or two. One of the things that synchronized with the General Election was the purchase of the *Pall Mall Gazette* by Mr. H. Yates Thompson, and his selection of Mr. John Morley as its editor. I had never seen Mr. Morley, but I had already had some correspondence with him. He had rejected, for the *Fortnightly Review*, an article of mine which pleaded the cause of Irish Home Rule, and illustrated its pleas with the struggle of Poland. Morley dismissed my allusions to the then desperate hopes of that country as "moonshine", and rejected—very properly, I daresay—my article as rhetorical rather than practical.

The memory of that rebuff did not daunt me. I wrote to Mr. Morley, and proposed that I should get the appointment of Parliamentary chronicler. To my surprise I received a summons to the *Pall Mall Gazette* office in Northumberland Street; met there Mr. Yates Thompson and Mr. Morley; was appointed, and received what to me then was the princely salary of £12 a week, with, above all, certainty of work and income for an indefinite time.

The experiment proved very satisfactory to both sides; it was hard work for me, and had to be done under tremendous difficulties, as will presently be seen. I was one of the most indefatigable Members of the House of Commons, speaking in season and out of season, leading or following in scenes of violence, embroiled in all-night sittings, and in all the other tremendous drudgery as well as excitement of the times. And when it was all over—

sometimes in the midst of it—I had to sit down and write my chronicle. With the characteristic disinclination of a journalist to begin one moment too soon, I usually put off my article till midnight, when a large dish of tea in the tea-room gave me a renewal of clearness of mind and of activity. Sometimes I did not begin until later than that.

I lived for a while at the Westminster Palace Hotel, in Victoria Street, so as to be always close to that great battle-ground in which I was taking so prominent a part, through the long watches by night as well as by day. At four o'clock on many a morning I went into the room which was at that angle of the hotel which faced Westminster, and there, a lonely figure and amid the silence, while the hundreds of occupants of the hotel were asleep, I wrote for a couple of hours, and had my article in the *Pall Mall* office by six or seven o'clock. I did not use the typewriter in those days. It was not a very easy article to write. It had to be descriptive and it had to be dramatic; but it had always to assume an air of an impartial though picturesque chronicle. I succeeded so well that, though the article excited a great deal of attention, its authorship remained a secret.

The House of Commons in which I started found itself in a very unfortunate position. As Lord Beaconsfield had not resigned till the General Election was over, the appointment of the new Ministers had to be postponed till after the meeting of Parliament. The appointment of the Ministers involved their re-election, and in the meantime their absence from Parliament.

Lord Beaconsfield resigns, April 21, 1880

I need not go into the tangled story of intrigue which was organized by many forces to keep Gladstone out of the Premiership. Lord Oxford published some time before his death a letter of the late Sir William Harcourt in which the possibility of Gladstone's becoming Premier was dismissed with contumely. Stories were current in London society as to pronouncements even more vigorous against Gladstone. The Queen, as has since been revealed, was violently opposed to the Premiership of Gladstone. The *Daily News* had then as editor a very brilliant and very cynical and rather saturnine figure in the late Mr. Frank Hill. He was a Gladstonian, and when Harcourt, with his usual somewhat provocative self-confidence, proclaimed to Hill that he knew several men who would refuse to serve under Gladstone, Hill drily replied that the noughts might revolt against the figure one, but could not get on without it—which was a humorous but true description of the situation. Gladstone had conducted almost alone the tremendous campaign against Disraeli. Gladstone had won the victory and become the idol of the democracy, and he was the inevitable head of the new Government.

The absence of Gladstone and all the other Ministers had left the House of Commons without a leader. The only man of serious Ministerial position was Sir Charles Dilke, who had accepted the office of Under-Secretary for Foreign Affairs. His acceptance of this office was partly inspired by his desire to pave the way for the entrance into the Cabinet of his friend and fellow-Radical, Mr. Chamberlain, who had become a member of the Cabinet as President of the Board of Trade—tremendous, and it was held in many quarters dangerous, promotion for a man who had avowed Republican leanings, and had actually advocated Irish Home Rule when every Liberal, including John Morley, was still dismissing it as an impracticable dream. Sir Charles Dilke might have assumed the leadership, but he would have had to shove Lord Richard Grosvenor out of the way. But Lord Richard Grosvenor was the Chief Party Whip, a position which gives authority in exceptional circumstances. I never enjoyed the personal acquaintance of Lord Richard Grosvenor, but all I have ever heard of him makes me believe that he was a thoroughly honest and high-minded man, and, above all, that he was the most loyal of supporters to his chief.

But he had no Parliamentary gifts, and he was during those days of a Ministerial interregnum faced with difficult problems that required both dexterity and Parliamentary promptitude. When things were in an impossible tangle, Lord Richard Grosvenor's solution was to move the adjournment of the House, which put an end to all further debate, and dismissed the House of Commons, laughing but impotent, and relieved.

The New Parliament, April 29, 1880

Now let me get back to the House of Commons itself and the first impressions it made upon me. I have already compared it to a restless and changing sea; I add a somewhat different and apparently incongruous figure—shall I compare it to a chess-board? The game has not begun, but the pieces are on the board and soon they will be brought into constant and even violent action. When you took your first look at the new House after it had settled down from the schoolboy pranks of the swearing-in, you might be struck with the tameness of its appearance. You could not help noticing, of course, the generally joyful swagger of the Liberals, flushed with their new and triumphant victory.

There were many palpable Nonconformists among them, and the long hair which some of them affected and their very serious, not to say fanatical, expression gave me the idea of how formidable a body they would be in the coming struggle. I still remember that one of the members who gave me this impression was Powell Williams, a very decent fellow, but not a fanatic except as a very faithful, and indeed servile, supporter of Mr. Chamberlain—as, indeed, were all the Members for Birmingham, with the exception of Jesse Collings, and he fell ultimately under the same spell.

And now there is the House of Commons as it was at the beginning of its career. Those unacquainted with the ups and downs, the unexpectedness, the confusion of every House of Commons would have prophesied for it a continuous career of triumphant and unbroken success. The Ministry had then an immense majority of a hundred in the lobbies; it had come fresh from a country exasperated beyond all patience with its predecessors and their innumerable follies, not to say crimes; it had the loyalty of most of the followers of Gladstone, who at this period were almost blindly devoted; and, above all, it had Gladstone.

No description of the Parliament of 1880 and of subsequent Parliaments would be true to the facts if it did not put in the forefront the immense power of Gladstone. Literally, even when in hopeless opposition, he dominated the assembly, and his domination was physical as well as mental. Be the House ever so full, however many good-looking men in face and figure there might be in it, Gladstone physically, with the beauty and the impressiveness of his face and figure, stood out different from and above them all. He had, in the first place, an immense head, the full size of which, of course, was brought out more by the fact that by 1880 he was very nearly bald, and the head was large both in front and at the back; so that, if size of head meant corresponding size of brain, Gladstone's head could have easily taken the first prize. As to which I may here insert a curious little anecdote told me by the late Mr. M'Ewan, a great and wealthy Edinburgh brewer, who was for some years a member for his native city—Mrs. Ronald Greville, known to this generation as one of the greatest London hostesses, is his stepdaughter. He was a daring, plain-spoken man, and once, meeting Mr. Gladstone, was so free from awe, even of that awe-inspiring man, that he told him that he had first seen him many years before at an Anglican meeting in Scotland, and that frankly he was rather disappointed then by his physical appearance, and, above all, by the smallness of his head—which was in great contrast with its splendid magnitude of this later day. Gladstone not only took the somewhat bold statement with good-humour, but said: "You were quite right; my head was then small"; and he revealed the curious fact that his head had, as life went on, steadily increased in size and that he had to get his hatter to increase, by at least two inches, the size of his hat.

Gladstone in 1880, *aet.* 71

The next remarkable thing in the appearance of Gladstone was his extraordinary eyes; they were large, black, and flashing; sometimes there came into them a look that was almost wild. As is known, he took a long walk every day, and this had become with him so great a habit that—as he told me himself—when he was Chancellor of the Exchequer and was working fifteen to sixteen hours a day, he would still walk home, and, if it were raining, he would take a hansom, change into waterproof clothes, and still take his usual amount of walking exercise. The blackness and the brightness of the eyes were brought into greater relief by the almost deadly pallor of his complexion. The nose might appear to be a little too large, but, on the other hand, it seemed to be quite in symmetry with the massive countenance and head. The chin was large.

Similarly with the figure: he had broad shoulders, a deep chest; he walked very erect even to almost his latest days. I have been told by some of his intimate associates that the legs were not perfectly shaped, that there was even a slight approach to knock-knees. I never observed it myself, but whether that be so or not, as he walked up the floor of the House he seemed to be enveloped by a great solitude, so unmistakably did he stand out from all the figures around him. I must add to this description of his extreme physical gifts the wonderful quality of his voice. It was a powerful voice, but sweet and melodious, and it was managed as exquisitely and as faithfully as the song of a great *prima donna*. If the speech were ringing, it came to your ears almost soft by that constant change of tone which the voice displayed; it could whisper, it could thunder. As his oratory, like the best House of Commons methods, varied from indignation to light raillery, so did the tones of his voice. The gestures were all graceful—so graceful that sometimes, as I have said, you saw the legs mark a passage as well as the arms. Now and then he came to the House a bit excited, probably by some occurrence outside or in the Cabinet, or in the diplomatic correspondence, and he shouted for a few minutes, and when he shouted he became less effective than usual; but this rarely lasted for more than a few minutes, and ordinarily he had a majestic composure. I have seen many great figures in my nearly half-century of life in the House of Commons; but, with all respect to the greatest amongst them, the House of Commons without Gladstone seems to me as great a contrast as a chamber illumined by a farthing dip when the electric light has failed.

And now let us turn to his intellectual side. At this period of his career he conveyed the same impression of what might be called "over-lordship" of the whole House. He could on occasions, especially when violent attacks were made on his Government, answer with great orations in which he smote his enemies and roused his supporters to wild enthusiasm. If anything were wanting to demonstrate this supreme power of his as an orator, it was to be found in the poor show always made in such debates by Sir Stafford Northcote, the leader of the Opposition. That very estimable but rather weak man made a poor figure in the House. These defects of his incurred, and even justified, the wild exertions of the Fourth Party. As he lay crunched under Mr. Gladstone's tornado, Sir Stafford used to look a somewhat pathetic figure. Captain O'Shea—who, contrary to the general opinion, was a very clever fellow, and rather witty—summed up the effect of this constant and painful contrast between the two protagonists of the parties in saying to me once: "It is cruel; it looks like hitting a woman".

Gladstone's Budget Speeches

To these great oratorical qualities Mr. Gladstone added surpassing gifts in dealing with facts and figures, with the clauses as well as the principles of any measure for which he was responsible—for instance, in making the Budget statement. There was no nook of the vast area of things which he had to deal with that he did not picture in the Budget speech.

These powers were exhibited in another way in the session which came after this, in 1881 when he was the sponsor for the vastly complicated and intricate Land Bill which he passed through the House of Commons and afterwards into law.

Mr. Gladstone's management of the Budget debates exemplified his multifarious powers of dealing with details. Nothing in his Parliamentary career was more striking as an exhibition of that truly marvellous readiness, mastery of detail, and far-reaching patience which were among his most marked endowments. It was a subject worthy of never-failing wonder to see this Minister, loaded with all the crowding responsibilities of the Premiership, discussing the question of worts with practical brewers like Mr. Watney and Mr. Bass; the rival claims of publicly and privately made beer with farmers like Mr. Pell and Mr. Hicks; of Irish and Scotch whisky with Mr. O'Sullivan; specific gravity with Mr. Wiggin, an accomplished chemist; the currency with Mr. Hubbard, a past master of finance; licences wholesale and retail with Mr. Callan, as representative of the publicans. The Budget Bill is a document of portentous length—to the ordinary eye as lacking in interest as *Bradshaw's Railway Guide*, and to the unfinancial mind as devoid of significance as the columns of the Money Market. But every line, it need scarcely be said, contains some provision a change in which might reduce or increase by millions the interest of some of the many national industries. It was marvellous to watch this greatest of Chancellors of the Exchequer as, with this portentous volume of the Budget in his hand, he, hour after hour, in the sweltering and even trying atmosphere of the House of Commons, followed every amendment, rejected or accepted every suggestion, and with his own hand marked in with his pen every alteration, from the omission of a clause to the change of "the" to "an".

I have already said, that after a very short experience of this splendid and apparently united and invulnerable army behind Mr. Gladstone, there came almost immediately that disintegration of Parliamentary forces which party conflict and powerful personalities are able to bring, and these forces came into play almost in the first hour after the Parliament was opened. The silent pieces—I revert to my simile of the chess-board—were rushed at once into the activity and the passion of the game; and foremost of the new combatants was Lord Randolph Churchill.

Lord Randolph Churchill, 1849–1895

Lord Randolph Churchill, confronting the new House of Commons, realized that his hour as a Parliamentary genius had come. His face had become familiar to me from my old place in the Press Gallery, for he was a Member of the Parliament of 1874. He played an eccentric rather than a promising part in that Parliament, and gave promise of eccentricity, impudence, and courage rather than of serious ability. He had already, however, shown that he was daring, and no respecter of persons. His father, until 1880, was Lord-Lieutenant of Ireland—a very dexterous, very handsome, and very conciliatory man. The small world of Dublin was moved to its depths by a speech of his unaccountable son, which somehow or other seemed to indicate a certain sympathy with the young Irishmen, like Parnell, who were then beginning the revolution that was to sweep so many things away from the old Ireland. Lord Randolph had also scandalized people by making a speech in the House of Commons in which he denounced a measure by the Government of which he was supposed to be a supporter and of which his father was a member. At mere denunciation he did not stop, but referred pointedly to "the nonentities with double-barrelled names" who were responsible for such legislation.

The responsible Minister was Mr. Sclater-Booth, a very respectable man, with a large body and a large face both of which suggested pomposity; his mantling cheeks were a response to the audacious youngster's unexpected attack. The impression that Lord Randolph Churchill first made on me was that he was a young man of fashion rather than a serious politician. He was very well dressed—indeed, almost over-dressed; he wore, if I remember rightly, a frock coat, but it was not in the sombre black then of almost universal wear, but of a beautiful blue. His shirts were always coloured, and what added to this appearance of dandyism was the amount of jewellery he wore. I remember very distinctly a ring which was American and not English in shape, for it was in the form of a Maltese cross, and it was set with brilliant stones. Mr. Winston Churchill recently showed me on his own hand a ring that had belonged to his father; but that was small and simple and not the ring I saw, which was of unusual shape and glitter. It was the shape that was affected a good deal at that period by American gentlemen and ladies, and I took it for granted that it was a present from the beautiful American bride whom Lord Randolph had married a short time before.

His moustache was long, and curled up a little at the ends, a little like the moustache which became the fashion in Germany in the days of the ex-Kaiser. The most remarkable feature of the face, however, were the eyes; they were large, bright, challenging, protuberant. It was the shape of the eyes and of the moustache that suggested to the caricaturists of the period to represent Lord Randolph very often as a King Charles spaniel—or a Pekingese.

There was another peculiarity of the face which I immediately observed, and which accounted for much that happened afterwards. He had a most peculiar complexion, not white, not red, but rather a mahogany-brown. The idea occurred to me even thus early that it was the complexion of a man of imperfect health. The figure was slight and very alert, and just a little over the middle height. Altogether, he looked rather like an eager, impudent, self-assertive boy. If one wanted to be severe and prejudiced, one might, looking at him at the time, have regarded him rather as belonging to the frivolous young men of the period, who loved a rat fight and were more at home in the stalls of the Gaiety than in the councils of the mighty.

I assume that during the years when his position as a supporter of an omnipotent Ministry left little for him or any other private member to do beyond these occasional wild excursions to which I have alluded, his mind must have been forecasting the day when events would enable him to play a larger part in the political life of his country, and open up to him a useful and brilliant career as a great Parliamentary figure. It will be seen before long that his forecastings of future eminence were more than justified, and that the eminence came not slowly but with a rush, and was fully deserved.

Sir John Gorst, 1835–1911

He had by this time two faithful friends who had evidently made a compact to work with him. The first and more important of these was Mr. John Gorst, as he then was. Gorst was, and looked, the family lawyer. Cold as ice in manner and in mind, he had had considerable training as organizer of the Tory Party in close association with Lord Beaconsfield, his chief. He spoke always in frigid tones; but he was always, as we say, on the spot. He went right to the heart of his subject and to the heart of his opponents, so that every sentence uttered in this cold voice was a barbed and poisoned arrow. He remained imperturbable amid the hubbub that his incisive rhetoric created. His vigilance was marvellous, and there was not an opportunity of criticizing or embarrassing or goading the Ministers upon which he did not promptly seize. In many respects, while Churchill was the shouting champion, this cold, self-possessed, experienced man of the world appeared to be the real inspiring brain of the Churchill group.

The third member was quite a different type. Sir Henry Drummond Wolff was the son of a missionary, originally Jewish by birth and creed, but in course of time an ardent Christian and a highly popular and esteemed missionary, who also made a brilliant marriage with a daughter of the great Walpole family. Before his entrance into Parliament, Sir Henry had had considerable experience in diplomacy, knew a great deal of many parts of the world, and especially of the East, which in the previous six years had been the battle-ground between Gladstone and Disraeli. He had not much gift of speech, but he was alert, with a good deal of knowledge, and now and then—though the bulbous blue, laughing eyes rather denoted his essential good-humour—he could also throw his barbed arrow at a Minister. I once saw him make Mr. John Bright bitterly angry by one of these barbed arrows.

To these two supporting Lord Randolph, there was added now and then a very different and a very important third. I believe Mr. Balfour (as he then was) has disclaimed ever being a member of the Fourth Party, but he was a semi-detached member off and on for years. He had none of the recklessness of the other three; he was rather bound to the peace by the fact that his uncle, the Marquess of Salisbury, was leader of his party, and that Sir Stafford Northcote, the then leader in the House of Commons, was to a large extent the mouthpiece of his relative. Churchill always struck one as like that character in one of Balzac's novels who seemed to care for nothing in the world, not for God nor man, reckless of all things except his own devouring ambitions and his determined resolve to dominate his fellow-men. Mr. Balfour was never made of such material.

Lord Randolph and the "Fourth Party"

With the earliest incidents in the new House of Commons, and especially in that unsteered course it was following in the absence of its leaders at their bye-elections, Lord Randolph saw and seized his great opportunity. One of his first acts was significant of what followed. Those acquainted with the inner life of the House of Commons will know that there is not a bit of furniture in it that has not its history and significance. The gangway, for instance, which breaks the continuity of the benches on both sides of the House, used to mark a man's political views. Members of the more moderate type sat above the gangway, especially on the Liberal side; those who desired to be regarded as more extreme, or belonged to the Radical section of the mixed Liberal Party of that period, took their seats below the gangway. The front benches, of course, were occupied by the Ministers and the ex-Ministers; but there was one spot, the first seat below the gangway on the Opposition side, which was a sort of Parliamentary Alsatia, marked out by tradition as the ideal position for that type of critic of the Government who was vehement, unsparing, reckless.

There was some rivalry between the self-assertive Irish Members and Lord Randolph Churchill for this favourite seat, but in the end Lord Randolph's claim was universally accepted. For five long years, every night, every day, there was directed on the Treasury Bench, and especially on Mr. Gladstone, the fire of Lord Randolph and his friends from this favoured spot. The attacks were ceaseless; sometimes clever, sometimes effective, sometimes frivolous, but the fusillade never stopped. At first Churchill and his fellows-in-arms were laughed at; afterwards they created impatience and disapproval. The disproportion between the smallness of their number and the abundance of their activities made their attacks still more resented. An Irish Member, named Callan, invented for them a nickname which stuck—the Fourth Party—an allusion to their number rather than their position; and a witty lady borrowed from the vocabulary of Oscar Wilde the "Two Two Party".

What helped to make the Fourth Party was the hopelessness of the official Conservative leader, Sir Stafford Northcote. His appearance, with his long beard, his big glasses, behind which peered rather dim eyes, suggested the veneration due to lucid and respectable old age rather than the allegiance that would have been given to a provocative and prompt leader who could confront that towering Titan who was then Prime Minister and leader of the House of Commons.

Another thing which helped the Fourth Party was that, for some months after the meeting of the new House of Commons, the ordinary leaders of the Tory Opposition seemed to have gone on strike. Some said they had been tired out by their long years as hard-worked Ministers under the rule of Beaconsfield; others thought that they still resented the outburst of popular condemnation with which they had been hurled from office. Anyhow, the front Opposition bench was usually empty except for Sir Stafford Northcote.

A little anecdote of the period will illustrate the relations between Sir Stafford and his unruly followers. Perhaps on account of his long beard, these disrespectful youngsters knew Sir Stafford Northcote by the nickname of "The Goat". One night he was invited to dine at Lord

Randolph Churchill's neat little house in St. James's Place, where the charm, the disturbing beauty, and the keen wit of his American wife added to the attractiveness of these little gatherings. In front of the place where Sir Stafford was seated was a bit of china in the shape of a goat.

Lord Randolph in 1880, *aet.* 31

At this time of Lord Randolph's life, there was little evidence, beyond the hard work in the House of Commons, of his putting too severe a strain on a constitution that I had already come to regard as frail. Now and then, however, he appeared frankly nervous, especially when he stood up to face the awe-inspiring eyes of Gladstone, a confrontation made the more nerve-racking by the fact that there intervened but a few yards between his seat below the gangway and Mr. Gladstone on the Treasury Bench. One day while he was hammering away at Gladstone, he rather shocked those who heard it by saying, "Wolff, bring me a glass of brandy", which Drummond Wolff immediately proceeded to do.

Lord Randolph and Labouchere were the first men I ever met who were the slaves of the cigarette. Neither one nor the other seemed to be able to remain in his seat in the House more than half an hour or so at a time, before he was off to one of the smoking-rooms with a cigarette in his mouth. I remember, as one of the things that struck me, that Lord Randolph had a cigarette-holder with a piece of jewellery in it, altogether like the cigarette-holder that a devoted and especially an American wife would present to her husband.

Anticipating some years later on, when we arrive at the time that misfortunes began to gather around his head, Lord Randolph impressed my mind with the belief that his nervous system could easily be broken down. There came a restlessness, and even a look of terror, into those great, protuberant eyes of his. His resignation from the Government brought him into temporary, if unavowed, good relations with us of the Irish Party. A Tory Government was in power, and he had every willingness either to conquer a place in it again or to destroy it.

I was stupid enough one day, after his tragic resignation, to take a seat by his side in one of the smoke-rooms of the House of Commons, and to suggest something in which he could co-operate with us of the Irish Party. I was surprised, even shocked, by the look of something like terror that came into his eyes, and the feverish and anxious way in which he looked around to see if there were any of his enemies and ours looking on. And, of course, as will be seen later in the story, when he found himself in the last impossible desperate position, the wearied brain and the never-strong nervous system broke down, and madness was the dark ending.

And now I come to the episode which gave Lord Randolph and the Fourth Party their first great opportunity. It was after nearly all the Members had taken the oath and picked out their seats, when there came the incident which all had dimly anticipated.

Charles Bradlaugh, 1833–1891

The benches were crowded with these young, eager new Members; but the floor was empty, and then, walking up this empty floor was a strange figure of a man who threatened to create something like a violent and, as the majority thought, fatal break with the past. As the House gazed at this strange, new, menacing figure, everybody was conscious that he startlingly looked the part. I had seen Bradlaugh several times before; I had always felt something like a shudder as I realized how lonely he looked in a world that hated and dreaded him. He had fine height, a great frame, a deep chest, broad shoulders; even his limbs suggested the masculine and powerful athlete. In the course of a trying and rather poverty-stricken youth he had enlisted, and had spent some time as a private in the Army; and he retained still some marks of the man who had been a soldier.

The face was as striking, as formidable, and, to those who hated and distrusted him, as menacing and as odious as the powerful body. Some of my *dramatis personae,* as I have said, seem to come out of the pages of French literature; Bradlaugh seemed to come direct from the French Revolution. The Revolutionary leader to whom he seemed to me to have the closest resemblance, physically as well as mentally, was Danton. There was the same short, abruptly ending nose, its abrupt shortness aggravated by the long upper lip. The eyes were very striking—large, brilliant, with quick changes of expression; when he was angry they became menacing: the eyes of a man who in a revolutionary epoch would send another, or go himself, to be guillotined. And this face, clean-shaven, brought into relief the immense, powerful, combative jaw. Before Mr. Bradlaugh had entered the House he had written many things, which now supplied his enemies with ammunition against him. He had published a vehement pamphlet on the history of the House of Brunswick, but perhaps what created most prejudice against him was his association with Mrs. Besant in defending their publication of a pamphlet under the title, "Fruits of Philosophy", by an American named Knowlton.

The epoch of which I am writing had not yet heard the name of Marie Stopes. The doctrines which she has set forth were then practically new and were held in abhorrence by the public opinion of the time, so that Mr. Bradlaugh came to the House covered with the odium of disloyalty and the moral uncleanness of birth control. Furthermore, though Mr. Bradlaugh at the time was rarely, if ever, reported in the daily papers, it was well known that more than once when interrupted by rowdies who threatened him, he had with his own strong arm cleared the hall and defended his rights.

These were among the many causes that accounted for the fierce hostility to Bradlaugh; but, after all, the underlying explanation was party passion, and what at the moment seemed to be party interest. An additional reason was that there were among the assailants of Bradlaugh some remarkable personalities who saw in the struggle over his rights an excellent opportunity for pushing their own Parliamentary fortunes. The first of these, to be sure, were the members of the Fourth Party. It would be insulting the intelligence of my readers if I suggested that any of the three members of the Fourth Party—Lord Randolph Churchill, Mr. Gorst, or Sir Henry Drummond Wolff—was inspired by profound religious feelings. Lord Randolph, so to speak, was a man about town; Gorst was a sceptic and a cynic; Wolff was the son of a converted Jew, and had the man-of-the-worldliness of one who had lived much abroad in the exercise of diplomacy.

Bradlaugh's Claim to affirm, May 3, 1880

There was a fourth among the most eloquent assailants of Mr. Bradlaugh. I remember still the surprise with which I heard the ringing cheers with which a member of my despised and detested Party was received by the most orthodox Tories, as, in vehement language, Frank Hugh O'Donnell defended the sacred rights of Christianity against the grim assailant who stood at the Bar claiming to take the seat to which a constituency had elected him in full knowledge of his religious opinions. But so it was, and among the loudest of the supporters of O'Donnell was Mr. Chaplin, temporarily devoting to his religion the time he could spare from his bets and his stable.

As to O'Donnell, I was not surprised. Here, again, was a figure from Balzac: one of the self-confident adventurers, like Lucien de Rubempré, who regarded life as a struggle between the world and his will to succeed. As I have already told, O'Donnell and I were at College together, and there as a young man he proclaimed his views of life. He had a handsome but very provocative physique and manner. A great athlete with a powerful frame, he rather provoked criticism by the manner in which he pushed out his chest. His air of arrogance found its climax in a single eye-glass which he always wore, and which he handled with dexterity; this arrogance of appearance and manner added enormously to the effectiveness and the provocativeness of his defiant and often very effective speeches.

Never did I know a man who started life apparently with such a determination and inner certainty that he was going to win. One day, as boys, we were discussing our future—we were equally penniless at the time; his father, a fine old gentleman, was a ranker who had held a commission and was in retirement on a pension—and when I wondered what we might be at forty, putting out his chest he replied that at that age he would be the leader of a political party.

He followed me to London, and, after the manner of

Irishmen, who are usually good to each other, I gave him a share of my bed and my two small rooms, but ultimately he took the single room in the attic above mine. When I returned to my room from my office, I usually found him there. At that period, as I have already told, part of my business was to read the French and German papers. Among these was the *Pester Lloyd*, a paper which, though published in Budapest, the capital of Hungary, was printed in the German language. In its columns I found one day a long obituary notice of a man called Eötvös. I had never heard of or seen the name before. The article in the *Pester Lloyd* gave a full account of the man and his career. I passed it over to O'Donnell, who could read German as well as I, and recommended him to make a free translation of it and then send it to the *Spectator*. It was just the kind of article that would suit a paper whose foible at that time was omniscience. The article was accepted. If I had had a little more regard to my own interest, I would have sent such an article there myself; it would have helped to give me a good footing in the Press, and might also, perhaps, have helped me to avoid that long period of misery and unemployment which I have already described. In a way it became at once the making of O'Donnell.

Soon after, he got an order for an article from the *Tablet*, a great Catholic weekly; and then somehow or other he managed to get into the office of the *Morning Post*, which then, as now, was a strongly Conservative journal. He had my papers from the *Daily Telegraph* office at his disposal, and he was able to become an authority on Continental politics. The paper was somewhat carelessly edited at the time, and O'Donnell, in describing the struggles for autonomy of the Yugo-Slavs and the Czecho-Slovaks—names then unknown in England—was able to deal many an indirect blow for Irish autonomy, while the fine Tory proprietor of the *Morning Post* and his editor remained quite unconscious of the use that was being made of their paper. Now and then he supplied material to Parnell, who was ignorant of any politics outside Ireland. It was the part that he was thus able to play in inspiring Parnell that really led to the miserable downfall in which his career ended. He never could get rid of the idea that it was he who had created Parnell, and in this way he became in secret the vindictive and jealous enemy of his chief. He was to learn in time that conflict with Parnell was a losing and fatal struggle.

Mr. Newdegate: a Hot-gospeller

Another figure in the Bradlaugh struggle I must describe. Mr. C. N. Newdegate was a man who would be at the present time incredible. He had made himself notorious for many years by a bitterness of spirit against the Catholics which had made him more or less a laughing-stock; but there was something about the laughing-stock that commanded respect, especially as he looked the part so completely. He was a tallish, thin man, all black; his hair was black, his short beard black, his clothes always black, his expression always black. Nobody ever listened to him, or, if they stopped to listen, they remained only to laugh. A singular incident connected with him will indicate his position at the time. There was in the Press Gallery a very respected chief of the reporting staff of one of the daily papers. He rarely went into the reporters' box himself; it was his business to select the men of his staff to do the job. Whenever, however, Mr. Newdegate got up, this man, ordinarily the most composed and leisurely of fellows, would be seen to rush to one of the reporters' boxes, and as long as Mr. Newdegate was speaking, he hammered away at his shorthand. The explanation was that Mr. Newdegate's harangues found hospitality in the columns of some weekly—the name of which, I think, was the *Rock*—which was so ultra-Protestant that the hot-gospelling of his speeches supplied the kind of stuff they wanted. Let me add, to try and complete the picture, that, though he never spoke to any of the Irish Members, the grim face now and then relaxed to something approaching a smile as he listened to the dithyrambics of Frank O'Donnell or others of the Irish Party who joined him in the denunciation of Bradlaugh.

Mr. Newdegate's pursuit of Mr. Bradlaugh never ended. He organized legal action after action, which harassed and impoverished poor Bradlaugh. It was one of the secret tragedies of Mr. Bradlaugh's life that he was rarely out of the courts, and that legal costs mounted and mounted. During most of his life he was in a hopeless financial position, weighed down by a gigantic burden of debt which even the generous help of his friends rarely brought down to a final balance.

The scenes towards the close of the Bradlaugh struggle were the bitterest of them all, when again and again the bigots on all sides—some of them on the Liberal side—gave a majority against him. Bright had made fine pleas for religious tolerance, though he himself was archaically orthodox. Mr. Gladstone was even finer, considering his intense orthodoxy, though it must have been a task which he did not find at all to his taste; but he performed it, and I remember one oration in particular, which for dignity and persuasiveness he never excelled. I may remark, on this famous oration, that it was the last time, in my experience, that a Parliamentary orator dared to impose upon the House a long quotation from Latin. The passage was from Lucretius. It was delivered superbly, but very few understood it, and I do not think that Gladstone ever again brought a long quotation from the classics into his argument.

Labouchere Motion defeated, June 21, 1880

There was Committee after Committee on the Bradlaugh case, and finally the Committee reported that Mr. Bradlaugh might be allowed to affirm, with the qualification that the lawfulness of this act should be subject to the decision of the Law Courts. It was then that Mr. Labouchere made his first serious appearance in the House since he had re-entered it after some years of absence. The duty of defence of Mr. Bradlaugh naturally fell upon him, as colleague in the representation of Northampton. He was not quite the man to undertake the job. His face, very flushed, for the first and perhaps the last time in his Parliamentary career, betrayed his nervousness; besides, he had already established his reputation in the House by satirical rather than serious writings in his paper called *Truth*. The Opposition, anyhow, refused to take him seriously; he spoke amid a disturbing chorus of mocking laughter, and when the motion came to a division, only 230 voted for Mr. Bradlaugh, and 275 against. In the majority against Mr. Bradlaugh were many members of the Irish Party; but on the other side were a minority from that party, Parnell and myself among them.

And then once again the House was in a hopeless morass. This led to a curious piece of something like acting by Mr. Gladstone, which showed his marvellous power of finding the exact and the dramatic means to meet a situation in the House of Commons. On the day after the defeat and when the struggle was to be renewed, Mr. Gladstone took his place, as usual, on the Treasury Bench;

but two or three things were at once remarked by the House, always quick to seize the significance of things. First, he did not occupy his usual seat as Leader of the House, which is by immemorial custom immediately opposite one of the two boxes that stand on the table in front of the Speaker; and even more picturesquely did Mr. Gladstone signify his position. He came down to the House in a frock-coat, not of the usual black, but of the ultra-grey, amounting almost to cream colour. If I remember rightly, he also wore a whitish-grey tall hat: when summer came, Mr. Gladstone was the most summery in dress of all the men in the House; he might, indeed, pass for an elderly dandy. It was also remarked that he took his seat holding his walking stick in his hands, and with his gloves on. All this was intended to proclaim that, as he represented not the majority but the minority of the House, his responsibility for its future action with regard to Mr. Bradlaugh devolved not on him but on Sir Stafford Northcote, as, for the moment, the only authorized exponent of the majority of the House. This, of course, gave great scandal to the now triumphant Tories and the recalcitrant Liberals, and there were jeers and some insulting ejaculations, which Mr. Gladstone received with unperturbed smiles.

Bradlaugh expelled from the House, June 23, 1880

And now for the last scene. Refused the right to affirm, Mr. Bradlaugh fell back on his right to take the Oath. He claimed to be heard at the Bar of the House. After some delay, the right was given him. What is called the Bar of the House was brought out from the two sockets in which it reposes, and Mr. Bradlaugh was allowed to speak from behind it. The speech, according even to his enemies, was a masterpiece, dignified, calm, well reasoned—indeed, unanswerable. Neither Sir Stafford Northcote nor Mr. Gladstone would interfere, and there was nothing left for the Speaker but to inform Mr. Bradlaugh that the House had called upon him to withdraw. Mr. Bradlaugh refused to go.

Never shall I forget the painful scene that then ensued. I had seen Mr. Bradlaugh and spoken to him as he stood in the Lobby—prepared to make this tremendous challenge. Dressed as usual in a glossy black frock-coat, wearing his tall and well-polished hat, beaming all over, he looked like a triumphant and almost sleek figure. Not many minutes after this I saw the same man, with his hat off, his face distorted by passion, his shirt torn, as he was being expelled by the constables and the officers of the House. He was pushed and jostled till he was driven into Old Palace Yard. He fainted, but soon recovered. There was a dangerous moment when the large crowd that had assembled outside, and were his ardent supporters, might have, at a word from him, invaded, and perhaps scattered, the House of Commons; but Mr. Bradlaugh wisely abstained.

I will not go through the almost innumerable stages through which Bradlaugh had to pass before he was finally vindicated. The close of this, as of so many of the stormy struggles of English life, ended quietly and unexpectedly. A new Speaker had been elected in succession to Mr. Brand, in the person of Mr. Peel. Mr. Peel ruled that there was no justification for refusing the admission of Mr. Bradlaugh to the House of Commons. He thereupon took his seat, and soon was regarded as a moderate member of the House. But the struggle had undoubtedly done a great deal to weaken his health. He had an attack of erysipelas immediately after his violent expulsion from the House. He had worked with furious energy for five years arguing in law courts and going long journeys to address crowded meetings, and his comparatively early death was undoubtedly precipitated by this long and very discreditable conflict.

CHAPTER IV

The rise of the Irish Party—Root problem of the land—My elders tell me of the Famine—The Land League—Workhouse boy's rise and fall—Discarded Irish M.P. as Society favourite—Michael Davitt of the One Hand—Daniel O'Connell's "Placemen"—Keogh's treachery.

The Irish Party in 1880

THE great new real force that was to dominate the House of Commons for five years, to embarrass the new Government, and ultimately to bring that powerful Government, with the great Gladstone at its head and a majority of more than a hundred, to the dust, was the new Irish Party. It was the beginning of the Irish Revolution which ended, among other things, in the transfer of the soil of Ireland from the Norman conquerors to the Celtic owners after more than six centuries of struggle, and finally, and later on, in the bestowal on Ireland of the right of self-government. It speaks strongly of the utter ignorance of Irish conditions which then prevailed, even among many Liberal politicians, that this new Party at first did not attract much attention: it was regarded for a while as almost negligible. Its very existence, indeed, and, above all, its formidable strength, were as much, if not more, a surprise to Mr. Gladstone than to anybody else in the ranks of the Ministry.

Mr. Gladstone had, to a certain extent, "a single-track mind", to use the phrase of the late President Wilson. For years he had bent all his energies, all his reading, all his speeches, to his tremendous campaign against the Eastern policy of Lord Beaconsfield. He himself afterwards confessed that during this period he had practically forgotten Ireland. If Irish politics are full of thunder-claps, it must be largely put down to this fundamental error in the English mind of ignoring Irish appeals and Irish conditions till they are thrust upon English attention with violence. Perhaps there was a further reason for this ignoring of the young men that were serving under Parnell, in the fact that the vote which substituted Parnell for Shaw as leader of the Party had resulted in a division of the Home Rule forces: more than half of the whole strength of the members sat on the Ministerial side of the House, thereby proclaiming their allegiance to Mr. Gladstone and his Ministry.

At our first meeting in the Mansion House in Dublin, where we had elected Parnell as our leader, we had an animated discussion on the question of where we should choose our seats in the House of Commons—a debate in which I also took part—and by the Parnellites it was resolved that the only consistent course for us to adopt was to sit on the Opposition side of the House as a proclamation of our equal independence of all English political parties, and our permanent opposition to them all until Home Rule sent us back to a Parliament in Dublin. A few of us realized how far this determination was to bring us later on, but I was not one of those. I had worked with Liberals for many years, especially because of my strong views in favour of Gladstone's campaign for the rescue of the Eastern Christians from the yoke of massacre and tyranny by Turkey. I regarded a large number of the Liberals as friendly to Ireland, which, indeed, they were. I remember once saying to Parnell that a speech of his would make Mr. Forster, the Chief Secretary for Ireland, unpopular, which I did not then regard as desirable. "So much the better", said Parnell, which opened up to me the curious and rather doubtful prospect of a collision with a great party which I believed, on the whole, was inclined to do justice to my country. I soon found out that I was wrong, and by a succession of steps and of events I was driven to the same conviction as that of Parnell and of many of my colleagues, that we had two special duties to perform. First, we had to destroy the section of our Party that sat on the Ministerial side as the worst kind of political enemy, the false and feeble friend; and secondly, it was our business to destroy the Gladstone Ministry. Ultimately we succeeded in both these objects, and I still think that it was not only the inevitable, but the best policy in the interest of our country. These two duties were imposed upon us, and almost at the very start of the Parliament, by the extraordinary state of things that had arisen in Ireland.

I intend in these memoirs to confine myself, so far as possible, to the proceedings and personalities of the House of Commons, referring to conditions and events in Ireland itself mainly so far as they influence and explain these proceedings. But I must make some references to the conditions in Ireland of which our Party were to carry the offspring.

The Irish Famine, 1846–1847

It would take me too far from my purpose to write at any length on the secular land problem in Ireland, and especially during the period of the old Irish Famine, from 1846 onwards. I dealt with the subject at length in an early book of mine called *The Parnell Movement*. I give extracts from that book about the Irish Famine of 1846 onwards, but I have put them in an Appendix so as not to interrupt my narrative. All I can do here is in a few and hurried sentences to get into the English mind what the Irish Famine meant to the Irishman. I was born in 1848, two years after the first year of the potato failure and of the Famine. In my boyhood there were plenty of middle-aged men who had lived through the Famine and seen it close at hand. From the stories I heard from their lips I was able to get a more vivid picture of what the Famine really meant than in all the hours I spent over the study of its events.

Here is one story told to me by a native of the county of Kerry. Passing, as a boy, with his father and mother, along the road from his native village to Tralee, the capital town of Kerry, he saw himself the corpses of a whole family; first, of the younger children, who succumbed earliest; then of the elder children; and finally of the father and mother themselves. Such tragedies were to be found on almost all the roadsides of Ireland. There was a campaign of wholesale eviction on top of the Famine. To all parts of the world the doomed race fled in their hundreds of thousands, bringing with them their half-starved and often diseased bodies. They brought a visitation of cholera to Liverpool, and a like visitation to Glasgow. Carlyle has some tremendous sentences on this last episode. Those who could scrape together the few pounds necessary to take them to the United States fled there, bringing the same stories of famished and diseased bodies: corpses lay on the sidewalks of Broadway. I heard a speech once in the town of Grand Rapids, Michigan, from an Irish-American which illustrated that epoch of Irish history. He was prosperous and a reasonable man, and he wound up his speech with a peroration in which he begged of me to give my exertions to complete that union of hearts, as it was called, which was the new policy inaugurated by Gladstone between Ireland and England; but before he got to that point he told this story. "My father and mother", he said, " and my three sisters sailed on a boat with four hundred Irish on board. By the time the boat reached New York, three hundred out of the four hundred had died, including my three sisters." The sentence has remained graven on my memory.

When Englishmen and reconciled Irishmen like myself are inclined sometimes to deplore the fanatical hatred for England of the men and women of the Irish race in America, it must always be realized that these are the memories of things that were told at the knees of their parents or grandparents. Up to a short time ago they had learnt little of English or Irish history since: they always thought of the Ireland of 1846 and of the England of 1846, two countries that have ceased to exist. I sum up with these few words the story of the Famine: in 1845 the population of Ireland was upwards of eight millions and a quarter; by the triple process of wholesale eviction, death by famine, by the coffin-ship—as many of the emigrant vessels to America came to be called—the population had decreased in less than fifty years to four millions and a half.

To realize, then, the policy to which the Parnellite Party felt themselves compelled to resort in 1880, this background in their mind must always be remembered. And the symptoms of the old Famine were already present in 1880 and in the preceding years. For three years there had been an affrighting reduction in the potato harvest, and, as in 1846, there had been a renewal of the policy of eviction. The minds of the Irish Members were haunted by the horrible spectre of the renewal of the old terrible days. They might well be forgiven if they thought that there was a fresh possibility of another and a final wreckage of the Irish population and the end of all things.

The Land League founded, *October* 21, 1879

In one Irish county, Mayo, the conditions were worse than in any other county in Ireland. It was not by accident then, that the new land movement found its root in Michael Davitt and in the county of Mayo. There used to be a familiar saying in those days that when a man of Mayo was asked where he came from, especially in America, his answer always was, "From County Mayo, God help me!" At a small town in Mayo, the first great meeting held in favour of the new land movement had met with a stern resistance from the last body from which such resistance would be expected. Dr. MacHale, the then Archbishop of Tuam, the diocese in which part of Mayo stood, had passed through most of his life as an especially ardent and extreme Nationalist, and had been called by Daniel O'Connell, who had a genius for the invention of appropriate and useful nicknames, "the Lion of the Fold of Judah". But the lion at this time was old and toothless, and under the control of younger men. These did their best to frown upon this new and extreme development, but it were as vain to try and arrest it as to stop the flow of Niagara.

Parnell, though at first a little doubtful, had ultimately grasped the significance of the new movement, and it was at a meeting in Mayo that, by an inspiration which occasionally came to him, he invented a fateful slogan. Going to this meeting he had thought over the grim tenacity with which Biggar, then his chief and almost only supporter, had carried on the obstructive warfare in the House of Commons, and the phrase came to Parnell: "Keep a firm grip of your holdings!" The slogan proved most effective. In the days of the old Famine of 1846 the peasants had walked out from their homes, as a rule, without resistance, and turned, as in the case of Davitt's parents, their weary feet towards the first port that would save them from their ruined country and enable them to start work in another. The new slogan entirely transformed this attitude. Nearly every peasant was now determined to fight for the house and the fields of himself and his ancestors.

So the new organization called the Land League was founded. Behind it was a good deal of the money that Parnell had collected in his very successful American tour. This new League, which immediately had Parnell as its chief, was able to establish branches with whirlwind activity in every town and in every village in the South of Ireland, and the members of each branch were determined to resist eviction, even at the cost of bloodshed. Thus, while Mr. Gladstone was thinking of Bulgaria and Montenegro, there had arisen in a country within a few hours of the shores of his own one of the most formidable revolutionary movements that Ireland in her long history had ever created.

The first duty, then, which fell to the Parnellite Party was to represent and transfer the spirit of this mighty revolution from the fields of Ireland to the floor of the House of Commons. At that time the Party had two small rooms, appropriate to the modesty of its financial position, in King Street, a small street long ago replaced by great public buildings, but convenient as very close to the House of Commons. Here we met immediately after the reading of the Queen's Speech, and of course our duty at once jumped to the eyes. That terrible question which was at the back of all our minds had been ignored while Ireland was panting for deliverance; a friendly Liberal Government was blind and dumb. It was at once resolved that we should force the question on the attention of the Government by proposing an amendment to the Queen's Speech. By universal consent the amendment was entrusted to Mr. John O'Connor Power, who had been a Member of the previous Parliament—one of the few who stood out from the ruck of Irish placehunters.

Workhouse Boy's Rise and Fall

I pause a moment to try and draw a portrait of this very remarkable figure. His origin was humble; he undoubtedly spent a portion of his childhood in the workhouse in the town of Ballinasloe, and his name was to be found in page after page of the books under the charge of the secretary to the guardians. It will give some idea of the fanatic devotion of the members of our Party to each other, that one of them, of whom something will be heard later on, called Matt Harris, who lived in Ballinasloe, and had been an old friend of O'Connor Power, feeling that this painful episode in the childhood of his friend might be brought up against him in an approaching election, got up one night with a razor in his hand, burgled the office of the Board of Guardians, and with his razor cut out every page that contained the name of O'Connor Power. O'Connor Power and he had in former days been associated as active members of the Fenian body. They had both largely, under the new flame of hope in Parliamentary agitation which Parnell and Biggar had created, dropped out of their old faith in revolutionary methods. Long, however, before this conversion of O'Connor Power, he had done his share as a revolutionary leader. Somehow or other he had become a house painter, and had assumed the *alias* of Flemming. Under this name he had gone from town to town in England and Scotland—often on foot, because he had not the money for railway or tram fare—addressed meetings, usually small, and enrolled men in the Fenian organization. In time, he had been detected by the authorities, and had served some months in gaol. He told me how he used to have to distribute over all the twenty-four hours the small amount of food he was allowed; if I remember rightly, he used to keep over from his supper a couple of potatoes for his breakfast. He had very great gifts of speech, and I never knew a member of our party who had a more perfect and instinctive knowledge of what was called "the tone of the House of Commons". Not by a demi-semi-quaver did he ever depart from the regular gamut of appropriate Parliamentary speech. In addition, he was a man of great courage, great self-confidence, and great force of character; but he had the tremendous defect of a very irritable and fierce temper. He had a powerful but a very ugly face, the ugliness accentuated by the marks of a severe attack in childhood of smallpox. Smallpox was in those days a mark or form of class inferiority; only the children of the very poor ever bore its traces. When O'Connor Power was in one of his fits of rage, these little marks of smallpox would become white, and his face looked ugly and ferocious.

It was this long training, spread over many years, of O'Connor Power in the rough and the smooth of Irish politics, the risks he had to run, the punishments he had undergone, his profound knowledge, his temper, which was cautious when he was not in one of his rages; his profound contempt for the ignorance and, as he thought, at the same time the insanity of Parnell, that made him from early days, after the creation of the Parnellite Party, a source of division. To add to all this, he had no profession. For a while he had managed to read up enough of history to give him the meagre job of a professor of history in a poor provincial college; he had to give this up when he went into Parliament, and I am afraid that sometimes the poor fellow, with all his brilliant abilities, his power of impressing and moving the House of Commons, found a difficulty in paying for his dinner amid all the luxury-making of the Palace of Westminster. Such were the difficulties of poor men before the days of Parliamentary salary.

The Irish Amendment, May 20, 1880

I may as well complete the sketch of his career here. He was profoundly distrusted by such men as Biggar and Egan, both intolerant and fanatical, because he had not always joined in what he regarded as the wild antics of Parnell and Biggar in the previous House of Commons. Biggar, who in addition, like most prosperous Belfast business men, had great contempt for penniless men, regarded O'Connor Power as no better than a traitor, and ultimately hounded him out of the Irish Party, inflicting on it a tremendous loss in Parliamentary spokesmen. O'Connor Power drifted over to the Liberals, stood twice as Liberal candidate, was fiercely assailed by his own countrymen as a traitor to the cause, and mainly by them was defeated. Later on, when passions were supposed to have cooled down, and when Michael Davitt, who had been one of his enemies, had been softened by natural good temper into favouring his re-admission, O'Connor Power put himself forward again and again as a candidate for entrance into his old Party. But he had made too many powerful enemies, and for the last twenty or thirty years of his life he was an uneasy ghost, haunting the National Liberal Club, with his great gifts unused and his heart broken. He had one piece of luck; he married the widow of a wealthy instrument-maker, and hunger, at least, was banished from his door. London society, with its usual ignorance of Irish character, began to take O'Connor Power to its bosom as a favourable contrast to the wild men who were then in control of the Irish Party. O'Connor Power was able to live up to this reputation of sweet reasonableness, for he had a suave manner and soothing tongue, and the pauper boy's name—to the horror and contempt of his old associates—used to appear in the list of the guests at the house of Lady Jersey and others of the then ruling *salonnières* of London.

How little they really knew the man; how little Englishmen and Englishwomen ever understand Irish character! One night after we had all risen and protested against the re-arrest of Michael Davitt, O'Connor Power retired with me to the Smoke Room, and then, with those little wells of white in his pockmarked face, and in a voice hoarse with passion, he said to me, "If I were in control of things, three of these Ministers would be dead by to-morrow". This was the old ferocity that lay behind the smooth-tongued guest of the fashionable ladies of London.

When Mr. O'Connor Power stood up to move our amendment denouncing the omission of all reference in the Queen's Speech to the Irish land problem, the first expression one saw on the faces of the members of the Government was one of unfeigned surprise. The events in Ireland ought to have prepared them for such a motion, but it was all new and strange and unwelcome to them. We made out, however, so good a case in the stories of the dreadful increase at once of the potato failure and of the evictions that we forced the Government to take action, and they consented immediately to bring in an emergency measure to suspend evictions. It was called the Irish Compensation for Disturbance Bill, and all at once the Government, elected on the issue of foreign policy, and backed by the majority of more than a hundred, found itself in the morass of a very contentious Irish Land Bill. This made an unfortunate position for the Government. They roused the passions of all their opponents. Powerful enemies in their own Party, the members of the Fourth Party, and all the representatives of the landlords' interests, in England as well as in Ireland, in the House of Lords and in the House of Commons—all these forces at once rushed into furious opposition, and the debates were prolonged and stormy. It was my first lesson in the fragility of Governments and of big Parliamentary majorities.

The Lords reject Land Bill, August 3, 1880

What made the situation worse for the Government was that they got grudging assistance from the Irish Party, though it was under pressure from them that they brought in the measure. Parnell, in that frigid and yet passionate voice of his which made men's blood run cold, denounced Mr. Forster, the then Chief Secretary for Ireland, with the quotation from Scripture: "Unstable as water thou shalt not excel!" Cursed by their enemies, and but mildly supported by the Parnellites, the Government nevertheless pushed the Bill through. It was immediately rejected by an overwhelming majority of the House of Lords—282 to 51. Among the more extreme of the Parnellites, this defeat was welcomed: the Revolution in Ireland was on its way; it was, they thought, bound ultimately to succeed—as it did. And this temporary measure might have proved only a curse in disguise, for it might cool down the Revolution, and so prevent the ultimate victory of what the Land League had now openly professed as its policy—namely, no more chaffering with rents, but the creation of a peasant proprietary no longer in the presence or under the terror of the landlord, of the rent office, of the bailiff, or of eviction.

And here I have to bring on the scene one of the most remarkable and potent personalities in modern Irish history. Michael Davitt began life with a bitter experience that to a certain extent shaped and stimulated all the subsequent actions of his life. He was born in the village of Straide, in County Mayo, where his father occupied a cottage and a small farm, earning a very scanty living from fields that belonged to the very specially barren and ungrateful soil of many parts of the county. The Davitt family had occupied the farm and the cabin for generations. Their landlord, like so many other landlords of the period, was obsessed by the idea of turning the arable land into pasture, as more profitable and less troublesome to him. The remorseless decree of eviction came to the Davitt family.

In those old days some of the desperate tenants insisted on going back, in face of the forces of the Crown and the legal rights of the landlord, into the homes from which they had been expelled. A remedy to this form of lawlessness was found by burning down the cottages. At four years of age Davitt was one of the children of the family that left Ireland for ever and turned to another country in search of a livelihood. They had to walk the miles that stood between the cottage and the port from which they were to embark, and Davitt's recollection remained vivid to the end that, as they started on this sorrowful exodus into the unknown, the last sight on which their eyes dwelt was the burning roof of the cottage of their fathers.

They had no money. Davitt stated in one of his speeches in later life that, when his parents and their children arrived in Manchester, his mother had to go out and beg in the streets for the money to feed her children. The family settled down in Haslingden, where the children got employment in the mills. This gave them bread; but at the age of eleven Michael had to pay a terrible penalty, for his right arm was caught in the machinery of the mill, and was so terribly injured that there was nothing for it but to amputate it, in spite of the protests of the little fellow himself.

Michael Davitt, 1846–1906

One of the pathetic stories Davitt used to tell of his early youth was the conflict between his mother, the doctor, and himself, and an old Irishwoman who was acting as help in the house, as to whether this operation should take place or not. The superstitious old woman had some hereditary idea that when Davitt reached heaven there would be some trouble among the saints as to whether a maimed man could find a place there. Davitt himself shrank from the ignominy, but, in the end, the opinion of the doctor and of the mother prevailed. One of the poignant recollections of my life is of Davitt with tears in his eyes describing how for months he had wounded the heart of the most excellent of mothers by refusing to speak to her in revenge for having allowed him to lose his arm.

Davitt now had to leave the mill and he next found employment as a letter-carrier. Among his warm friends were the postmaster and the postmaster's daughter. Davitt was a very handsome man, more than six feet high, with a powerful though not very large frame. He looked like a Spaniard rather than an Irishman: the hair was coal-black, so were the moustache and beard; the nose was regular, and he had very remarkable eyes—under heavy black eyebrows—dark, luminous, which gleamed on very small provocation, with menacing wrath and uncontrollable excitement.

He had a very melodious and powerful voice. One thing he had learned from his English training, and that was great powers of industry. When he had become a speaker, he used to write out with his left hand—he had taught himself to write very clearly with that hand—every word of every speech he made, and the different parts of the speech were titled and docketed as though he were preparing a financial report. In spite of the quickness of his temper and the warmth of his temperament, he had acquired something of the Lancashire outlook and manner. He spoke usually, unless in moments of passion, slowly, deliberately, prosaically, rather than rhetorically. But while he was still a youngster that hot and violent temperament made him listen eagerly to the agents of the Fenian movement, who, at this stage and before the rise of Parnell and a new form of Irish Parliamentarianism, held that only by armed rebellion could Ireland achieve her rights.

His energy, ability, and passion soon sent him to the higher ranks of the Fenian organization, and he was soon entrusted with the duty of buying and importing arms into Ireland. His associate was a Birmingham gun-maker named Wilson. Ultimately, of course, he was detected; he was tried, and this tall, kindly, impressive figure, whose picturesque appearance appealed to the newspaper chroniclers of the period, was sentenced to twenty years' penal servitude.

Davitt in Prison, 1870–1877

Of all the disgraceful chapters in modern Anglo-Irish history, there is none quite so disgraceful as the treatment of political prisoners. The line adopted by successive British Governments, Liberal as well as Tory—at the very time when Gladstone, by describing the sufferings of Neapolitan prisoners, was helping to arouse Europe and to liberate Italy—would have excited horror if applied to any other country struggling to be free. Davitt spent many an hour in describing to me the horrors through which he went during the seven long years, with a second period of two years later on—horrors which were shared by the ordinary criminals. I have heard the same story from many other Irishmen.

It was easy for an Irishman in those days to find among his companions men who had gone through prison. One man, James O'Connor—afterwards a Parliamentary colleague of mine—described how in the Isle of Wight he and another prisoner, both of somewhat small physique, used to gather snails for two stalwart fellow-prisoners, and how these men in their hunger used to eat the snails without even waiting to take off the shells. Davitt told me of a half-silly creature who would rush to the bones that came out in the sewage and try to gnaw off some of the bits of gristle that might be left. And then, of course, there was the grave-like silence to which these hapless victims of politics and of the criminal law were condemned through long years of days and nights. How Davitt lived at all and retained his reason it is difficult to say; be sure those years left their mark. Apart altogether from his excitable temperament, he was wayward; he lived in waywardness; and, as will be seen later on, he died of his waywardness.

But, with these reservations, he was one of the most lovable of men. He was perfectly, impeccably straight, an idealist, and good-natured, except when a fit of temper and misunderstanding, and a certain intolerance, drove him into a hostile political, and therefore personal, attitude. He and I were estranged for some years, but we became reconciled, and then warm personal friends; and among the many men I have met in politics there is not one of whom I have a more tender and affectionate memory.

At the end of the first seven years of his imprisonment, Davitt and many other of the Fenian prisoners were released. They got an uproarious reception wherever they went. There was a grim reminder of what they had gone through in the tragic death of Colour-Sergeant M'Carthy, one of their number, at a breakfast given to him and Davitt in Dublin after their release. The prison treatment had made him incapable of standing the excitement, and he died suddenly.

Davitt's early experiences, and especially that sight of his burned home, his long meditation in prison, his omnivorous reading—especially of the history of his own country—had burned into his brain a fiery flame of determination to bring to an end the terrible land system of which he had been, with many millions of his race, such a pathetic victim. Events lent themselves to his taking up this mission with some hope just after his release from prison. Ireland was in the throes of that series of bad potato harvests to which I have already referred. The potato then, as in the previous great famine of 1846, was the thin partition that excessive rents left to the peasants between them and starvation. With the decrease of the potato crop there came, as in 1846, a corresponding increase of notices of eviction. "They fell", Gladstone said in one of his speeches, "like snowflakes over the land." A different population, however, confronted the spectre of another famine and of another reduction of the population of Ireland; this was partly due, of course, to the spread of education. But here it was that another young Irishman began to play a momentous and even a decisive part.

Daniel O'Connell's "Placemen"

To understand the gravity of the task before Parnell, it is necessary to know something of the degradation to which Irish politics had been brought during a generation of rampant self-seeking. Himself unpurchasable, it was O'Connell's persistent idea that his followers were justified in taking office under the Crown. Every post of power in Ireland was then held by the enemies of the popular cause. The Lord-Lieutenant, the Chief Secretary, all the judges, all the barristers, all the sheriffs, all the men in any public position great or small, were Protestants, and most of them were Orange Conservatives. O'Connell, in the hope of breaking down the rigid fences of ascendancy, encouraged his followers to take office. The class of men from whom O'Connell had to draw his members was particularly susceptible to marks of Government favour. A member of Parliament was obliged to have £300 a year to be a borough, and £600 a year to be a county member. The landlords were almost to a man on the side of existing abuses, and the greater number of the members of this body whom O'Connell was able to recruit to his ranks were *déclassés*. They were usually men of extravagant habits and of vicious lives, and politics was the last desperate card with which their fortunes were to be marred or mended.

The result of this theory of O'Connell's was the creation in Ireland of a school of politicians that became her dishonour and her bane. This was the race of Catholic place-hunters. In exact proportion to their success and number were the degradation and deepening misery of their country. For years the struggle for Irish prosperity and self-government was impeded mainly through them, and the hope for the final overthrow of the vast structure of wrong in Ireland showed some chance of realization for the first time when they were expelled for ever from Irish public life. This chapter of Irish life can be summed up in the name of one man in particular, William Keogh. It is a picturesque chapter, but it would interrupt my narrative, and I have put it into the Appendix.

The Dark Years

The years which followed the treason of Keogh were among the darkest in Irish history. The landlords saw their power once more unquestioned by popular leaders and unopposed by popular organization or popular hopes. The oppression practised on the tenants at this period knew no limit of age or sex or circumstances; it penetrated into the smallest as well as the largest affairs of the tenant's life. The rent was raised year by year. The building of a mansion in London, a bad night at the card-table, the demands of a generous and exacting beauty, or the loss of a great race, remote as they were from the concerns of the Irish farmer in his cabin and on his patch of land, influenced and darkened his destiny; and year after year his rent steadily kept rising. When at last successive generations of folly and vice swept the old landlord into the maelstrom of debt, the change of landlord meant in nearly every case a rise of rent, and a master penurious perhaps where the old proprietor had been spendthrift, but as grinding and as greedy. With the advent of Parnell's party, that power was for the first time to be seriously challenged by the elected representatives of the people.

CHAPTER V

Parnell's ancestors—Sir John the incorruptible—"Old Ironsides" of the American War—Parnell's American blood—His youth at Avondale—Servant's heartrending memories—His mother and sisters—His relations with Mr. Tim Healy—The mission to America—Mr. Healy's likes and dislikes—The contradictions of genius—His powers as a Parliamentarian.

Parnell, 1846–1891

CHARLES STEWART PARNELL, as everybody knows, came from an ancient and historic family. His great-grandfather, Sir John Parnell, who was a great-nephew of Parnell the poet, was one of the few men of the old Irish Parliament who went unscathed through the fiery furnace of the almost universal corruption by which that Parliament was brought to an end. He held the high office of Chancellor of the Exchequer for many years; but, in spite of this dependence on Government favour, he remained inflexible in his hostility to the destruction of the old Parliament.

Sir Jonah Barrington, who has written the best account of these times, and was by no means a charitable observer, compiled a "Red List" in which he summed up his impressions of the Irish politicians of his time. Opposite the name of Sir John Parnell he put the one word, "Incorruptible". The family had come to Ireland from Congleton, in Cheshire, during the reign of Charles II. Sir John's son Henry, Parnell's grand-uncle, was also a Member of the Irish House of Commons, and also resisted the destruction of the Parliament. Henry was elected to the Imperial Parliament; advocated there everything that would increase the liberties of the country: was against the Corn Laws, supported short Parliaments, extension of the franchise, vote by ballot, and, curiously enough, as his relative of our times did afterwards, the abolition of flogging in the Army. He attained high office, for he was Secretary for War in Lord Grey's Ministry of 1832, and Paymaster-General in the Administration of Lord Melbourne from 1835 until his death in 1842. In 1841 he was created the first Baron Congleton.

It will thus be seen that Parnell's ancestry was both distinguished and consistent, and it was this historic heritage that did a great deal to recommend him to the confidence of the Irish people. His father, John Henry Parnell, was the grandson of the Sir John Parnell I have mentioned. He inherited a fair-sized property, and he was free to take a trip to America, which had important consequences both for himself and his family. He made a brilliant marriage with Delia Tudor Stewart, whose father, Commodore Charles Stewart, was a historic character, for he had taken part in the war between England and America in 1812, and his boat, the *Constitution*, captured two English battleships.

He lived to a great age, surrounded by the aura of this romance of his youth. He had been received with every form of public honour on his return to his country. In Boston he was met by a triumphal procession, in New York presented with the freedom of the city and a gold snuff-box, in Pennsylvania he was voted the thanks of the Commonwealth and presented with a gold-hilted sword.

Commodore Stewart: "Old Ironsides", 1778–1869

After this he had another historic adventure, for he was sent to the Mediterranean, where there was a great amount of discontent, amounting almost to a mutiny, among the American sailors. Stewart was not the man to falter in such a state of things, and by severe measures he soon brought back discipline to the American crews. In his patriarchal years he passed by the name of "Old Ironsides", and, with all this air of romance about him and bringing back the glories of a receding past, became something like a national idol. At one time, indeed, he was among those spoken of as a candidate for the Presidency. He retained his youthful vigour even when, in his eighty-fourth year, Sumter was fired upon. He immediately wrote a letter to the papers demanding to be put back into active service. "I am as young as ever", he said, "to fight for my country."

Here is a description of this famous sailor's appearance and character:

"Commodore Stewart was about five feet nine inches high, and of a dignified and engaging presence. His complexion was fair, his hair chestnut, eyes blue, large, penetrating, and intelligent. The cast of his countenance was Roman, bold, strong, and commanding, and his head finely formed. His control over his passions was truly surprising, and under the most irritating circumstance his oldest seaman never saw a ray of anger flash from his eye. His kindness, benevolence, and humanity were proverbial, but his sense of justice and the requisitions of duty were as unbending as fate. In the moment of greatest stress and danger he was as cool and quick in judgment as he was utterly ignorant of fear. His mind was acute and powerful, grasping the greatest or smallest subjects with the intuitive mastery of genius."

I think it is not pushing things too far to say that there was a close resemblance between Parnell and his grandfather. I have always held that both in appearance and to a large extent in character Parnell was much more American than either English or Irish. He had at once that combination of masculinity and of courage and of nerve which are more American than English or Irish. He had that imperturbability of manner and impassivity of face which also are not characteristically English or Irish.

His family was somewhat nomadic. Parnell himself used to say that he thought he had been born in Brighton, and certainly a good part of his early life was passed in England. He was at school in Yeovil, Somerset; Kirk-Langley, Derbyshire; in Oxfordshire; and he went to Cambridge University, which also was the university of his father. This was the reason why he had a pronounced English accent, which was one of the things that put considerable difficulty in his way when first he was appealing, as a strong Irishman, to the support of the Irish people.

The Irish Rebellion of 1798

But, all the same, the permanent background to his mind and to his early training was Irish. His father's house was at Avondale, in the county of Wicklow, and in one of its most beautiful spots; you could almost hear from his house the sound of the Meeting of the Waters, which Moore has made immortal in a poem. Moreover, he was surrounded by, and kept on familiar terms with, the peasantry. When I tried in conversation with him to find out the origins of his public opinions, so hostile to those of his class, nothing impressed me more than his tale of his acquaintance with Hugh Gaffney, a gate-keeper at Avondale, who was old enough to have seen some of the scenes of the Rebellion of 1798. One of Hugh Gaffney's stories was of a man who was taken by the English troops in the neighbourhood during the Rebellion. The sentence upon him was that he was to be flogged to death at the end of a cart. The interpretation of the sentence by Colonel Yeo, the commander, was that the flogging was to be inflicted on the man's belly instead of on his back. Gaffney saw the rebel flogged from the mill to the old sentry-box in Rathdrum—the town nearest to Avondale—and heard the man call out in his agony, "Colonel Yeo, Colonel Yeo!" and appeal for respite from this torture. He heard Colonel Yeo reject the prayer with savage words; and finally saw the man, as he fell at last, with his bowels protruding.

When Parnell told this story in his usual tranquil manner, the thought suggested itself to my mind that at last I had reached one of the great influences that made him the man he was, and that in this poor gate-keeper was to be found the early instructor whose lessons on British rule and its meaning imbued the young and impressionable heir of the Parnell name and traditions with that hatred for British domination in Ireland which characterized his public career.

Another of the influences which doubtless produced the opinions and the acts of Parnell was his heredity. As has been seen, he inherited a long and consistent tradition of adhesion to Nationalist views from his ancestors. The ancestors were not forgotten. On an occasion when I spent a night at his house in Avondale, characteristically Irish in its look of neglect and decay, I could not help remarking the tattered banners that hung from the ceiling of the lofty hall, all belonging to the period and the struggles that immediately preceded the destruction of the Irish Parliament in 1800.

He did not, I should add, get any of his inspiration from reading. I doubt if Parnell to the very end of his days could give you anything like a correct account of any epoch of Irish history; indeed, to most young Irishmen of his time, Irish history was taboo. I do not remember ever reading a word specially devoted to Ireland in the school books of my own boarding school, which, being under the control of Catholic priests, certainly was not inspired by anti-Irish feeling. I cannot pretend even now to know in anything like accurate detail the history of many epochs of my own country.

Parnell had, in no sense of the word, any literary taste; there are not half-a-dozen records of visits to a theatre; the only quotation from Irish poetry he is ever recorded as making were the well-known lines—"First flower of the earth, first gem of the sea"—and my recollection is that he quoted even those wrong, substituting "jewel" for "gem", and "ocean" for "sea".

This lack of interest in anything literary was partly the result of a very decided bent towards science and mechanics. If you met him on a Saturday you generally saw a copy of *Engineering* or some such journal under his arm. He was always trying experiments on the metals in some mines on his property and projecting schemes for their development—which came to nothing. He had also, I have heard, some aptitude for the study of such commercial problems as the development of railways, and he could give an accurate and penetrating account of the financial position of the great railroads of the United States. I never saw any sign that he had ever read a single novel or a single drama.

Finally, among the great influences of his early days was that of his mother, and of her I will speak more fully later in this book. He was extraordinarily like her, physically as well as mentally, and they had in common a certain eccentricity that was the thin barrier between insanity and reason. I met her for the first time on that first missionary visit of mine to the United States in 1881.

At the moment of Parnell's career which I have now reached he was at his best, both personally and politically.

His hours of work were extremely long, and one must include his constant attendance at the all-night sittings which he had already inaugurated in the House of Commons. He was just as feverish and as enthusiastically active outside as inside the House. Similarly, after his American campaign for money and support, those who were with him—including Mr. T. M. Healy, who played so important a part in his life later on—described to me the extraordinary exertions which Parnell took without hesitation and without complaint. I know what lecture missions in America are, with the terrifically lengthy journeys, the big meetings, and all the rest. Missions of that kind have killed various men—they almost killed Bradlaugh, they killed Max O'Rell, they killed Ian Maclaren, and they shortened Mark Twain's life. Parnell went through them with fortitude.

Mr. T. M. Healy in 1880, *aet.* 25

As this is the first time I have brought the names of Parnell and Mr. Healy together, I may indicate here the nature of their early relations. Mr. Healy had gone out to make his living as a clerk at an early age. Beginning in Ireland, he had gone to Newcastle to one of the clerical departments of the railway. His perfect knowledge of shorthand, his energy and indefatigable industry, had made him a very welcome secretary. That he once collected tickets from railway passengers is one of the imaginative additions to the early career of a man afterwards celebrated which is quite common, but it is not true.

Mr. Healy was connected by marriage and by long friendship with Mr. John Barry, who also was for many years one of the considerable Irish population that works in Newcastle. A change of occupation by Mr. Barry, which made him the chief commercial traveller for a very prosperous Kirkcaldy firm of linoleum manufacturers, had taken Mr. Healy's relative to London. Apart from the ties of relationship, Mr. Barry had realized the great gifts of this young man, and brought him to London as the confidential secretary to his firm. Mr. Healy was also connected with the family of the Sullivans, of whom the chief members were Mr. Alexander M. Sullivan, a brilliant writer and an even more brilliant speaker, and Mr. T. D. Sullivan, who won a genuine reputation as a poet, and especially as a maker of popular ballads. This family connection was one of the reasons why Mr. Healy's pen was employed in writing the London correspondence of one of the Dublin newspapers of which the Sullivans were the proprietors.

Mr. Healy was a born journalist: he had certainly then an extraordinarily brilliant pen, especially as a not very merciful critic of men of opinions contrary to his own. Parnell, when he started his career in the later 'seventies, was largely prejudiced by the absence of all support among the popular journals of Ireland. The *Freeman's Journal*, under the control of Mr. Edmund Dwyer Gray, who was essentially a constitutionalist and a devoted adherent of Isaac Butt, not only did not support Parnell's new policy of obstruction, but actually opposed it—and, still more, opposed Parnell. There was a very ugly controversy between Parnell and Dwyer Gray in these early stages, in which Gray accused Parnell, when the Irish Party refused to follow his lead, of calling them "Papist rats". It was only, therefore, in the columns written by Mr. Healy that any defence was to be found of Parnell's policy. When the bitter controversy afterwards arose between Parnell and Mr. Healy, attempts were made to deny the service that he had rendered to Parnell at that critical moment in the

Mr. T. M. Healy

(From Sir Benjamin Stone's *Parliamentary Pictures*)

To face page 102

latter's career; but they were not fair. Undoubtedly Mr. Healy did a great deal to help the early career of Parnell. He did even more at a later date to ruin that career, but that is a story for future pages.

Parnell was always the most slatternly of men. It used to be said that when he was called from his belated and feverish attempts to prepare a speech in the library of the House of Commons, he lost half his papers in the short distance between the library and his place in the House.

The reception he got in America was wildly enthusiastic and unanimous beyond all his hopes. He lay helpless and overwhelmed under the vast mass of correspondence and of subscriptions and of demands for meetings that came from all parts of America. He thought of Mr. Healy, and sent him a cablegram to London asking him to come to America. It was characteristic of the Healy of that period that he was on his way to the boat at Queenstown on the afternoon of the day he received this cable. He immediately created order out of chaos, organized Parnell's meetings, sent out the summonses for a great Nationalist convention in America—which was virtually the beginning of the Parnell Movement—and slaved and wrote with equal facility in hotels and in railway cars. Never did a man have such an assistant. Yet the strange reward which these incomparable efforts had created was that Parnell came back from America suspicious and indeed hostile to Healy.

I never was able to discover the real grounds of the silent but unconquerable aversion from Healy which Parnell ever afterwards displayed. He did not as a rule speak frankly of his likes and dislikes, and, as will be seen, I did my best to remove this fatal estrangement between the two men. Until the split, the only time I ever heard Parnell give frank expression to his feeling about Healy was when I was consulting and helping him to make his speech immediately before the General Election of 1880. Parnell and I were then—as indeed always up to the split—on the best of terms. He knew that I had no desire to be anything but a private member of the Party; the idea of leadership—for which I knew my entire unsuitability—would have made me look with fear and horror had such a position ever been offered to me; and this was one of the reasons, I think, why Parnell had such confidence in me. But at that time I had both admiration and affection for Healy, and I certainly did everything I could to discourage Parnell's dislike and suspicion of him. On one occasion Parnell said to me that Healy was a selfish man; I gave a deprecatory reply, and Parnell turned on me, not fiercely but certainly very determinedly, and asked me if I thought him a man who formed his opinions lightly. There I left it.

Parnell and Mr. Healy, 1880–1885

During the years from 1880 to 1885 there was no visible estrangement between the two men, though I must say that I now and then saw a certain inclination in Parnell to underrate the services of Healy—which at that time were very great, especially during the discussion of Gladstone's Land Bill. But both the men, if they felt bitterly to each other, managed to conceal their feelings; and Healy could very well be described as one of the most faithful followers of Parnell, and Parnell was just enough to allow that in the debates on the details of the Land Bill Healy led our campaign much more assiduously and effectively than himself.

I dare say the relations of Parnell and Healy were not improved by the appointment of Henry Campbell to be Healy's successor as Parnell's secretary. Campbell was quite an honest and sincere man, so far as I ever could see, but he was an Ulster man with something of the Ulster man's narrowness. He was a partisan essentially, and of course so far as his great chief was concerned, a blind partisan; he had already formed a very strong suspicion of the disinterestedness of Healy; he saw before others how Healy was fighting for a big representation of his friends in the nominees we elected at our secret meetings in Morrison's Hotel; and once at least, if not twice, Campbell dragged me over from London to take part in these councils with a view to correcting what he regarded as Healy's deliberate intention to pack the party with men on whom, either from some relationship or from co-operation in legal or other proceedings that were constantly taking place, were attached to him at any rate in some form of association.

This produced some slight coolness between Healy and myself; but that passed away. When the Galway election, with O'Shea as Parnell's nominee, came, the fury doubtless existing in Healy's mind, from the unjust and ungrateful treatment of him by Parnell after his great services in America, at last burst out into the violent flame I have already described.

As will be seen later on, Healy was the real and the most effective, and indeed most ruthless, opponent of Parnell in that struggle, and anybody reading only his public utterances during part of that time would describe Healy's pursuit of Parnell as fierce and vindictive and, part of the time, indecent. And yet in this strange and mixed character you never could count from day to day or even from hour to hour on Healy's changing moods. One of the most interesting and puzzling features in the character of this remarkable man was this changefulness of mood. He could give a stab to an opponent's heart (he often did that to

Parnell) at one moment, and in the next—as is seen even in the letters that he wrote at the time of the fiercest collisions in Committee Room 15—there were moments of hesitation, and even of something like remorse. Over and over again in the candid letters he wrote to his father or his brother occurs the phrase, "I am sorry for Parnell". These moments of repentance and self-reproach were a constant feature of his character.

One evening in the House of Commons we had a fierce debate on the conduct of a sub-inspector of police in a riot at Wexford. The poor sub-inspector was belaboured during a whole night's debate by all the members of our Party, and charges of brutality were hurled against him. And then came Healy's speech, and in the middle of the speech Healy dropped in a statement that the sub-inspector had lived with his present wife months before he married her. The story, if true, had never been told in public before, and much as we desired to strike down the sub-inspector, this shocked us, and a foolish Tory member emphasized the charge by repeating and denouncing it.

I met Healy the next afternoon; he seemed extremely depressed. I invited him down to the lower smoke-room, where members of the time used to find relief either from the boredom of sitting for hours saying nothing and waiting only for the division, or for some of the other worries of life. I proposed that we should take an Irishman's characteristic relief in a good drink. Healy accepted the proposition with evident gratitude, and when I left to him the choice of the drink we should take—we were both sober men—he mentioned lachrymae Christi as a wine he had often heard of but never drunk; and we had our bottle of lachrymae Christi.

Upheavals of Contradictory Sentiment

There are other and almost incredible stories of these tremendous upheavals of contradictory sentiments in this curious nature. Once Alfred Illingworth, a typical, dry, and self-contained Bradford man, told the story of his meeting Healy coming panting down the staircase of a hotel, his face covered with blood. Illingworth, shocked and surprised, asked Healy what was the matter; and Healy told him he was trying to catch up with the man who had so brutally assailed him to tell him that he forgave him.

There were other occasions which I do not recall at the moment of Healy's strange and sudden alternations of mood. I used to sum up that side of his character half-humorously by likening him to a wife in Bedlam who, when she received a visit from her husband, might either kiss him or stab him, or both.

It was another characteristic of this strangely temperamental creature that he could be moved to tears publicly and unexpectedly, and on several occasions he interrupted proceedings by violent outbursts of tears. This was put down by his enemies to hypocrisy; it was wrong psychology; it was part of his strange and ill-balanced temperament.

It was part of the tragic irony which is constantly found in political life, that events placed a man of temperament so uncertain and so contradictory in a leading position in the great struggle between Parnell and his associates during the subsequent strife, mainly in Committee Room 15. There could not be two personalities more destined by their inner psychology for such a struggle. If Healy were changeable as to mood, Parnell had the disadvantage at once of an inability to understand other men, and of an inner and temperamental and gigantic self-confidence which made it difficult for him to yield to any man.

There was one other conspicuous feature in the character of Mr. Healy: that was his absolute physical fearlessness. It is no exaggeration to say that every moment in his struggle with Parnell he carried his life in his hands. But Healy never flinched. I realized the full meaning of the peril to him by a little incident that took place at a committee meeting when he and I sat side by side. I observed that he took his seat with a little awkwardness, and then I realized that he carried a revolver in the back pocket of his coat.

He used to walk alone from the office of the *Nationalist Press*—the anti-Parnellite organ which he had taken a great pride in founding—until his friends insisted that they should accompany him and prevent this foolhardiness. On one occasion I believe a small gang of rabid Parnellites who came on a visit to Healy practically threatened his life. He defied them and told them they had come to the wrong man; and he went steadily on with his violent campaign against Parnell. He was assaulted twice—but again he went on.

There was only one man of whom Healy ever showed any fear, and that was Parnell. Parnell used to say: "Healy is all right as long as he is afraid of you". It was not a just judgment; but it is true that when Parnell directed upon Healy the frozen glare of his brilliant and mysterious eyes, Healy wilted. It was probably his sense of this inner weakness in the presence of Parnell that added venom to his hatred of him.

Mr. Healy's Gifts as a Parliamentarian

In adding something of an estimate of Mr. Healy's gifts as a Parliamentarian, I have to begin by saying that in some respects his reputation was higher than his deserts. No man had a quicker insight into the details of Parliamentary life. The saying is well known that only three people knew Mr. Gladstone's fearfully complicated Land Bill of 1881, and Mr. Healy was one of these. It was Mr. Healy who inserted into that Bill the clause which came to be known as the Healy Clause, which protected to a large extent the capital and labour invested by the existing tenants in the improvement of their holdings. I remember well when the Government accepted Mr. Healy's amendment, his turning to me and whispering that that had saved millions to the Irish tenantry.

But in general I regarded his judgment as faulty; he was too impulsive and too excitable, and had not really a clear outlook, to be trustworthy as a guide in big affairs. His faults of temper, which was sometimes mulishly morose and obstinate, often led him into astonishing positions. I remember when the day was approaching for Gladstone's proposing his second Home Rule Bill, we all agreed that when Gladstone entered the House he should receive the reception that his courage and fidelity after so many disappointments entitled him to, and it was decided we should all stand up when he entered the House as the most popular shape we could give to our admiration for the most heroic enterprise of even Mr. Gladstone's life.

Healy, dissatisfied with some of the inner negotiations with Gladstone, absolutely refused to comply; and when all the members on our benches stood up, he obstinately held on to his seat with the characteristic scowl on his face. But Parliamentary reputation and popularity in speech do not depend entirely, indeed I might almost say hardly at all, on the intellectual merits of the speech. The House of Commons dearly loves humour, sarcasm, and personality, and all the other things that give it that relief and that amusement which the most serious meetings of men instinctively demand. By his wit, sometimes by his extravagance, by his power of withering personality, Mr. Healy could always interest the House of Commons; and the result of it was that the House was always eager to listen to him.

Without the prestige which Ministerial position gives to the speeches of Ministers, Mr. Healy was able almost always to fill the benches of the House and to be heard with amusement and delight. In that respect Mr. Healy was one of the greatest Parliamentarians of his time. One would have thought that he did his best to cool this enthusiasm, for neither his manner nor his appearance was calculated to win him sympathy. He stood with bent shoulders, with very bright eyes gleaming through the glasses he had always to wear, and with the most foreboding expression he could give to his face, from the scowling brow to the small, beautifully shaped, but venomous-looking lips. This made him always, even when he had to speak alone, without any party to support him, or even friends—except perhaps his brother—a man who could fill and dazzle and amuse and shock the House of Commons.

CHAPTER VI

A variety of members—The old gang—When Parnell began—The murder of Lord Mountmorres—Wild gatherings on the Irish hills—Captain Boycott—Orangemen's harvesting expedition—A veteran's indiscretion—Our flight from a platform.

The "Nominal Home Rulers"

I HAVE mentioned the fact that the Irish Party, on returning to the House of Commons, after the election of Mr. Parnell as their leader, had broken into two parties. Mr. Shaw and many of his friends—indeed, the majority of the so-called Home Rule Party—took their places on the Government benches, while all the Parnellites sat, for reasons I have already given, on the Opposition benches of the House. This might very well seem an extreme measure. O'Connor Power severely criticized it, and pointed to the united ranks of the Liberals on the Ministerial side of the House as an example to us of how men of the same party, though of different shades, could remain united. But any other policy, I think even now, was impossible. The supporters of Mr. Shaw were really, as they were afterwards called by Mr. Gladstone, in a very apt phrase, nominal Home Rulers. The phrase stuck to them and helped to destroy them. They had most of them swallowed the policy of Home Rule as the shibboleth of the hour, which meant nothing and would lead to nothing. One of the gang was an Englishman, who, though he lived in Ireland, was thoroughly anti-Irish. Another of them had not been quite sober for twenty to thirty years. Many of them, if not most, were office-seekers.

There was one whose history was characteristic of the type. The inheritance of a small patrimony in some farms brought him in something like £800 a year, which was really almost prosperous independence for an Irish member in those days. He was able to get in for his native place time after time. He announced quite definitely his objective, which was to be the Governor of one of our great Dominions, with a quite princely salary which that position involved. So he capitalized his income. When he came to London he spent money lavishly, taking, among other luxuries, a box at the Opera. He confidently relied on the precedence of several generations, that loyal service to the Liberal Party would make his looked-for reward certain and inevitable.

Another member, who belonged to the legal profession, was looking with the same certainty to a fat job that would substitute the certain income from the Government for the precarious fees of his profession. Meanwhile, he was preparing for a more prosperous time by having a pint of champagne before him at luncheon and at dinner, and not infrequently in between. I was sorry for the poor devil, especially a few years afterwards, when he had been driven out of Parliament and, without a job, he haunted the lobby of the House of Commons penniless and in rags. These men were bad enough, but they were not quite as bad as the members of the generation that preceded them.

Let me tell how an Irish member answered an Englishman who contrasted the disreputable Irish representation, myself included, with the more respectable men of a previous period. The Irishman admitted the contrast, though not quite in the same spirit, for this is what he said: "There were four Members of Parliament, personal intimates and political associates: one was a forger, and committed suicide; the other was a forger, and was expelled from Parliament; the third was a swindler, and fled; the fourth was made a judge". It was this hopelessness of the honesty and the effectiveness of Parliamentary representation that was really the origin of the Fenian revolutionary movement, and the greatest of all the achievements of Parnell was the restoration, slowly and with many obstacles, of the faith among Irishmen, that Parliamentary and constitutional agitation was a weapon that could be confidently regarded as potent to reform the land system and win self-government for the country.

Parnell's Political Beginnings, 1875–1880

It required a man of consummate political genius to remove this deep-rooted sentiment of cynical disbelief in Members of Parliament, and more especially in those who called themselves Liberals and demanded Liberal reform. There is no achievement in the life of Parnell which is more remarkable and more surprising than his success in a few years in producing this extraordinary transformation in the attitude to constitutional agitation of nearly all the Irish people. Shallow and ignorant observers of Parnell's attitude in those early days of his were always describing him as a revolutionary. At the start of his movement he used the revolutionary forces. Without their honesty, their self-devotion, and their high spirit, he could not have drawn Ireland out of the slough and disparagement into which all the dishonesty and corruption of some thirty years of Irish life had sunk the people. Parnell was elected to the House of Commons in 1875, and it took him less than five years to restore Irish faith and hope in Parliamentary methods. Parnell, instead of creating and maintaining, had reduced the revolutionary movement to a mere shadow of its former self.

It looks incredible that Parnell was able to do so much in so short a period of time. Up to the election of 1880, all that could apparently be said about him was that, by a policy of violent obstruction, he held up the House of Commons, had created scenes, had driven Ministers and big majorities to impotent fury, had introduced the eventful phenomenon of all-night sittings, and now and then, by methods like these, was able to wring from the badgered and helpless Government some small concession. He had the instinct of genius for the kind of thing that would appeal to his people. He was a simple and straightforward man by nature, but there was not absent from his mind a sense of the histrionic. I have told already how O'Connor Power, who hated and underrated him, used to repeat as an instance of the younger man's folly that Parnell had once proposed to him to come down to the House of Commons arrayed in the historic garb of Lord Edward Fitzgerald or Robert Emmet, two of the martyrs of Irish liberty, and so compel the House to expel him after a course of tumultuous scenes. The scenes which Parnell created did not quite reach this form, but they were histrionic enough to make that appeal to Irish sentiment which was required to rouse the country from its hopeless somnolence and black despair.

These personalities, however, powerful as they were, did not produce the terrible situation in Ireland. All kinds of things, some of which I have already indicated, combined at what proved to be the psychological moment, as in other countries and in other revolutions, to mark the hour as the last day of slavery and the dawn of emancipation. I have already described how the Land League swept from village to village, gathering force, strength, and adherents with every hour. The passion grew by what it fed on, until in the end there was in Ireland an outburst of revolutionary feeling that in its intensity was on the same level as that of the Parisian mob that dragged the King from Versailles.

Murder of Lord Mountmorres, September 25, 1880

As is usual in all the sudden revolutions of long oppressed classes, violence of act followed violence of language. All *jacqueries* in history have been cruel, and the Irish *jacquerie* was no exception. The old landlordism in Ireland had only one final weapon against it—that of assassination. It was a terrible, but it was an ineffective weapon, as the success of the landlords and of the British Government in exiling more than half of the Irish population proved; but still, it was in the tradition. There were all over the country the relics of the old Ribbon societies, as they were called, which carried on this deadly war against the landlords; and they burst once more from their long lull of impotence into ominous activity.

The first instance of the re-creation of this force was a sensational murder. Far away in a small village in the west of Ireland there was a landlord called Lord Mountmorres, whose small property left him with almost as scanty an income as that of the penniless peasants by whom he was surrounded. From all I have heard, he was rather a harmless person, hail-fellow-well-met in market or public-house with his tenants. One morning, within half a mile of his own house, he was found shot dead, with six revolver bullets in his body. The cruelty of this murder was emphasized by the painful and tragic incidents which followed, for a cottager near the spot where the body was found would not allow it to be brought into his house for a doctor to make assurance that the victim was dead.

The crime sent a shiver through Ireland, and still

more, of course, through England. The bitter opposition by which the Government of Gladstone was assailed by the landlord party was enormously helped and increased by this murder. Lord Randolph Churchill went ramping around the country, and—though in less inflated language—Lord Salisbury and Sir Stafford Northcote joined in the chorus of violent denunciation both of the Government and of the Irish leaders. Not the centuries of oppression which had gone before, but the immediate incidents of this revolutionary movement and the inaction of a Liberal Government were, with characteristic superficiality, described as the causes of this outburst of violence, the roots of which lay in six centuries of history. Gladstone was held up as the chief culprit.

These denunciations at once of the Ministers and the Irish leaders were accompanied by the demand for the only alternative policy which the Tory leaders had to propose—namely, the policy of Coercion. Ireland was lawless in the throes of civil war, making demands which the Tories denounced as confiscation, but most of which they themselves have translated in a later period into law. The Government had to stand between these two policies: Ireland demanding the abolition of rent and of landlordism and the creation of a peasant proprietorship, and the Tory Opposition challenging all attempts at reform and offering the bleak alternative of Coercion.

This produced a revolt in the more Liberal section of the Ministry and in the Liberal Press. Mr. Bright was against Coercion, at least as the last word, and so was Mr. Chamberlain. The general feeling among Liberals was that an attempt should be made to meet the tragic situation in Ireland by the offer of real remedial land legislation. But the revolution by this time—it might be called the sanguinary revolution—had got beyond both enemies and friends. There was thunder and lightning and tragedy in every breeze that blew on the Irish hills.

Parnell's Monster Meetings begin, September 19, 1880

The effect of this revolution had been as violent on Parnell, and indeed on all Irish politicians, as on the British parties. Up to the foundation of the Land League the Irish demand for land reform had not got beyond what were known as the "three F's"—Fixity of tenure, Fair rent, and Free sale—and up till then any measure which offered these things to Ireland would have been joyfully accepted as almost the last word in the emancipation of the tenants. The Land League transformed this ancient demand into an anachronism which was only mentioned to be denounced and rejected. Parnell possibly began as an advocate of the "three F's", but under the circumstances I have already narrated had been swept on by the Land League, and perhaps also by the tempestuous and wildly enthusiastic receptions which he got at the crowded and tumultuous meetings through which he swept from one part of Ireland to the other.

Everywhere the people prostrated themselves before him. The man who, but a few months before, had been reluctantly and by a small majority elected as leader of a disunited party, was quickly raised by the tempestuous voices of the multitude into the irresistible and adored leader of a nation-wide and revolutionary movement. In speech after speech he adopted the Land League programme, and rejected any form of compromise which still left rent and the landlord. It may be added that neither then nor at any other time did the Irish Party propose the expulsion of the landlords without full compensation, and their plan, after years of struggle, was put forward and finally adopted—that the State should advance the purchase money to the landlords, and the tenants should pay back to the State the purchase money by instalments spreading over a certain number of years. There was no justification for any party in attributing the confiscation of estates and the "expulsion" of landlords as the aim of Parnell.

In one of his speeches he declared: "What was wanted was the will on the part of the English people to settle the land question, and the object of the agitation was to produce this will. Once minded to settle the question, once convinced that a settlement could not be evaded or postponed, they would settle it. He would not bind himself down to any particular mode, but he agreed that an arrangement by which the landlord should be converted into a fixed rent-charger, or by which the tenant, after paying a fixed annual sum for thirty-five years, should at the end of that time become absolute owner, would be a fair arrangement," and so on.

Every speech he made at these wild gatherings and in this intoxicating atmosphere was severely scrutinized, especially with a view of convicting him of the encouragement of the crimes that were now beginning to be daily more frequent and more terrible. Parnell treated accusation and appeal—especially from his political opponents in England—with a scorn that was characteristic of the man. Whether he in his heart liked or disliked the English people as a whole, it was always difficult to say. It was an Englishwoman, after all, whom he loved and who loved him, but the very core of Parnell's being was pride, Satanic pride, which led to his return of scorn for scorn of the other race which claimed the right to govern—or rather, misgovern—his own race. Perhaps I should add as another ingredient in this mental attitude of Parnell that he was naturally of a suspicious—perhaps even a cynical—temperament. He always suspected Englishmen. That side of his mind was part of his undoing when his own fate came to be in the balance.

Isolation of Captain Boycott, September 23–November 26, 1880

He had a tremendous sense of his personal dignity, and with all his apparent imperturbability there were very tempestuous depths in his strange soul. He astounded me one day—it was in one of the dining-rooms of the House of Commons, when he was perfectly tranquil—by saying that he had made up his mind that if any policeman or any other official of the Crown were to make an assault upon him, he would shoot him.

Another tragic and sensational incident of the time which brought home to the world the gigantic figure of Revolution that was now stalking over Ireland was of a very peculiar character. A gentleman named Captain Boycott occupied a large farm in County Mayo, and was also the agent of Lord Erne. One of the advices tendered by the Land League was that rack-rented tenants should offer what they considered a fair rent, and if this was refused they should pay nothing at all until the landlord came to a better frame of mind. Lord Erne's tenantry acted on this advice, and Captain Boycott retorted by serving them with notices of eviction. The people determined to bring him to his senses by a system to which he afterwards gave his name, and which has passed into the practice, and also into the vocabulary, of all the countries of the world—namely, the boycott. Not a man would work for Captain Boycott, not a household servant would remain with him, not one would sow or reap or carry any of the fruits of his farm. The shopkeepers would not sell to him, the post-boy would not deliver his letters, the blacksmith would not shoe his horse, the laundress returned his dirty linen. The newspapers grasped the tragic picturesqueness of this lonely figure, and descriptive and sensational articles began to appear in all the papers—English as well as Irish. A body of militant Orangemen descended from Ulster to his relief, under the protection of seven thousand soldiers and police. In spite of all probabilities, they were allowed to come and return without any interference beyond the boos of women and children. The Orangemen remained a fortnight, and when they departed, amid the ostentatious indifference of the people, Captain Boycott and his family went with them, on his way to England, and Mayo knew him no more. Parnell calculated that every turnip saved had cost the Government a shilling. The formidable display of cavalry and foot for the protection of one farm had only gone to show what a losing battle the Government was fighting against the Land League.

Parnell's Speech at Ennis, September 19, 1880

It was a speech of Parnell that was supposed to have helped to apply this new and most effective weapon to all people connected with the landlords throughout the whole of Ireland. In the most famous of his speeches, that at Ennis, he summed up this policy.

"We have been accused", he said, "of preaching Communistic doctrines when we told the people not to pay an unjust rent, and the following out of that advice in a few of the Irish counties has shown the English Government the necessity for a radical alteration in the Land Laws. But how would they like it if we told the people some day or other not to pay any rent until this question is settled?

We have not told them that yet, and I suppose it may never be necessary for us to speak in that way. I suppose the question will be settled peaceably, fairly, and justly to all parties. If it should not be settled, we cannot continue to allow this millstone to hang round the neck of our country, throttling its industry and preventing its progress. It will be for the consideration of wiser heads than mine whether, if the landlords continue obdurate and refuse all just concessions, we shall not be obliged to tell the people of Ireland to strike against rent until this question has been settled."

"And if", he added, "the five hundred thousand tenant-farmers of Ireland struck against the ten thousand landlords, I should like to see where they would get police and soldiers enough to make them pay."

"When a man", he said, "takes a farm from which another has been unjustly evicted, you must shun him on the roadside when you meet him, you must shun him in the streets of the town, you must shun him at the shop-counter, you must shun him at the fair and in the market-place, and even in the house of worship, by leaving him severely alone, by putting him into a moral Coventry, by isolating him from the rest of his kind as if he was a leper of old—you must show him your detestation of the crime he has committed; and you may depend upon it, if the population of a county in Ireland carry out this doctrine, that there will be no man so full of avarice, so lost to shame, as to dare the public opinion of all right-thinking men within the county, and to transgress your unwritten code of laws."

Thus, then, even the shallowest observer of Irish conditions must have seen that the Government and the Parliament had to deal with a movement nation-wide, violent, and, as it turned out, irresistible. The feeling in England mounted inevitably with the feeling in Ireland, and thus there were at the same time the cyclone of the Irish revolution and the cyclone of party passion in England. It looked as if the two nations were approaching a bloody conflict, which would be nothing short of civil war.

Parnell at Galway, October 24, 1880

It might perhaps lighten this tragic narrative if I tell a little anecdote of one of these meetings in which I took part. Parnell, I suppose, felt that he was under some obligation to me for the very energetic support I had given him in my first Parliamentary session, and accordingly agreed to come and address a meeting of my constituents in Galway. I was only beginning to learn the realities of the Irish situation at the time, and I made a speech which cannot have been of much importance. I have forgotten what I said, and I do not think it worth my while to look it up, for there were two speeches much more important.

One was that of Parnell himself. It was a speech that passed into history, because he answered the charge that by concentrating on the land movement he had forgotten the national demand for Home Rule. He then used the phrase that he would not have taken off his coat to fight for the land if he did not think he was fighting at the same time for Home Rule.

It was on that occasion, too, that he lent his sanction to a nickname that had just begun to be applied to Mr. Forster. A police circular had been unearthed which recommended the police not to use the deadly bullet in conflicts with the people, but buckshot. Granting that these collisions should take place at all—and, of course, they should not with proper and prompt legislation—the intention of the circular was undoubtedly humane; but it was not so interpreted, and "Buckshot" Forster became the favourite appellation for the unfortunate Chief Secretary.

But there was another speech which attracted a great deal more attention. I have already introduced the name of Matt Harris, who was among the most effective and zealous leaders of the tenantry in the west of Ireland. I knew him from my childhood, for he was a native of Athlone, like myself. He was a man of wide culture, of great reading. He could have had a prosperous business as a builder, but the violence of his political opinions and his temperament drove him into politics, which, curiously enough, at that time ruined him with some of the people among whom he lived. A good many priests of the time, as in other times, were as extreme in their opinions as the people around, but some of the elder men were suspicious of this new movement, and poor Matt Harris, who might have got a good many valuable contracts as a builder of chapels, was more or less boycotted by the older clergy of his county, and had many a dark hour of pennilessness in the intervals between his political activities.

He was fortunate enough to have a splendid and courageous wife, who set up a little business of her own, and kept from the door of her children and herself the wolf of hunger which the politics of her husband had brought to them. The curious thing was that he was a man of intense humanity of spirit. He told me that he had suffered for months because he had felt compelled to drown a dog which he was afraid was about to go mad. It was certainly true that at an earlier date he had specially opposed the Ribbon lodges and their policy of assassination. But for some reason or other he lost his head on this occasion, and, having described how he had saved many a landlord's life in the old days, and having seen as the only result of this policy the eviction and the expatriation of millions of Irishmen, he told the people that if they shot down the landlords like partridges in September, he, Matt Harris, would not say a word.

Flight from a Platform

Parnell and I looked at each other blankly when we heard this terrible speech. I need not say that it was condemned by all the sane people on the platform, including the chairman; and the uncharitable view was taken—which was quite wrong—that Matt made the speech in the hope that the new Coercion Act, already looming in the near future, would put him in gaol and add him to the martyrs of the cause.

Parnell and I had retired to the back of the platform, having delivered our souls. "What had we better do?" said I to Parnell, for we felt that controversy would only have aggravated the situation and perhaps given more prominence to the wild speech. "We had better hook it," said Parnell. The use of a popular phrase of that kind by Parnell struck me by its strange contrast with the consummate dignity of his personality and demeanour. We dropped down from the platform and went to our hotel. Within a few minutes crowds of people, and priests among them, came to report to us this ugly incident. Parnell listened to them with an air of well-simulated innocence, and most of them went away with the idea that he had not heard the speech.

Once after, when Parnell was the subject of a prosecution, the stout, impartial, purely business-like English shorthand-writer who was taking notes for the Government was examined with regard to this speech. My feelings can be imagined during the pause which occurred when the shorthand-writer was asked by the Attorney-General prosecuting for the Crown whether Mr. Parnell was present when this speech was delivered. The shorthand-writer replied that he thought Parnell had left. It was a perfectly honest answer on his part, for he was sitting with his back to Parnell in the position which we occupied at the end of the platform. I should add that, the very next week, Matt Harris made a speech in which he made a complete apology for the violence of his language.

Such, then, was how the session of 1880 and the recess passed. Everybody knew that the disappearance of the stormy debates in the House of Commons did not mean that anybody or anything was remaining still. On both sides the forces were visibly gathering for a violent and terrible struggle the moment the doors of the House of Commons were again open. There were hurried and frequent meetings of the Cabinet; a Crown prosecution was undertaken against Mr. Parnell and some of his most prominent colleagues; the meetings in Ireland were increasing in numbers and in violence of temper. It was perfectly clear that in the next stage of the struggle the Government and the Parnellites were to come to deadly grips. Coercion was in the air.

CHAPTER VII

Parnell at his best—While "Lord" Biggar slumbered—Poor meals in Westminster Bridge Road—Disguises at the fair—Biggar in breach of promise—Long-distance speeches—Mr. Sexton's lightning arithmetic—Mr. Dillon's fervour.

A Fateful Session begins, January 7, 1881

THE year 1881 was a marvellous year for the young and small Irish Party. It did very remarkable things at subsequent times in later epochs, but that year will always retain its position as the high-water mark which they, or any other small party, could reach in resolution, in tenacity, and in success. As will be seen in most of the divisions, the Irish minority varied from twenty to twenty-seven; it rarely got to thirty. They were practically deserted by the so-called Home Rulers on the Ministerial side, led by Mr. Shaw. They got an occasional vote and speech from the small group of Radicals in the Ministerial party; but virtually, and especially as passion grew more intense and their unpopularity reached something like frenzy, these English auxiliaries were swept away from them, and they could count on, as a rule, only twenty members for active work. Yet even this small, insignificant group were able to hold up that great assembly whose members were virtually united to a man against them; to thwart all the plans of a Ministry led by the greatest Parliamentarian in the history of the House of Commons, backed by a majority of 100, increased at vital moments by all or nearly every member of the Tory Opposition. It was a fight of twenty men against six hundred.

This is, perhaps, the time to give a sketch of some of the men who carried on this historic fight.

Parnell I have already sketched. At this time he was in full possession of that inexhaustible energy, that tireless industry, and those steady nerves which were the characteristic features of his earlier years as a politician. In order to be nearer the scene of incessant action in the House of Commons, he took a room in the Westminster Palace Hotel, as I did, and he was in his place as steadily throughout the long day and night sittings as any member of our Party. His mind was still uncorrupted by the sense of dictatorial power, and he assumed none of the airs of leadership. He sat even in an inconspicuous seat. The leader of the Opposition in the House of Commons, unless he is on the side benches, where he sits behind one of the boxes on the Speaker's table, generally sits on the first seat of the bench among his followers. As the Irish Party arranged themselves, however, the first seats were occupied by Mr. Sexton and Mr. Healy; Parnell usually sat on the third seat, and I sat next to Parnell.

I may say here that I was convinced, from my first days in the House of Commons, that the leadership of Parnell was the centre-stone in the arch of our fortunes; that I regarded every attempt to displace or overthrow him as a dagger aimed at the heart of Ireland; that I used every power and influence I possessed as a writer in newspapers to exalt him; and that I was only too ready to regard with suspicion anybody whom I could think of as an enemy or a possible rival. I confess that sometimes I made mistakes and misunderstood men.

The bitter quarrel which parted for a season Michael Davitt and myself was largely due to something I had written which suggested that Davitt had spoken slightingly of Parnell. Davitt was the best and most unselfish of men, but I have remarked jealousies in the old politicians like O'Connor Power and others who had given Ireland years of service before Parnell was ever in the House; and Davitt had something of this feeling of jealousy of the man who, to him, as to them, was a modern and recent upstart. Davitt could certainly place his seven years of penal servitude in comparison with the years of a country gentleman in easy circumstances which filled Parnell's life before he entered the House of Commons. Besides, Davitt had some class prejudices. He regarded landlords as a class apart, and looked on Parnell as a landlord and the son of a landlord. In the beginning of the campaign for Land Reform, he found Parnell rather wedded to the old idea of a war against eviction and rent, and not to a war for the greater purpose of getting rid of landlordism and securing peasant proprietorship.

Davitt, in his years of study and meditation in his convict cell, had gradually become something of a Socialist, and his belief in the writings of Henry George amounted to piety. His solution of the Land Question was Nationalization, a policy which was not only wrong in principle, but almost insane if preached to a following three-quarters of whom were small farmers anxious to possess their acres.

The Father of Parliamentary Obstruction

I come now to some of the other great personalities in the mighty struggle of the session of 1881. First I must call up the figure of Joseph Gillies Biggar. There could not have been a more typical Belfastman than Biggar. He was the son of a very successful Belfast merchant. Henry Lucy, in his days of violent vituperation, used to say that when Biggar rose to speak there was a faint smell of a kippered herring! This was a rude way of saying that Biggar was in the provision trade. I do not think kippered herrings, but rather cattle, sheep, and pigs, were the things he disposed of. How a man brought up in these circumstances could have become a violent agitator it is hard to believe. In later life—I suspect, from political rather than theological reasons—Biggar became a member of the Catholic Church. I have found this difficult to explain, except that he had the feeling that this change of religion would bring him more into accord with the sentiments of the people he loved.

For a man who had not a particle of wildness in his mind, who was essentially by nature and upbringing business-like, it seems a hard thing to say, but he certainly was a fanatic. In political opinion he was fanatical enough to have joined the Fenian conspiracy—a rebel and somewhat hopeless movement, with a risk of imprisonment, and even of the scaffold. Then, like so many of the Fenians, he began to have faith in the effectiveness of constitutional agitation. He was returned to Parliament, in the election of 1874, for the county of Cavan. At no time had he the gift of speaking. His speeches were just like his letters, terse, direct, and business-like—great things in business life, but not good material out of which to make the eloquent and endless speeches which the members of his Party were expected to deliver when our policy was that of obstruction. It was said that when he made his first election campaign he used to carry the manuscript of his speech in the inside of his tall hat.

His physique was like his character in its extraordinary contradictions. He had a fine, well-shaped face, with regular features, a well-shaped nose, and very bright eyes; he had powerful limbs; but all this was spoilt by a prominent hunch-back. In Ireland they used to have the curious nickname of "lord" for a hunchback, and once an

Irishman (who, unfortunately, was also hunchbacked) was, long after Biggar's death, recommended to a Northern constituency as "the son"—which he was not—"of that great Irish Parliamentarian, *Lord* Biggar". There was something of the same contradiction in Biggar's qualities. He was hard sometimes, and showed a little arrogance when brought in contact with the poverty-stricken. He was essentially ruthless. Some of these figures in the Irish movement have a certain faint resemblance to those of the French Revolution, and, different though they were in upbringing and race, Biggar always suggested to me the replica of the spirit of Marat. I rather think that if Biggar, like Marat, had had the services of the guillotine at his disposal, the lives of his political opponents would have been seriously in danger.

He had also a great deal of the "nearness" of the typical Belfastman of Scottish descent. Whenever we had to discuss the question of salary for a very poorly paid official, Biggar was adamant against any increase. Once we were determined to make such an increase if we could, even if it meant a long struggle. Fortunately, just as the business came on, Biggar fell into one of those deep slumbers which occasionally overcame him, and were the forerunners—though we did not realize it—of the sudden death in which his life unexpectedly ended. We hurried up the proceedings, and by the time Biggar woke the salary had been increased and we had gone on to other matters.

He was the ruthless enemy of anybody who deflected by what he considered a hair's-breadth from his own strict gospel, and he could make no allowances. He was responsible for the deadly hatred with which that brilliant character, O'Connor Power, was pursued for years, and which caused him ultimately to be thrown out of Irish politics. As an instance of his contempt for the natural pride very strong among Irishmen, especially among the poor, this incident was narrated to me. Three-quarters of our Party had to be assisted from our Party funds. This was a matter held so delicate and so sacred that very few of the members of the Party knew who were and who were not the recipients of this very necessary dole.

The "Nearness" of Mr. Biggar

I may say here that I never knew, to the last day, anything about the allowances of the Party, or which members received this aid. Parnell might have known, but if he did, he did not interfere. To which I must add that Parnell, though personally absolutely indifferent to money, was also inclined to be "near". I remember he reproached me once for proposing too large a salary for somebody; he said my ideas were warped by having lived for so long in a rich country like England. There was a meeting of the Party in the Mansion House in Dublin during these years to discuss the programme of the coming session. I was not there, but this is what occurred. Among Biggar's peculiarities was the practice of never using blotting-paper. As treasurer, he drew out the cheques for the members of the Party and scattered them all over the desk in the Mansion House. This was terribly humiliating to the poor fellows whose pecuniary dependence was thus exposed.

I have already told the story of how Biggar once lent a ten-pound note to a colleague who was suffering from a bad cold that necessitated his having a short trip to Brighton, and how, when the money was not almost immediately returned, Biggar reminded his friend of the debt, giving as his excuse for asking for the money that if he were promptly paid it would be a recommendation for a future loan, if such necessity arose. And yet here, again, comes one of the contradictions. He had a sister or two, and I have heard that when they spoke of his generous kindness to them, they did so with tears of gratitude in their eyes.

At one time, owing to some trade complication, he lost part of his capital, and he resolved to meet these losses with a direct reduction of his expenses. Before, he used to dine in the House, and even there the price of his dinner was not large. As part of his new economy, Biggar used to leave the House for an hour or so, walk across Westminster Bridge, and take his meal in one of the poor eating-houses in the somewhat squalid neighbourhood of Westminster Bridge Road. Another story I have heard of him, which I will give though it seems to me rather incredible. He took it into his head that when he went to cattle fairs he was charged exorbitant prices because of his notoriety. So he went to these fairs in disguise. The hunch on his back, as well as the constant portraits of him in the papers, made such a disguise quite palpable. I have heard an amusing description of how, dressed up as a poor peasant, Biggar would be pointed out with a smile and a jeer by the shrewd farmers who were endeavouring to press their cattle upon him at their own price.

He had violent passions, rather coarse in their choice, and on this point he was quite unabashed. On one occasion he was the unsuccessful defendant in an action for breach of promise. So little did he feel the humiliation of the proceedings that he wrote a monumental letter to the great Sir Charles Russell accusing him of incompetence in the conduct of his case. It must have been the first, and was no doubt the last, time that that great counsel, of so arrogant and hot a temper, was subjected to such an insult. What I believe happened was that Biggar wished questions to be put to the plaintiff full of gross insinuations, which could scarcely be proved, against her character, and which, if asked, would have added enormously to the amount of damages awarded to her by the jury. One of the defences which Biggar urged against the charge of having made a promise of marriage was that there were impediments in the way, the main "impediment" being the number of children he had already to provide for. The word "impediment" caught on the public mind, and it was now and then used with an eye to Biggar. Any other man of his notoriety might have died under the ridicule and disrepute of such proceedings, but Biggar said himself that "no man could go down who had the courage to face his enemies". At the large dinner given on the occasion when Parnell was to receive a big cheque which was subscribed by the country, Biggar stood up after Parnell had taken the cheque, to say a few words. At that a large number of the ladies in the gathering left the room. Biggar did not mind, and went on his tempestuous way unmoved.

Mr. Biggar's Four-hour Speech, April 22, 1875

He was the most fearless man I have ever known. It was almost incredible that this little hunchbacked man, slow of speech, with no power of appealing to the House of Commons, should stand up there and continue unmoved when nearly six hundred men were shouting words at him of execration and contempt. One of the Coercion Bills to govern Ireland against her will was under discussion. Biggar got up and made a speech of four hours. It was by such an achievement that he first attracted the attention of his countrymen. This was really the beginning of the policy of obstruction which his Party followed with such success years after. Biggar, and not Parnell, was the true author of the policy of obstruction, though, by a curious coincidence, this performance by Biggar took place on the night that Parnell took his seat in the House of Commons for the first time. This was the germ from which Parnell was able, later on, to create the formidable policy of his great Party. I happened to be in the House at that time, though in the Strangers' Gallery and not on the floor. Such a feat by some members of our Party would not have been a remarkable achievement, but this little man, with no rhetorical resources, actually managed to carry out this project of holding Bills back. Time after time attempts were made to confound him, but no one could. Then the Speaker complained that he could not hear the words of the Hon. Member. Biggar had been speaking from a seat *below* the gangway, and he calmly walked to a seat *above* the gangway, so that he might meet, as he put it, the convenience of the Speaker, and he began his rigmarole all over again.

Biggar, of course, gave enthusiasm to Parnell's new and violent policy, but his feelings toward that great leader were always extraordinarily mixed. When the famous O'Shea Election of 1885 came on, he was one of the men who dealt at Parnell the first deadly blow, from which, in reality, he never quite recovered.

If anyone had drawn the contrast of Biggar in that election posing as an apostle of sexual purity, with that well-known story of his earlier life, he would have replied that he had never sacrificed political principles in any of his transient passions. Of course, such a collision as at Galway would have made, between any other men except Parnell and Biggar, deadly enmity. But Parnell could be curiously indifferent to attacks upon himself, and if anyone criticized Biggar in his presence, Parnell would always say that "no one minded Biggar".

There was a certain grotesqueness in Biggar's individuality as well as in his policy, but deep down within him he had a positive affection for his leader. Not long after Parnell had got into his terrible imbroglio, and his health had begun to fail, he used to come, sometimes after weeks of absence, to the House of Commons, looking deadly ill, with his face drawn, the back of his neck narrow, his complexion ghastly. One day when Biggar had seen Parnell in this condition he turned aside and wept.

Sometimes this grotesque image has come to me in describing the attitude of Biggar to his cause, as that of a Belfast Quasimodo to an Irish Esmeralda.

Mr. Sexton's Long Speech, January 26, 1881

Mr. Sexton, the next man in my portrait-gallery, was quite an opposite type. If Biggar were a Northern of Northerns, Sexton was a Southern of Southerns. He had the southern sensitiveness, the southern versatility, the southern eloquence. I have known in the course of my forty-seven years in Parliament many very great Parliamentarians. The greatest, unquestionably, in my judgment, was Gladstone. I would put Sexton in no inferior place to that of the very next to Gladstone as a Parliamentarian. He had a most singular combination of gifts. He could rise to heights of eloquence that touched even the unsympathetic ear of a hostile House of Commons; he could reason out a case with close-knit logic; he had a power with words that seemed something like magical. It was perhaps a defect of this command of language that his speeches were now and then weakened by prolixity; but even in prolixity he could be impressive.

On one of these terrible all-nights I am about to describe, he spoke for three hours—from a quarter to five until twenty minutes to eight. The House to which he spoke consisted of about six to eight members, most of them fast asleep. One of the members who listened to him throughout was a Cabinet Minister—George Shaw-Lefevre in those days: the venerable Lord Eversley in ours. Mr. Shaw-Lefevre reported afterwards that he had listened to every word of Sexton's long speech, and found them all fascinating and not one of them redundant.

Lord Gladstone in his recent book—*After Thirty Years*—has expressed equal admiration. He says—

"Sexton's speeches, however long, were perfectly phrased and admirably reasoned. . . . At one all-night sitting he spoke after 2 A.M. for three hours. The House and galleries were almost deserted. . . . Next day I met Herschell, who was in a state of enthusiasm about Sexton's speech. . . . He had listened to the whole of the speech, which he said was an intellectual masterpiece. Yet the speaker had an audience of about a dozen men, and the speech was not reported in any newspaper."

Of another speech of Sexton's, Mr. Gladstone wrote with equal eulogy.

"Mr. Gladstone's estimate", said Lord Oxford in his last book, "of his (Sexton's) powers is noteworthy. Writing from the House of Commons to Lady Frederick Cavendish shortly after her husband's assassination (May 1882), he says, 'Sexton just now returned to the subject, with much approval from the House. Nothing could be better either in feeling or in grace; the man is little short of a master.' "

Side by side with this extraordinary power as an orator there was in Mr. Sexton another gift which is very rarely allied with great powers of speech. He had an extraordinary mastery of figures, and in mental arithmetic he was far beyond any man in the House. This talent was developed in him while he was little more than a child. His schoolfellows afterwards used to tell how they or the masters would pitch at him a great bundle of figures, and how, quick as lightning, he would give the proper answer.

This gift was immensely useful to him as a Member of Parliament. Once Sir George Trevelyan, then Chief Secretary for Ireland, produced a long and complicated Bill, crammed full of figures, dealing with the question of police salaries and police pensions. Rising immediately afterwards, Mr. Sexton was able to repeat and to analyse all the figures of this statement, which it had taken the Chief Secretary many laborious days to master.

"Vice-Leader of the House"

Finally, he had inexhaustible industry. Other members might be usually present in the House, and some of us had to be almost always present—but Sexton was never absent, except when he went out to take a hurried meal or to indulge in his one relaxation, a cigar. He was not visible until the House met, but he worked at home for hours before he came to the House. He read every official paper that had any connection with Ireland. In a microscopic but very regular handwriting there would be in his pocket innumerable pages of notepaper on which there were comments on all these papers. So he went into the conflict of debate with all his armoury ready. So great was the ascendancy which he ultimately obtained over all parts of the House that, in later years than those with which I am dealing now, his rise immediately after Mr. Balfour, the Leader of the House, was regarded as most fitting. A caricaturist accompanied his portrait with the title, the "Vice-Leader of the House"; and so, indeed, he was. Even Mr. Balfour, with all his fierce antagonism to Mr. Sexton and his Party, always listened to him with respect, and yielded to his representations when it seemed to him possible.

There was a strange contrast between these immense powers and extraordinary authority and the physique and, I may add, the habits of the man. He was of small stature, his beautiful hands and his feet were as small as those of a woman, his body had not upon it an ounce of superfluous flesh; the face, long, thin, high-coloured, with a beard all round, was chiefly remarkable for the eyes, which were large, expressive, sometimes so blazing that they seemed to obliterate the rest of his face. The head was large; a friend satirically described Mr. Sexton once as consisting of a big head balancing a small body. His habits were those of an ascetic: this mighty Parliamentary figure lived in two small shabby rooms in the desolation of Tatchbrook Street, one of the mean streets of mean Pimlico. He rarely took any food beyond a cup of tea and toast until the dinner hour in the House of Commons. Even the tea and toast he did not always take the trouble to enjoy. I remember, after a committee meeting one night in the House of Commons, when we had got to the end of our business and to seven o'clock, Mr. Sexton remarked with a smile that he could now go and take his breakfast.

He had one devastating defect, and that was supersensitiveness. Other men much less gifted, but much less sensitive, were able to confront and to defy the hailstorm of calumny and attack, but he found it in the end intolerable. At a time when he might have been most useful to the Party, and when any constituency in Ireland would have been proud to have him as their representative, and immediately after he had been elected leader of the Party, he retired from the House of Commons, and it knew him no more; one, I think, of the most tragic incidents in all those years of our Parliamentary conflict.

Of all the wrongs which Mr. Healy's want of judgment,

personal bias, and want of self-restraint inflicted on the Irish Party throughout his career, his expulsion of Sexton from Irish political life was one of the greatest.

Like most of his friends, I have not seen Mr. Sexton for years, though we were for most of our time warm and intimate friends. In fact nobody has seen Mr. Sexton. I understand that, living still in his modest house at 20 North Frederick Street, Dublin, which he has occupied for more than half a century, he spends most of his time in reading; but he takes a nightly walk, and he does this so regularly that people say they could time their watches by his punctual appearance. He takes his long walks usually, I believe, alone. He has an income, I am glad to say, from some commercial companies over which he presides. But this lonely figure, unrecognized by anybody and out of Irish politics for so many years, with all his great genius useless to his country, and all his great achievements forgotten, —this lonely man is, I think, one of the most tragic of all the tragic figures in the Irish movement.

Mr. John Dillon in 1881, *aet.* 30

When we met in the House of Commons in 1880, there was one distinguished figure absent from the benches. Mr. John Dillon had accompanied Parnell on the historic trip to America, and had delayed his return. In his absence, and at the expense of half-a-crown for some telegrams, he was returned unopposed for the county of Tipperary. When he did take his seat, he was a very striking addition to the figures on our benches, and for a time stood out almost from every other member of the House of Commons. Very tall, very thin, with a long, thin face, coal-black hair and eyes, he was another who looked rather like a Spanish than an Irish figure. Painters and sculptors and men of letters raved about the beauty of his face, and especially of his eyes. Henry Holloway, the great artist in mosaics, chose him for one of the saintly figures in a window he had to make for a church. George Meredith glows over his eyes in one of his letters.

But under this apparently fragile form there was a burning passion. Though he looked usually impassive and tranquil, the fires of this temper were always there. He represented almost the extremist opinion in the Party, and, fearless and indefatigable, he never hesitated to express these opinions in the clearest, and sometimes in violent, language. Seated, he seemed the most tranquil of men; on his legs he could become the most fervent and even most violent. He differed from many of the members of the Party, and especially from me and also from Parnell, in his views of the demands of the situation. He looked to the revolution in Ireland as certain to be ultimately victorious, and he was against all compromise that might interfere with its, as he thought, certain triumph. To the majority of us he was as the men of the Mountain in the French Revolutionary Convention to the men of the Gironde.

Like Sexton, his industry was phenomenal. Every morning of his life he read innumerable journals; every one of them was marked with a pencil on the pages that he thought might be useful in debate. He was extraordinarily well read, and had a fine library of his own. For a certain time his activities were in Ireland rather than in the House of Commons; nearly every revolt had him as one of its leading figures. Again and again he had to face prosecution for his acts and speeches, again and again he had to go to gaol, and in some exciting scenes even to risk his life. He looked always the same deadly calm man when he was not speaking, but faced all these as the necessary incidents of an Irish politician's life.

Since I wrote these lines about him he has passed away—one of the bitterest bereavements of my old age. He had come over to London to see a specialist; the intimacy which always united us was renewed; he lunched and dined with me every day he could spare. Then one day he said to me quite equably that he would be with me next week if he were not in another world; he spoke as dispassionately as if he were speaking of somebody else. Next week came; he was subjected to an operation; he lingered for a few days, and then he died. Of all the many fine creatures in our world I put John Dillon as the noblest.

Mr. William O'Brien in 1881, *aet.* 29

William O'Brien came from a family at once of rebels and of almost permanent invalids. On the very day an elder brother was born the police had a warrant to search his father's house for arms. This elder brother afterwards became one of the most active members of the Fenian movement. He took part in raids for arms, in raids on police barracks; he was sent to gaol under the suspension of the Habeas Corpus Act: this imprisonment helped to kill him. Another of William O'Brien's brothers and a sister were attacked by the same disease—consumption. The brothers died on the one day; a fortnight afterwards the sister died.

William O'Brien himself was threatened with the same fate in his early days, and it was only a trip to Egypt which saved him. He entered into journalism, and migrated from Cork to Dublin. He had given, from his earliest articles, the proof of a brilliant and, when needs be, a vitriolic pen. When Parnell thought it necessary that a paper should be founded as the mouthpiece of the great organization which had come into existence, he naturally chose William O'Brien as its editor; and thus was founded *United Ireland*, a newspaper which perhaps was more influential than any other paper in Ireland.

It was a paper which revealed the character of its editor — ruthless, eloquent, inspiring. On it devolved more than on any other Irish paper the conflict between coercion and Lord Spencer. The state of Ireland at the time was desperate; at the mercy of one man, the Lord-Lieutenant, with all the powers of coercion which the Legislature had bestowed upon him, with the power to arrest, to try by his paid and dependent resident magistrates, and on appeal by partisan County Court Judges, every member of the popular Party.

There came thus one of the conflicts which were frequent in Irish history, and which are inevitable and have occurred in every oppressed country fighting against a stronger alien power, namely, the resort to criminal acts. On the one hand there were murders, and on the other executions; it was a regime of the revolver and the rope.

This deadly conflict was practically symbolized and to a large extent carried on by the two figures of Lord Spencer on the one side and Mr. O'Brien on the other. Lord Spencer struck with his Coercion Act and Mr. O'Brien with his pen, and thus Mr. O'Brien advanced to be one of the most powerful and popular figures in the country. Every word of his articles was read with feverish interest and with an immediate response. For a time he wielded almost as much power as Parnell himself. There was no enterprise, however absurd, there was no risk, however great, that he was not willing to face.

One example out of many I may give of this. There were several of the dependents of Dublin Castle, and some even of its police officers, who were suspected of the hideous crimes of sexual degeneracy. O'Brien opened a campaign against one of the most prominent of these officers. On the result of that trial depended to a large extent for the moment the fortunes of Mr. O'Brien, of his paper, and even of the movement. It will give some indication of the resolute character of the man that he went into this conflict, very hopeless apparently at the start, with the determination to win or to die.

Mr. O'Brien often told me that if the trial had gone against him he had made up his mind to commit suicide. As he was a man of intense religious faith, it will be understood what a terrible resolution this involved. But the trial ended in a triumph for Mr. O'Brien, and he shook Dublin Castle to its foundations by exposing it to the world as the refuge and the shelter of men of the most degraded vices.

I always think that one of the paradoxes I have seen of Irish life is the spectacle of this omnipotent journalist in his hours of work. He had a small salary—about a quarter of what he might claim—something like £4 a week. He lived in a single room in a popular and not very dear hotel. It was in this room that he wrote most of the brilliant articles which were setting all Ireland aflame. Many an evening I have seen him sitting at the table in this small room, with the light of a single candle by his side, with his nose almost in the paper (he had always very short sight), and amid these homely, not to say squalid, surroundings issuing the articles that were like thunderbolts on the listening Irish world.

Lord Spencer in 1881, *aet.* 45

The conflict went on for years with varying fortunes, but it ended in the victory for O'Brien; for, as will be seen,

Lord Spencer became a convert to Home Rule, and was one of its most faithful and effective supporters. Mr. O'Brien, of course, like most strong characters, had the defects of his qualities. He was self-willed and intolerant; to him might be applied the famous phrase of an American journalist about a great American politician, Senator Conkling; like Senator Conkling, Mr. O'Brien divided mankind into his slaves and his enemies. In a later period this defect made him a source not of union but of disruption; but nobody could, in his worst aberrations, suspect him of any motive except that of honest though narrow conviction.

He was the most wayward of men, and in his estimates of individuals the most self-contradictory. The day on which you agreed with him you became in his speech and writing a being of almost celestial merits; your honesty was only equalled by your genius. The following day, if you disagreed with him, you might become a loathsome traitor.

He never attacked me bitterly, though we disagreed. He was kind enough to suggest several times that if I had been in Imperial instead of Irish politics, I would have been a strong candidate for the Premiership—a ridiculous exaggeration which only amused me. For years he and John Dillon had been the warmest of friends; until Dillon differed from him, and then Dillon became a most sinister figure in Irish politics; and once even O'Brien almost incited a mob to attack him when he was passing in a rival procession through the streets of Cork.

The violence and foolishness of his temper frequently suggested to him impossible and perhaps fatal adventures. One of his proposals, for instance, as set forth in the excellent biography of him just published by Michael MacDonagh, was to kidnap the then Viceroy, Lord Spencer, and his Chief Secretary, and hold them as hostages in the Dublin mountains until the Government agreed to drop coercion as well as to remedy the grievances of the police. Of course, such an attack would have met with immediate defeat, and probably O'Brien and all those along with him would have been shot down by the police.

Another incident in his life which has the element of comedy in it—but William O'Brien had very little sense of humour—is characteristic of the man. There was some incident in the land war on which he poured forth miles of print in his paper. He desired that this should be debated in the House of Commons. Mr. Balfour, then leader of the House, was very civil, but with all the illimitable demands on the time of the House, he, like every other leader, was in an impossible position. O'Brien informed me that he intended to make a violent demonstration in the House itself if Mr. Balfour remained obstinate.

Affrighted by the folly and possible violence of which O'Brien was capable, I got into touch with the Speaker of the time (Mr. Gully), who was a friend of mine, and put before him the situation with the request that it should be conveyed to Mr. Balfour. My representations, after some negotiation, were accepted, and Mr. O'Brien got his opportunity.

And here comes the grotesqueness of this amusing situation. The time given to Mr. O'Brien was at an evening sitting beginning at nine o'clock and ending at eleven. The House met; the audience consisted entirely of Irish members—I do not remember that there was more than one English member present, and that was Mr. Walter Long, who, as Chief Secretary, had to listen and to answer; and it was to this spectral audience that Mr. O'Brien poured forth his hot philippic about the dreadful crimes of the Government. His comrades, of course, gave him an occasional cheer, but otherwise he spoke to the empty air.

I am convinced that Mr. O'Brien, who, in addition to his mental peculiarities, was very short-sighted, peopled the empty and almost silent chamber with interested crowds listening to every one of his words, cheering or deriding him; he filled the empty air with the phantoms of his own imagination, and honour was satisfied.

As a matter of fact, in order to get these two hours in this unresponsive and empty atmosphere, he had plotted with some of his more ardent supporters as to the form which his demonstration should take. It was decided to rush up to the Speaker's table; to seize the mace; to carry it from the House and smash it on the floor of the inner lobby! It might, he said to me, have meant penal servitude for himself and his comrades. And all this he thought worth while to get his two hours to address the empty air!

Since I began these memoirs William O'Brien has disappeared from this world—a beautiful and tranquil ending to his tempestuous life. It was on a Sunday evening: he had been to the Cathedral to the Sacrament in the morning; when he came home he was bright and cheerful, though a little weak. At nine o'clock at night, just as he was going to get ready for bed, he leaned his head on the back of his armchair, and peacefully passed away.

A Party of Young Men

Such, then, were some of the leading figures in the great conflict I am about to describe; other figures I shall allude to later on. These men were despised, underrated, hated. The comments in the British papers would make their readers think of them as illiterate rowdies; as a matter of fact, they were nearly all highly educated men.

Sexton was one of the finest Shakespearean scholars I have known, and he had been trained for many years as a newspaper writer. Dillon was, in some respects, the best-read man in English literature I ever met, and he had a fair acquaintance with French, German, and Italian.

And this was the Party in its infancy which was to produce such gigantic results. It did not look in the least like a party capable of such achievements. It consisted almost entirely of young men and of poor men. In those days there was no Parliamentary salary, and the leaders of the revolutionary movement in America had imposed on Parnell that none of the money which had streamed in in such a Niagara-tide as I have already described should be given to Parliamentary purposes. The members of the Party had no time, even if they had had the money, for self-indulgence; their lives were spent in the House of Commons until the vacation, and then in addressing the multitudinous meetings that were taking place not only in Ireland, but in England and Scotland. Most of them at the time were teetotallers.

I remember T. D. Sullivan, a veteran Irish Nationalist, when we sat at a dinner-table in a hotel in Liverpool, remarking that so many tumblers of cold water were the only drink by the side of these young men, and then he uttered the prophecy, which turned out to be true, that landlordism in Ireland had now against it a more formidable body of opponents than ever in the history of Ireland before.

It was perhaps not unnatural that men who at the moment were trampling underfoot the most sacred of English institutions, and practically defying and destroying the ancient House of Commons, should be disliked and misrepresented, and for some years vituperation was poured upon them by almost every journalist of the period.

Apart from the favourite charge—believed by a good many people, and perhaps not unnaturally—of being enemies of the Empire, the comrades and the subsidized servants of revolutionaries and assassins, we were reproached with our poverty; we were not only criminal, but low-born and vulgar.

And now, to explain this tremendous conflict of 1881, I will give a hurried glance at the curious political conditions of the time.

CHAPTER VIII

Mr. Gladstone's difficulties—Irish tactics—Circumventing the rules—Portrait of Mr. W. E. Forster—His dreaded Bill—Prolonged Irish debates—The longest sitting—The Speaker intervenes—The Irish members leave the House.

Irish Difficulties of the Government, 1881

OVER everything that occurred in the first session and in subsequent sessions of the Parliament of 1880 there spread the large, gaunt, inevitable spectre of the Irish Revolution. I hope my readers will keep that point constantly in their mind; it is the key to this strange enigma to which I have already alluded, of a powerful Ministry with a great majority and the greatest of leaders being gradually worn down, and with little but follies or mistakes to mark its history. And the Government was between Scylla and Charybdis. On the one hand they and the majority of their Party were convinced that the failure of the potato crop, the innumerable and cruel evictions, and the impossible conditions of the Land Laws in Ireland compelled a Liberal Government to bring in Liberal land legislation. On the other hand they were confronted with a civil war, with some terrible crimes and the subversion of all the authorities and laws of the country; with men preaching—rightly from their point of view—lawlessness, and the law paralysed in its attempts to deal with the situation. The one side of the problem required great land reform; the other, in the view of the Government, required a new application of the old remedy of coercion. There was neither of these policies that did not necessarily elicit violent hostility. Land Reform was violently opposed by the landlord party in both Houses of Parliament, and if that party were powerful in the Commons, the House of Lords, where it was omnipotent, showed throughout a defiant and arrogant determination to use to the utmost its powers against the Government.

To the landlord party at that stage of their political mentality, Land Reform, except the purchasing out of the landlords, was sheer brigandage. To this opinion forcible expression was given not merely by Lord Randolph Churchill and his guerilla warriors, but also by such notable men as the Marquess of Salisbury and Sir Stafford Northcote. There were not a few, even among the supposed supporters of Mr. Gladstone, and especially the small section still left of the old Whig Party, who did not view Land Reform with an unfavourable eye.

On the other hand, when the Government proposed Coercion, they were already warned of the fierce hostility and of the angry passions and the prolonged resistance they would meet from the Irish people and their representatives in the House of Commons.

Even in the Ministry itself there were plenty of cross-currents. Mr. Chamberlain, and still more his chief spokesman at that period, Mr. John Morley—who had become the editor of the *Pall Mall Gazette* in 1880—were warmly for Land Reform, and very tepidly for Coercion; and John Bright had the same point of view. Two other elements added to the confusion of this confused situation. First, the constant intrusion of the impossible Bradlaugh situation. Mr. Bradlaugh went on being elected and re-elected for his Northampton constituency; he burst in on the House of Commons, in one form or another, at regular intervals; and the confused state of parties which broke up the Government majority by the enemies of Bradlaugh in the Liberal Party made legislation or compromise impossible. It was a cul-de-sac; it came again and again, and again and again remained a cul-de-sac.

New Rules of the House

Secondly, there were, in the then rules of the House of Commons, inexhaustible opportunities for obstruction to delay and even to defeat the proposals of the Government. It was really the antiquated machinery of the House of Commons that made obstruction possible, and that gave to a small band of able and alert men the opportunity of holding up the Parliament—it might indeed be said, of holding up the Empire. The great Imperial Parliament, with all its centuries of tradition and authority, backed, of course, if needs be, by all the military and naval resources and the wealth of the great Empire, held up for week after week by twenty young men, would be an incredible phenomenon, if we did not know that it had existed. And on this question of the rules of the House, again the course of the Government was not clear. Much as they hated the Irish members, anxious as they were to put them down with a strong hand—some of them, indeed, would have had them ranged against the railings of Old Palace Yard and shot down, or taken to Newgate and hanged—this did not diminish their dread of any rules that facilitated and sped up the course of legislation in the House of Commons. For to most Conservatives and a quota of the Whigs who were nominal Liberals and ordinarily supporters of Mr. Gladstone, any machinery by which Radicals like Mr. Chamberlain could speed up Radical legislation seemed a great future peril.

Opposed in principle to nearly all change, they detected in the improvement of the rules of the House of Commons and the curtailment of its disorderly debates a subtle conspiracy to enable the House to rush legislation through, which they dreaded and condemned as confiscatory and revolutionary.

The Irish members were quick to see these flaws in the armour of their powerful enemies, and they could always be certain that, whenever they were embarrassing and obstructing the Government on everything but Coercion, they could rely on the open or partial support of the Opposition; and, above all, they could rely on Lord Randolph Churchill.

These were the conditions when the House met in January 1881. It met, too, after a very disturbed recess. A futile attempt was being made under the existing law to send the leaders of the Land League movement, from Parnell onwards, to a conviction in the law courts and a sentence of imprisonment. But everybody knew that these proceedings were bound to end, as most State trials in Ireland have ended, in futility and further contempt for the Government. The Ministry had also tried to gain some time, and perhaps some support, by a Land Commission to make an enquiry into a subject that had been enquired into by Commission after Commission for generations—an enquiry which the Irish Party, with the omnipotent revolution behind it, regarded as only an additional excuse for small projects and further delay. The House had soon an opportunity of coming to grips with this extraordinary situation.

On the very first night the benches were already crowded, and it was on the first few nights of the session that an important reform in the procedure of the House was first carried from precept into practice. For centuries it had been the unbroken law of the House that every member who had a question on the Order Paper should read it aloud. There the question was in print for everybody to see, and yet if a member attempted to ask the question without reading its terms, he was howled down by that strange and almost incredible love for ancient forms which is one of the characteristics of the House.

Mr. Joseph Cowen was the first to suggest that a member should be allowed simply to ask his question by referring to its number on the paper. There was some objection, and the Irish members were always certain to oppose anything that facilitated business; but for once they felt gracious enough to fall in with the reform, and questions from this time forward were not read, but simply indicated by their number on the paper.

The Shadow of Coercion

At last the evening came when Mr. Forster had to bring in that terrible Coercion Bill, the dark spectre of which had hung over Ireland and England for many months. The Bill amounted to a suspension of the Habeas Corpus Act, and left to the executive of Ireland the power, without trial and without anything beyond a vague allegation of criminal intentions, to put anybody in gaol—a startling abrogation of all the rights of British citizenhood, and especially coming from a Ministry with such veteran Liberals as Gladstone and Bright among its members.

Now, the foremost figure in opposition to the Irish leaders on the English side was undoubtedly Mr. Forster. It rather amuses me to-day to recall the feelings and the opinions with regard to Mr. Forster which were then common in our Party and still more among the Irish people. It was necessarily his part to have the main responsibility for the many acts of violence which the English authorities in Ireland had to perform during his administration. As will be seen, hundreds of homes were made hostile by the imprisonment of their relatives.

Large bodies of police night and day were necessarily employed in watching and in harrowing every countryside. The other Ministers, though they supported Mr. Forster—some enthusiastically, some very tepidly—were as responsible as he, but the Chief Secretary stood out as the main and dominating figure. It came really to this: that the policy of Coercion which he felt himself bound to propose and to carry out recklessly was embodied in his person; that with him it might well be regarded as standing or falling. There was not an hour in which his life was not in danger. How much it was in danger was not revealed till later on to a surprised and shocked world.

He had, in addition, labours that might have broken down the strongest of men, and ultimately did break him down. He had to rush backwards and forwards between Westminster and Dublin Castle—always a fatiguing journey, and in those times for him a very perilous one. His passions and his opinions were daily incited by the innumerable reports—some of them alarmist, and some of them, as it was proved, ridiculous—which were poured into him by his ubiquitous police.

These experiences did not tend to improve a rather fierce temper. So much did we among the Irish members participate in the feeling of hatred towards him that I heard one of our number—no less a person than benignant Justin M'Carthy—repeat a story that, while game-hunting in Greece, Forster had fired a shot which killed—of course accidentally—some unfortunate being, and that the hunter had walked off without taking the least notice. Of course the story was untrue—at any other time I would have added palpably untrue—but in the heat of party controversy everything against a political enemy is accepted almost in good faith with credulous ears.

All these feelings about Mr. Forster's character—though not of the unwisdom of his policy—have disappeared from my mind; and I now endeavour to sketch the man as I know him to have been.

Mr. W. E. Forster, 1818–1886

We regarded him as the last word in duplicity, in treachery, in bad faith, and in a love of tyranny for its own sake. It was a gross misunderstanding of an opponent, but it was partly justified by certain flaws in the character of the man. He was undoubtedly, to use a common expression, very downy. His adroitness was held, even by members of his own Party, to degenerate on occasion into something like trickery. The majority of the stern Nonconformists held for many years that in the Education Act, which he had carried through in a previous Parliament, he had battered the hopes and even the principles with regard to the control of the schools for which they stood, and many of them never trusted him again. His record in Ireland, of which we knew or remembered nothing previous to his Secretaryship, was a very clear proof of the affection and sympathy he had for the Irish people. He was one of the many Englishmen of the time who were deeply moved by the sufferings of the people in those dreadful years of the Famine. He had in his youth done good and self-sacrificing work for the Irish starving and dying in the Famine, and he was the head of a mission that went over to Ireland from England to distribute food among the starving people.

And here let me make an interpellation that has its solemn import. While the Irish people were being almost forced into death by hunger on the waysides of Ireland, and into wholesale emigration, through eviction, amounting to millions to all parts of the world, there was scarcely a pious home in England in which families were not practising self-denial in love and sympathy for Ireland. One of the friends of my early political youth was the late Henry J. Wilson—his son is now a member of the Labour Party in the House of Commons. I heard Mr. Henry J. Wilson describe how his parents, who belonged to a stern Puritan home, compelled him and the rest of the children to go without butter on their bread so as to save some money for the relief of the starving Irish. This is a tragic contrast which has gone almost without a break through the relations of England and Ireland. The English people as a whole, and when they had any knowledge of the facts, showed themselves full of love and sympathy for Ireland, while successive Governments remained with blind eyes and deaf ears even to the most poignant appeals of the people of Ireland in their agony and hunger and oppression.

Mr. Forster was a fine though rough figure of a man. He had great height, splendid shoulders and chest. He seemed to dress himself in somewhat extravagant fashion. No man had such big pockets to his coat, and it used to be said you could put a baby inside any of them. His red hair was always somewhat rough and dishevelled. There was a red lock which came down on the middle of his forehead and added to the uncouthness of the appearance. Frank Hill, the then editor of the *Daily News*, a sardonic spirit, used to say of Forster that he was "the best-staged Yorkshireman living"—a jibe that received additional point from the fact that, though Forster had spent most of his life in Yorkshire and was a Yorkshire member, he was Dorsetshire by birth.

Irish Amendments to the Address, January 6–January 20, 1881

The fight on Coercion was not slow in starting. On the very first night of the session Mr. Forster gave notice of his intention to move his Coercion Bill the next day. There was some skirmishing by Sir Stafford Northcote, his main theme being that the state of things in Ireland was the result of Government inaction. Mr. Gladstone made a powerful and temperate reply, and then I quote with some amusement now the following sentence from the *Annual Register* for 1881—

"Immediately afterwards, the House was practically emptied; and when Mr. T. P. O'Connor rose to speak there were only seven members present."

Parnell, of course, was the chief spokesman on our side, and he made a speech which a leading Tory like Mr. E. Gibson, the Member for Dublin University, described as being "adroit, intelligent, and sagacious". Parnell contended that the reports of outrages were grossly exaggerated. He admitted that he had encouraged the people to resist eviction—alas! what remedy was left to them when they were thrown on the mercy of the landlords by the rejection of the Compensation for Disturbance Bill by the House of Lords?

The debate on the Address dragged on, with some dissent from Sir Charles Russell and other Liberals. Sir Charles Russell supported Parnell's amendment, and summed up what was the latest apprehension of many who were of his way of thinking—that the Government were going to bring in strong Coercion and weak Land Reform. That really was the abiding apprehension which partly explained the ferocious opposition to Coercion by the Irish members. The debate then dragged on for seven nights, with the result that in a division, while the Government had the big total of 435 supporters, the Irish were able to muster the respectable minority of 57, which included eight English Liberal members. Even yet the Address was not voted, and further Irish resources of delay brought the debate over the ninth day. On the tenth day our Party proposed that evictions should be suspended, this debate winding up with a defiant declaration by Parnell that if Coercion were carried out, there would be a revolt in Ireland. The settlement of the land question would be taken out of the hands of the Government. "The first man that is arrested", he said, "will be the signal for the suspension of the payment of all rent in Ireland." Even yet our Party had not exhausted their resources. Other members proposed other amendments, and it was not until after eleven nights that the first stage in the programme of the Government was reached.

Mr. Forster's final speech—as, indeed, all his big speeches—was very well documented, and on the whole the anxiety to hear his proposals, of which the House in general had been given no notice, overcame the bitter passion underneath. Now and then, however, when Forster struck a fierce note in a raucous voice, there were loud cheers by the Conservatives and violent protests from the small group of Irishmen; but the first skirmish passed by with more tranquillity than might have been expected.

The Forty-one Hours Sitting, January 31–*February* 2, 1881

But the next manœuvre of the Government let loose the tempest. This was the proposal of Mr. Gladstone that the Coercion Bill should have precedence of all other business before the House. Then our men rushed into the debate, speaking to practically an empty House. Biggar was named and suspended, and then passions were let loose. Irish member after member proposed amendment after amendment. The debate was continued, but it had become aggravated by a provocative speech from Sir William Harcourt, who said the Government were determined to go on until the Prime Minister's motion was carried. It was quite clear soon that the Irish members were determined to persevere, and thus there came the first of the all-night sittings; the House did not adjourn till five minutes after two o'clock. There was worse soon to come, for this led on to the famous forty-one hours sitting, which stands out so conspicuously in Parliamentary history. It began by the declaration by Mr. Gladstone that they intended to finish the first stage of the Coercion Bill at that sitting. The announcement was received by an ominous cheer.

For a while things went on with some tranquillity, and even tamely, until Mr. Gladstone, replying to several questions which were put to him, repeated that he had every intention of pushing the Bill through in that sitting. Then the storm was not long in breaking forth. Parnell intervened with one of those speeches of cold bitterness which he could on occasion infuse into his utterances. Attempt after attempt was made to get the Government to some compromise; but they steadily refused. The English members who had occasionally interfered now lapsed into silence, so Irish member had to succeed Irish member. Appeals after appeals were made to us, but we remained deaf to them all. In succession almost every one of us made a speech. Some of us were able to hold on for even two hours, and Mr. Sexton made the speech of three hours to which I have already alluded.

By this time there was electricity in the air, and there

began to be rumours of some drastic and desperate action on the part of the Speaker. It is one of the mysteries of the House of Commons how these portents of big events, however carefully an attempt has been made to conceal them, gradually appear. They are part of that crowd psychology which we must always take into account when appraising the life of the House.

The Speaker had left the chair to take some necessary rest, and this added to the sense of dull unreality in which the five or six members, mostly half asleep, listened to the succession of Irish speakers, who were repeating the same arguments, almost the same language.

My own adventures on this fateful night will give some idea of the life the small Party to which I belonged had to live in those strenuous days. In order to be prepared for the debate, which might go on for several nights still, I went home to my room in the Westminster Palace Hotel. Sleep at that time was fortunately at my command, no matter at what hour of the day or night, and I was able to sleep quite tranquilly from midnight to close upon four o'clock in the morning. I then pulled myself together and got back to the House, to begin to prepare my contribution for the prolongation of the debate. As a matter of fact, I threw myself down on a sofa in a spare corner of the House of Commons—one could always find a quiet spot in that gallery which is above and behind the Chamber itself. For over two hours again I slept, to prepare myself for my coming effort. When I went down to the House I found Sexton speaking; Leamy and Biggar were to follow, and it had been arranged that I should follow Biggar. I had determined not to be too brief in my speech, and to give to the members, already tired out with their forty-one hours of sitting, still several hours more of impatience and waiting. Meantime Biggar had to pause for the replacement of Dr. Lyon Playfair, the temporary Deputy Speaker, by Mr. Brand. At once it was seen that something portentous was toward. It was still very early in the morning, and although the House had been almost empty during the last few hours, the Chamber suddenly became crowded; there was excitement in the very air. Everybody now knew that something very drastic was coming.

The Irish members were still undefeated, except that they knew that a heavy blow was going to be struck at them. The Speaker was evidently perturbed and nervous as he declared that, in view of the continued obstruction, he had decided to put the question immediately. He had the manuscript in his hand, which was visibly trembling. From it he read out the solemn and fateful declaration that he had determined there and then to bring the long debate to an end. In short, to make a *coup d'état*.

The Speaker's Closure, February 2, 1881

Never shall I forget the scene that followed directly after. From all sides of the House—except, of course, from our own little group—there was a thunder-clap of cheers, louder than any I had ever heard; but that was not all. One could almost detect amongst the raucous echo of the cheers the passionate frenzy which our prolonged resistance had created. That very painful moment has always remained vividly in my memory, especially the expressions on the faces of the members of the Tory Party, as they looked in triumph and hate at us, to whom they considered they had dealt a crushing blow.

For a moment we were staggered. It was Parnell's interval of rest, and one of us went over to rouse him from his bed in the Westminster Hotel. We had not yet made up our minds how to meet the staggering blow, and we could do nothing but silently take part in the division that was immediately called. Silently and sullenly both sides trailed into the division lobby.

Mr. Justin M'Carthy, that benign and striking figure, to whom was entrusted the lead during this time of storm and passion, rose to oppose the taking of the next division; the Speaker, however, stood firm. Loud shouts began to come from all parts of the House, and it was evident that Mr. M'Carthy was not going to be heard. It was then that Mr. O'Connor Power showed that sense of Parliamentary fitness of which he was always a master. Jumping to his feet, with that pock-marked face of his looking dark and menacing with rage, he shouted "Privilege! Privilege!" Beckoning angrily to his comrades to follow, he led an immediate retreat, and the Irish members walked in a body out of the House. We went straight away to what was then the Conference Room, and scarcely had we got there when Parnell appeared from the Westminster Hotel. He was fresh and smiling and composed, as we were not. Our feelings took expression in the greatest cheer Parnell had received from his followers for many a long day. In spite of everything, we felt that we had won.

It will give some idea of the courage, tenacity, and endurance of the little Irish Party that it received this deadly blow at nine in the morning; that at twelve, when the House reassembled, and after in most cases a sleepless and laborious night, they were once more all in their places. There was no sign of fatigue; still less any sign of being cowed or beaten. In question after question, in suggested motion after motion, they showed that they were ready once more to go on with the fight. Their voices were, perhaps, shrill; their nerves may have been a little jangled; but their spirits were still unsubdued.

CHAPTER IX

An angry House—Thirty-six suspensions—Serjeant Gossett's ordeal—Frustrating the new rules—Bobbie Spencer's *bon mot*—The Irish Land Bill—Fighting in the Transvaal—Afghanistan—The Marquess of Hartington.

Michael Davitt arrested, February 3, 1881

THE fierce passions which had been roused everywhere by the *coup d'état* of the Speaker and the forty-one hours' sitting had not yet died down when there came another and even more exasperating cause for fierce temper. I have already told of the part which Michael Davitt had played in the creation of the Land League. It should be noted that Davitt, though he occasionally used menacing language with regard to the part which Irish America might play in the struggle between the people of Ireland and the new Coercion policy of the Government, had steadily set his face against the crimes which were occurring with such frequency. Davitt at the time, perhaps because of this very denunciation, himself had to go in hourly danger of his life; he always had a revolver in his pocket.

The great intellectual powers which he had displayed in eloquent speeches, the enormous hold he had established on the confidence of his people, and, in spite of his hot temper, the very warm affection he inspired, had given a new conception of him to that of mere vulgar ex-convict, which is how he had appeared to Englishmen after his release from prison. Though he did most strongly advocate the abolition of landlordism, he did so, as a rule, in unexceptionable language—except on such occasions as recalled to him his early flight from the burning house of his fathers, and as he told of that enormous strength of the Irish movement in America of which he had seen demonstrations during his visit to that country.

There was one phrase, I remember, on which Sir William Harcourt was able to fasten when he came into the forefront as an advocate of the Coercion policy of the Ministry: it was a passage in which Davitt spoke of "the Irish wolfhound bounding across the Atlantic". This language was used at a time when there came into the movement almost an entirely new factor. It was the funds supplied by the Irish-Americans that started the Land League, and it was the funds supplied by the Irish-Americans that kept it going. With every new and violent incident in the House of Commons or on the country-side in Ireland, these subscriptions got a new stimulus. In one week it would be announced in Dublin that the *Irish World*, which was one of the main agents in raising subscriptions, had sent so large a sum as £4000 to the funds.

In addition, there had been created all over America as widespread an organization as in Ireland. I made a tour in America shortly after the period which I have now reached. There was scarcely a town—I might say scarcely a village—in the whole broad spaciousness of the United States in which there was not an active branch of the Land League; and each branch was engaged in fanning the flame and raising subscriptions for the Irish movement. Some of the Irish-American journals used very different language from that of the Irish leaders. In correspondence, if not in leading articles, the suggestion was made that the war between England and Ireland, as they put it, might be transferred from the soil of Ireland to the soil of England. The dreadful word "dynamite" began to be employed, and later on the preaching was turned into practice, and dynamite outrages began to be attempted in England. I need scarcely say that these incidents were a serious embarrassment and danger to the Irish Party, who relied for support on the organized passive resistance of the Irish country-side, and required no such violent methods—so dangerous not only to them, but to the two millions of Irish people whose homes and whose livelihood were in Great Britain.

Bombs dropped in the House

I remember distinctly at the time that I often left my house in the morning somewhat uncertain as to whether I should reach it alive in the evening. Such outrages as were threatened and attempted in England might very well have brought bloody reprisals. I must here candidly avow that never was I more surprised, might even say never more edified, than by the splendid self-control which the English people, including our English colleagues in the House of Commons, displayed under these tremendous provocations. One of these outrages had its scene in the House of Commons.

On Saturdays the public are admitted, with freedom and without any scrutiny, to view the House. On one such Saturday two bombs were dropped in the Palace at Westminster; one was laid in the space immediately leading down to the crypt of the House of Commons. It had very widespread results, for all the vast window facing Westminster Hall was smashed in every pane, and there was also some destruction on the floor of the House itself, some of the seats having been bombed. I went down to the House to see what had occurred, and I remember still my surprise at the perfect equanimity with which this terrible provocation was received. With the kind of speeches that were being made in favour of Coercion, and with the tide of public and Parliamentary feeling rising against us, this was a surprise; but so it was.

Davitt, in spite of such provocative phrases as that to which I have alluded, was sincerely anxious to keep the Land League within the lines of passive resistance, which had hitherto proved so entirely successful, and had undoubtedly created in Ireland an organization which could defy all the mighty agencies on the side of the Government. A phrase from Mr. Healy, afterwards quoted by Ministerial speakers, stated the case in his own picturesque way: "The law of the Land League has beaten the law of the British Government into a cocked hat".

These were the facts which made the next action of the Government the more inexplicable and the more provocative. On February 3 there was again that curious portentous whisper through the House, which anticipated some great coup. The House had not long to wait. Sir William Harcourt, the Home Secretary, was asked by Parnell whether it was true that Mr. Davitt had been sent back to penal servitude that morning by the suspension of his ticket-of-leave. Sir William Harcourt replied that, after consultation with the Law Officers and the Chief Secretary, he had come to the decision "that the conduct of Michael Davitt has been incompatible with the ticket-of-leave by which a convict enjoying the conditional favour of the Crown is permitted to be at large". To a further question by Parnell as to what were the conditions of the ticket-of-leave which had been violated, Sir William vouchsafed no answer.

The reply of Sir William Harcourt produced, as was natural, a very different reception in the different parts of the House. As a portent of vigorous action in dealing with the leaders of the Land League in Ireland, it was received with rapturous cheers by the majority of the Liberals and by all the Conservatives. On the Irish benches it produced violent excitement, and there was the feeling that such a sinister event should be marked by some dramatic expression of Irish resentment. There was a pause for a few moments before anybody took the initiative; but Mr. Dillon, whose courage and promptitude always rose to such occasions, rushed to the front.

Mr. Dillon suspended, February 3, 1881

The business before the House was a proposal by Mr. Gladstone for meeting the tremendous obstruction of the Irish members by new rules of procedure. He had risen immediately after the announcement of Sir William Harcourt. Mr. Dillon met the situation by standing up with his arms folded. Amid the general confusion, Mr. Gladstone was seen standing on one side and Mr. Dillon on the other, claiming his right to rise to a point of order.

The House, except the Irish members, shouted for action against Mr. Dillon; and the Speaker, in the terms of the new standing order that had been agreed to for dealing with obstruction, "named" him as "wilfully disregarding the authority of the Chair". Mr. Gladstone then moved the consequent resolution that he be suspended from the service of the House for the remainder of the sitting. Thereupon Mr. Dillon was asked to withdraw; but he again stood up, again demanded the right to address the House, and wound up by respectfully declining to withdraw except on the exercise of force.

This produced a scene somewhat like that which had so often occurred in the struggle over Mr. Bradlaugh. When a member disobeys the authority of the Chair, the person who is officially called upon to carry out the order of the House is the Serjeant-at-Arms. The Serjeant-at-Arms of those days was a universally popular figure: so popular, indeed, that, according to gossip, an alleged attempt by people high in authority to deprive him of his succession to the Serjeantcy, and to substitute for him a new man, produced such universal resentment that Gossett had been forced into the chair.

One of the secrets of his popularity was his creation—a creation that died with him—of what was universally known as the Serjeant's Room. This, of course, was entirely under his own control. It was he who either gave or withheld invitations to become one of the selected members who were free to use his room. It was part of the attractiveness of this more or less secret meeting-place that the generosity of his friends always supplied the Serjeant with the sound liquor that was more necessary then than nowadays to make a company agreeable and keep conversation flowing; and the little circle consisted, as a rule, of men who were in most cases equally remarkable for their enjoyment of a good joke or a good glass of whisky.

By this time, Gossett had served through a generation, if not two, as one of the officials of the House; could speak of historic and bygone celebrities like Daniel O'Connell, and Disraeli in his hot youth, with the familiarity of close personal acquaintance. He was a venerable wreck from the distant and historic past; a wreck, thin-legged, shaky.

In all his many early experiences the poor Serjeant had never had to confront incidents such as those which were now presenting themselves with maddening and unnerving frequency. First there was Bradlaugh, and now came the Irish members. The poor old Serjeant in his uniform, the thinness of his limbs exposed by the knee-breeches he had to wear, and with his sword and his tremulous hands, lent a comic and pathetic feature to these demands upon him to compel the withdrawal of members, many of them like Bradlaugh, young, or comparatively young, robust, and capable, with a breath, of blowing the poor old Serjeant off his feet.

He could, and sometimes did, call in the assistance of the young attendants of the House; and many of these had given him not only effective, but in some cases, it was thought, almost violent support when it came to the conflict with Bradlaugh. The Irish members, however, adopted a different course. Refusing to leave the House except on the exercise of force, they were content to await the approach of the Serjeant. Solemnly he tapped them on the shoulder; solemnly they accepted this as the force to which they had appealed, and quietly left the House.

Thirty-six Members suspended

Passion, however, had been so moved by the thunderclap of Davitt's arrest that the Irish members all found themselves compelled to follow the example of Mr. Dillon. One after another they came forward with some sort of dilatory motion. Mr. A. M. Sullivan, a very brilliant member of the Party, raised a point of order; but before he could go to any length he was interrupted by the Speaker. Mr. Gladstone attempted to resume his speech. But things had gone too far by this time for the Irish members to cease from their violent protest; and Mr. Gladstone had only risen, when Parnell rushed into the fray with a motion—borrowed from a precedent set by Mr. Gladstone himself in the case of O'Donnell, already mentioned—that Mr. Gladstone be no longer heard.

Thus every time that Mr. Gladstone rose there was some such motion from one or other of us. Parnell yielded to the force expressed by the tap on the shoulder from the Serjeant-at-Arms, and left the House amid a hurricane of cheers from his followers.

In turn our other members tried to intervene, and all declined to leave the House and take part in the divisions on the expulsion of their colleagues. Each was named; each was suspended; each refused to leave except compelled by superior force; each was tapped on the shoulder by the tremulous Serjeant; and each then left the House quietly, with one or two exceptions. Mr. Metge, a prominent young Protestant landlord like Parnell himself, was very excited, and remained in his seat till poor Captain Gossett had to be assisted by the attendants. The next stubborn resister was of a very different type, no less a person than the Rev. Mr. Nelson, a Presbyterian clergyman, with white hair, who was some seventy years of age.

The spectacle of Nelson and Gossett—one old gentleman attempting to resist the other—was ludicrous. It should be added that the Serjeant—the representative of force—was a much more benign-looking person than the belligerent pastor. As the attendants came in single file to assist in the work of expulsion, they suggested somewhat the depressed and perfunctory air of the theatrical "super".

During all this time Mr. Gladstone was in the unhappy position of waiting to make his speech in defence of the new rules for dealing with obstruction which had been more or less agreed to between him and the Tory Opposition. Even when thirty-two Irish members had thus been removed, he had to stand the attack of others who had come in, and he still had to move the suspension of four others, thus disposing of the whole available strength of the Party. In spite of this very trying experience, Mr. Gladstone's speech was as powerful as usual, and put the case for the restoration of its powers to Parliament with great effectiveness.

I notice the speech for two reasons. It is rather ironical to find that he wound up with these words: "Personally, my prospective concern in this arrangement is small; my lease is all but run out". Twelve years afterwards this very man was carrying through the House of Commons his second Home Rule Bill with a vigour that seemed in no way diminished, even by the heavy toll of more than eighty years of life.

The second observation I make is that, while I have felt bound to bring out the courage and tenacity of the struggle made by the small body of Irishmen to whom I belonged, I could not forget to note that there was real tragedy in the sight of this splendid Parliamentarian, filled with the best intentions, nightly fighting a struggle like this against a body of excited young men. Gladstone should have had a bigger and a better task.

Mr. Gladstone in 1881, *aet.* 71

In the end, like all the members of my Party, I came for a while positively to detest Mr. Gladstone, and I am still of opinion that his policy towards Ireland at this period was profoundly mistaken. Indeed, I have the strongest confirmation of this opinion in the revolt against it to which he was driven about a year afterwards, and which involved the sacrifice of Mr. Forster and the transformation of that gentleman from a friend and follower into a deadly enemy. But when I was most indignant with Mr. Gladstone, I could not help feeling in my heart of hearts a certain sympathy with the splendid old warrior. I still remember how, passing in the early hours of one morning through Old Palace Yard, I caught sight of the figure (it was about eight o'clock at the time) of the old man striding down to the House of Commons from his house in Downing Street.

He was a picturesque and appealing figure, with his white locks shaken by the wind, with a look of iron determination on his face, and with his brusque, youthful, and quick stride. But fierce political strife can permit no man any bowels of compassion for his opponents; and if there were any such weakening of my ferocious opposition and often ferocious personal criticism of Mr. Gladstone, it would have been destroyed by an event which soon followed the forty-one hours' sitting.

The rules for putting down obstruction were soon frustrated by the ingenuity of our members. We managed by various devices to keep the debate going, and the Second Reading of the Coercion Bill occupied four days. This was sufficient to force new rules against obstruction, and these were brought in by the Speaker. One of the rules was indeed very drastic; it enabled a certain hour and a certain day to be fixed as that which would terminate any debate, and allow the Speaker to put the question at issue to an immediate division.

At last the Coercion Bill got into Committee, and Mr. Gladstone at once showed the determination of the Government to take advantage of the powers that the new rules conferred upon them. He announced at the very beginning of the discussion that unless the Committee stage of the Bill came to a close that night he should move that it be concluded at twelve o'clock on the following evening. This proposition rather staggered the House generally, but especially the Conservative Party, and some of the Radicals expressed their dislike.

There was one scene in the discussion of the amendments on the Coercion Bill that is worth introducing as supplying the comic relief to a somewhat tragic situation. We had among the Irish members of the time a gentleman named Dawson. He had held every position the Corporation of Dublin could bestow, including the Lord Mayoralty. He had an abundant supply of resonant rhetoric, but he was a small, insignificant-looking man, given much to heroic gesticulation. On an amendment of ours that women should be excluded from the operation of the Bill, he found occasion—striking a heroic attitude—to say that if they came to seize his wife, they would have to do it over his dead body.

Bobbie Spencer in 1881, aet. 23

This led to one of the many *bons mots* of "Bobbie" Spencer. I saw "Bobbie" Spencer (later on, Lord Spencer) on the first day of the meeting of the new Parliament. He was twenty-two at the time, but he might have passed for sixteen, the face was so extraordinarily youthful. Its youthfulness and its conspicuousness were marked by perhaps the most dandiacal dress that ever the House of Commons in its modern day had seen. The especially notable point of his dress was a high collar, which almost went up to the top of his ears, and the rest of his clothes were according to this ultra-dandiacal fashion.

Though he was a manly fellow and really quite clever, there was something essentially child-like about his expression, manner, and dress, and people would never take him seriously. Now and then, rising amid an expectation of jeers, he suddenly was able to make the House laugh with him instead of at him. When, later on, the proposition was made to give the agricultural labourer the vote, he gravely began his speech with the words: "I am not an agricultural labourer"; and the contrast between poor, hobnailed Hodge and this exquisite dandy immediately jumped to the eyes; there was round after round of laughter, and the joke became historic. His *bon mot* at the expense of Mr. Dawson was this: Speaking of the lack of serious importance and, above all, of serious information in the barren conflict between the Government and the Irish obstructors, "Bobbie" complained pathetically that "there was only one piece of solid information he had received through all the stormy proceedings, and that was that Mr. Dawson was a married man".

At last the Coercion Bill was through the House. At a later period some of the substantial reasons which justified the Irish members in resisting it with such force and such unprecedented and brutal methods came to be realized. Their main point was that this attempt to cripple the Land League, with its comparatively open methods, led, when its leaders were removed, to the rise of other men and other methods. The secret society would take the place of the open; the deliberate and systematic assassin would replace the occasional and, on the whole, not very serious outbreak of crime, beyond that, of course, of intimidation by the employment of the boycott. In a few months these prophecies began to be realized, and they had a bloody and terrible harvest finally in the two hideous and disastrous assassinations of Phoenix Park.

In the midst of these wild scenes in the House of Commons, there came one of those episodes, half farcical, half tragic, which always seemed destined to play their parts in Irish history. For some reason or other the idea got abroad in the Irish Party that the Government intended to arrest and imprison Parnell. At that epoch of the movement the removal—especially in such a way—of its great leader seemed to some of his colleagues fraught with incalculable danger.

Parnell in Hiding

The leading figure in taking this view was, of all men in the world, James O'Kelly, that intrepid soldier to whom I have already alluded. This dare-devil (as he had proved himself time after time) was on this occasion cautious almost to timidity, giving his views for moderate instead of extreme courses. I used to call him laughingly the "Whig revolutionary". He strongly recommended temporary flight to Parnell, and Parnell accepted the advice for reasons of his own. Mr. Healy was entirely hostile to this course; he said himself, in his own picturesque way, that when he heard the footsteps of Parnell descending the staircase in the house in Doughty Street, where for the moment both were lodged, he imagined he heard the death-knell of the Irish cause.

Be that as it may, Parnell disappeared—it was supposed to Paris. For some days no word was heard of him. And here I must repeat that there was always in the minds of his followers, and even when he was apparently most triumphant, an undercurrent of apprehension. He was incalculable; he was mysterious—he came from a family with a bad history of both insanity and suicide.

This suspense could not be borne any longer, and several members of the Party (including Mr. Dillon and Mr. T. D. Sullivan) were sent across to Paris to try and trace the vanished chief. They went to the hotel where it was likely he would stop; they found there bundles of letters awaiting him and unopened. After a solemn consultation it was agreed that Mr. Dillon should be authorized to open the letters. It was not long after this process had been gone through that Parnell himself walked calmly into the room where his colleagues were awaiting him.

A well-known chief in Scotland Yard was reported to

have declared that if only he were required he could find our mysterious leader within a few hours—which meant, of course, that all Parnell's elaborate precautions for hiding his visits to Mrs. O'Shea at Eltham had failed before the watching of his movements by the detective department.

It was while these rumours of flight and the disappearances of Parnell were at their height that Sir William Harcourt brought about one of the most curious and really amusing episodes of Parnell's life. Sir William, in defending some portions of the new Coercion Bill, let himself go and was in one of those boisterous moods which were familiar to the House. Alluding to the disappearance of Parnell, he quoted with great effect a parody on a verse of Tom Hood's poem "Ben Battle", which runs as follows:

> Ben Battle was a hero bold,
> And wars he did delight in;
> But he fled full soon on the first of June,
> And bade the others keep fighting,

which aroused the anger of O'Gorman Mahon—the "Chieftain", as he was usually called. He belonged, as I have said already, to that generation of Irishmen in which the duel was a common episode of political difference, and such an affront in the gospel of his day—to which he still adhered—could only be met by a duel to the death.

Parnell had returned, and the first thing that happened was that a meeting was arranged between him and the O'Gorman Mahon, Mr. Dillon and myself. The meeting took place at a table in the tea-room of the House of Commons. The discussion was opened by the O'Gorman Mahon, who passed by any preliminary discussion as to whether a duel was necessary or not, and entered at once on those preliminaries for such an encounter with which his experience had made him familiar—as, for instance, where the duel was to take place, who were to be Parnell's seconds, etc. etc. We all listened silently until Parnell spoke; and then he announced that he did not intend to issue a challenge, he did not believe in the duel.

I will never forget the look of dismay and astonishment that passed over the leonine face of the old duellist; he was simply dumb with surprise, and even disgust. And so no challenge was issued. Parnell had one great quality as a leader—especially as a leader of a party so thrown open to attack as that of which he was the chief—attacks upon him left him quite cold. His only comment to me in private was, "Why should I take notice of the attacks of such a blackguard as Harcourt?" And so the incident ended.

Let me give very briefly a history of the Land Bill which, after the passage of two Coercion Acts, the Government at last brought in. It was a curious and a characteristic Gladstonian proposal; it went very far, but it stopped short of the solution which might have finished the whole question, and which ultimately had, though by easy stages and at long intervals, to be adopted by the common consent of all parties in the State—namely, the purchase-out of the landlords and the establishment of peasant proprietary.

Irish Land Bill introduced, April 7, 1881

Parnell subjected his followers to a very severe ordeal. He came down, without any notice and after some days of absence, to a meeting of the Party, and there he made to them the startling proposal that either they should abstain or vote against the clause of the new Land Bill which gave the tenants the right to appeal to a land court for the reduction of their rents. The proposal came with a shock to most of the members, and especially to old Parliamentarians like O'Connor Power. Ireland had been clamouring for a reduction of rents, and, above all, for preventing the system of rack-renting which kept the peasantry at once enslaved and pauperized. The tragic fact was that on most of the estates of Ireland the rents were being constantly increased, until there came ultimately the predestined ending in the potato as the only food. When the potato failed, famine or emigration were the only alternatives for the majority of the people.

And now here was an Irish leader actually proposing to throw away this apparently splendid triumph, after generations of agitation, of the great weapon against Ireland's two greatest perils! I was doubtful myself as to the wisdom of Parnell's proposal; on the other hand, I stood aghast at the idea of doing anything to oppose, and therefore to weaken, Parnell. I consulted Sexton, and his answer was that Parnell had acted badly, but that we were bound to support him.

I am not sure now that Parnell did act foolishly, because, in order to get peasant proprietary—our final and only practical solution—we were bound not to pledge ourselves in any way to anything which established the perpetuation of rents. The Bill was so complicated that it was with difficulty that anybody understood it. It was said that there were only three men in the House who really did understand it—Mr. Gladstone, Mr. Law (the Attorney-General), and Mr. Healy.

There was the first evidence with regard to that Bill of a fruitful combination between Mr. Healy and his brother, Mr. Maurice Healy. Mr. Maurice Healy was not a Member of the House then, but was in constant communication with his brother. Mr. Timothy Healy had become an expert shorthand writer in his early days, kept up its practice, and conducted a great deal of his correspondence with some intimates in that abbreviated method of communication.

His brother was so different from him in character that they could scarcely be taken as members of the same family. The one was short and somewhat inclined to stoutness, the other was fairly tall and spectrally thin; the temper of the one brother was hot, and that of the other icily cold. One brother was a master of rhetoric; the other was a most dreary speaker, but had an extremely acute mind.

Time after time Mr. Healy proposed amendments, while most of us stood apart, conscious of our ignorance of the complicated measure. One achievement in particular stood to the credit of Mr. Healy; he moved the amendment which insisted that consideration should be given by the law courts to the improvements in their holdings made by the tenants. The Government quickly assented to his proposal. Mr. Healy whispered to me, after this unexpected acceptance, that these words of his would put millions into the pockets of the tenants. And, indeed, so it proved to be.

There was some danger that when the Bill got to the House of Lords it would be mutilated and some bad changes be made; but, on the whole, the Bill was good enough to be accepted by both Houses.

Annexation of the Transvaal, April 12, 1877

It is one of the many proofs of how this Irish question overshadowed and almost obliterated all other questions, all other discussions, all other party issues, that two of the most important questions of British policy were dismissed in a few nights—not as many altogether as were spent in the progress of either the Coercion Bill or the Land Bill. The first of these questions was the Transvaal. I remember how surprised I was when, on paying a visit to Mr. Morley at the *Pall Mall Gazette* office, I found him very disturbed about the Transvaal. I could think of nothing, of course, but Ireland at the time, yet the Transvaal was a very serious question for the British Empire, and, above all, for the Ministry.

The annexation of the Transvaal had been carried out by Lord Carnarvon, with only a corporal's guard and a few officials; it was as unmilitary in operation as the change of guards on St. James's Palace. For a time it looked as if the Boers themselves were just as little interested in it, as if they were only onlookers at the dramatic setting of the annexation. With the vast interests involved in the gold-mines of the Rand, there were very powerful influences which favoured the annexation. There was also among the English population which the mines had attracted there a number of men who, naturally, welcomed the advent of the flag of their own country. There were also British officials who took a roseate view.

All these things doubtless helped to create in the Home Government a false sense of security, and when the new ministry came into office they found the situation very complicated and very difficult. There came, as a thunder-clap upon these roseate dreams of a satisfied and tranquillized Transvaal, rebellion. The rebellion, of course, would ultimately have been easily put down, but meantime there had been several humiliating defeats of British arms, notably that at Majuba Hill.

The Government were naturally perplexed and hesitant. The national pride of a great nation, defied and then beaten in the field by a small Republic, aroused a sense of humiliation and national resentment. But, on the other hand, the Government were confronted with the innumerable speeches made by the existing Ministry in their days of Opposition, and especially by the speeches of Mr. Gladstone, who had been one of the severest critics of the action of the previous Government in bringing about the annexation. The Opposition, as usual, had few of those difficulties that confront every Government. The Radical section of their supporters insisted, in season and out of season, on demanding from the Government the fulfilment of their promises in Opposition. Several damaging motions were made against the Government from below the gangway, where the Radicals sat. Chief among those assailants of the Ministry was Mr. Peter Rylands, the eager, almost fussy Lancashire Member who had been characterized and almost annihilated by one of those chance epithets in which Disraeli was so fertile—he spoke of him as a "didactic member". The name stuck, especially as it fitted the eager, somewhat voluble, somewhat fussy Mr. Rylands. Everybody liked him; most people called him "Peter", even his political opponents; but everybody laughed at him, and sometimes he laughed at himself.

Sir Wilfrid Lawson, 1829–1906

Sir Wilfrid Lawson, always a reckless supporter of everything extreme, and given to great recklessness of speech, was also on the track of the Ministry. Bearded, good-humoured, with laughing face, humorous eyes, and very often humorous speech, he rarely consented to realize all the difficulties of the Ministry and the complications of imperfect human conditions, and was always ready to say the most provocative and most inopportune things. When the Government of Beaconsfield had almost brought England into a sanguinary conflict with Russia, because of the approach of the Russian armies to Constantinople towards the close of the Russo-Turkish War, Lawson scandalized everybody by saying that he did not care whether the Russians entered Constantinople or not, as he much preferred them being in Constantinople to the Turks. Such a statement sounded very like high treason at a time when Lord Beaconsfield and his colleagues had brought forward all the old traditions about Russia, which had diseased the mind of the nation for several generations, the idea being that anything that increased the power of Russia in Europe or in Asia would mean the end of our rule in India, and perhaps the end of the British Empire. It was impossible to take even serious words like these from Sir Wilfrid Lawson seriously; he seemed so benign, the benignity increased by the long venerable beard, by the slight form, by the humorous conversation, by that spirit of irony which was so much in contrast with the vehemence of his opinions and of his speeches.

I remember once, when we were walking up Constitution Hill from the House of Commons, that he repeated to me an exchange of views with Sir George Trevelyan, a Radical like himself. It had been the rigid rule that no private vehicle should be allowed to ascend Constitution Hill, and the hansoms and four-wheelers of the period had to take the round on going that way to Piccadilly. The rule had been changed, and now hansoms and four-wheelers careered over the once sacred and secluded highway. "That", said Sir George, "is the one reform that you and I have seen carried out in our lifetime."

However, the shots that strayed from their light guns were enough to make uncomfortable a Ministry that contained Gladstone, Bright, and Chamberlain, and which was confronted with its own vehement discourses, made only a short time ago in the freedom of Opposition. In face of the soreness of the national pride, the Government changed its whole policy and practically admitted the claims of the Boers to the restitution of their self-government. There were some limitations, which were not seriously considered at the time—they were of the "face-saving" order; but by and by these unguarded provisos formed one of the terrible complications that led to the disastrous Boer War.

Another, and in some respects an equally important, subject also roused the vehement protests of the Opposition, and more than one attack on the Government and its policy. I need not here go into the details which led to the Afghan War and all its great cost to the nation in money and life. This policy was almost the direct invention of Lord Beaconsfield.

The Marquess of Hartington, 1833–1908

Such a policy was a disastrous one in the hands of the second Lord Lytton. I never knew him personally, and I think I saw him but once or twice. He was a man of considerable literary distinction, and one of his poems, though perhaps not noticed much in England, was learnt by heart by several of the lovers of poetry in America. His speeches and despatches had the hall-mark of literary attainments, but he had just that other side of the literary mind which made him a most dangerous man for the delicate situation in India. He was fully obsessed by that Russophobia which was popular for two or three generations among the leading British politicians. He had that touch of the grandiose that makes a man dangerous in problems so intricate as Asia. He looked to me also the kind of man that he was—a visionary; the face was handsome, but with that visionary look. Anyhow, the Government found it necessary to replace him by the late Marquess of Ripon, who was a realist, a strong Liberal, and of impeccable integrity. The very first problem the new Government had to decide was whether it should continue its occupation of Kandahar.

By the supporters of Lord Beaconsfield and Lord Lytton, this was regarded as a necessary outpost of the Empire, which would enable the Indian Government at once to have an easy approach to Afghanistan and to act promptly against any attempt at Russian aggression in that country.

I will not go into the arguments; it is sufficient for me to say here that the question was debated with great vehemence in both Houses of Parliament. For the purpose of this narrative, I will confine myself to what took place in the House of Commons, and especially the part played in that debate by the Marquess of Hartington. He was not a figure that was popular with the Irish Members: he had been Chief Secretary for Ireland under a previous Administration, and his tenure of that office had been marked by a very brutal collision between the police and the citizens of Dublin, and the conduct of the police was warmly defended and unquestionably upheld by their erstwhile head. Then, and until the end of his days, he was a vehement opponent of Home Rule, and undoubtedly the long delay which cost England and Ireland so much loss and so much suffering and injury—as people see now—was largely due to his malevolent influence.

He had good height, good features—almost a handsome face. He wore a long but rather jagged beard, and he walked with rather a knock-kneedness, which is sometimes characteristic of men who ride a good deal. His aspect was dull and commonplace, the eyes heavy-lidded and expressionless, and the under-lip as pendulous as that of the Hapsburgs. One of his peculiarities was to fall fast asleep on the smallest occasion. Even between the early hours of four and five o'clock in the evening he would be seen falling into a gentle slumber. He did so by allowing his head and neck to fall to his right shoulder; then he would be quite oblivious to what was going on, until someone roused him from this apparently uncomfortable position. It was one of the amusements, even one of the excitements, of the House to watch this strange lethargy, this rather hazardous sinking into sleep.

Obstinacy, intense courage, a Liberalism that belonged in its very roots to English Whiggery, caused him to be regarded always as representative of the most reactionary element in the Ministry. Mr. Chamberlain certainly so regarded him. Mr. Chamberlain's scheme for Radical social reform found in this obstinate adherent to the past a distinct enemy, who could not tolerate any new proposal. There had been open collision between the two men in the past when Lord Hartington was acting in a previous Parliament, and after the retirement of Mr. Gladstone as the Leader of the Liberal Party, a position to which he had been elected in opposition to Mr. Forster, Mr. Chamberlain one night denounced Lord Hartington publicly, and dismissed him as "the late Leader of the Liberal Party".

I was the spokesman of our Party in the rude language I occasionally applied to him. Once when he was left in charge of the House during the temporary absence of Mr. Gladstone, I made the rude observation that, "now that Don Quixote had left the House, Sancho Panza had taken his place".

The Occupation of Kandahar, January 8, 1879

He was sometimes a quite hopeless speaker. He and—I remember it with pain—Lord Frederick Cavendish, his martyred brother, had the very strange peculiarity that towards the end of their sentences you would suddenly hear something like a prolonged wail: it was an extraordinary form of that stammer and hesitancy in speech which is characteristic of so much English oratory. It was said of Lord Hartington, even among his own Party, that he had once been seen to yawn in the middle of one of his own speeches, and that when he was chaffed about it his retort, also with a yawn—so it was said—was: "Yes, wasn't it damned dull?" And yet I have to avow that in this speech on Kandahar I saw some great possibilities of effective debating power on the part of this hesitant and usually uninteresting speaker. The point of the speech was its realism and its straightforwardness. I remember one of the sentences that sounded like a blow of the hammer of Thor: it was when answering an argument of the Tory spokesman as to the importance and efficacy of our tenure of Kandahar. Lord Hartington replied: "We hold not one inch of Kandahar except that which we occupy with our arms".

One figure only I need mention among the protagonists in the debate in the House of Lords: that is the Duke of Argyll. He was a great but a somewhat eccentric figure—a short, stoutish person, which was brought into greater relief by the very high forehead and great mane of yellow hair, combed back from the brow. He had, I always thought, a certain resemblance in appearance to John Bright, who also was a shortish and full-bodied man. The Duke had also something like an approach to Bright's oratorical powers, and there was in his voice a suggestion of the melody of that of Bright.

In the big struggle on the Eastern Question which went on between Gladstone and Beaconsfield for so many years, the Duke of Argyll struck some of the deadliest blows. A famous speech which began: "My Lords, you are beginning to be found out", rang through the country, and helped to bring Beaconsfield's Government to disaster. He made one of his most powerful speeches in the Kandahar debate. In short, the debate in both Houses laid the final torch to the pile on which was burning the romantic and gloriose, but senseless policy of the dreamers, Beaconsfield and Lytton.

CHAPTER X

Mr. Forster puts through the Coercion Act—His shout of joy—Some Irish police leaders—Gladstone's threat and Parnell's answer—Parnell arrested—Bloodshed in Dublin—Seventeen thousand evicted in a year—The Land League suppressed.

THE real thing which at this time obliterated the interest in the Eastern Question was the obsession of Ireland. It spread like a ghost over every other preoccupation, and the worst of it was that any attempt to lay the ghost seemed to make it more dread, more menacing. Mr. Forster, pursuing his policy with the deadly self-satisfaction of his angry and defiant temper, and his unmoved and increasing self-confidence, aggravated the situation by every word he uttered. He celebrated the passage of the Third Reading of his Coercion Bill with something approaching a yell of triumph, which shocked many Liberals, and found open condemnation in some Liberal papers. I quote one—

"We do not see much ground (said the *Pall Mall Gazette*) for Mr. Forster's uncouth exaltation; it is true that Irish Members have tried to stop the Bill, but we do not know if this is a good reason why the Liberal Member should feel particularly triumphant because he has passed a measure over the heads of all the Liberal representatives of the country concerned."

Coercion Act passed, February 25, 1881

"I should not object", Forster said, "to appeal from the Hon. Members opposite to the people of Ireland. I am sure", he added, "I could venture to appeal from the Hon.

Members below the gangway opposite to their constituents." You might imagine from his words that his destruction of the Irish leaders and the Land League was close at hand. He backed all his opinions with a series of prophecies with regard to Ireland which were, to those who knew the country, merely childish ignorance. Not we, but he, represented Ireland; we were only the impudent, violent, and senseless minority that misrepresented the real public opinion in Ireland. As a matter of fact, of the many factors that helped the creation of the great Party we ultimately became, nothing contributed more than that determined fight we had made in the House of Commons. It enabled all who knew nothing of the Irish peasantry up to that time to understand the state of opinion in that country, and the Forster regime only proved that we were the determined mouthpieces of the passion which it had strengthened and aroused.

This aggravation of things in Ireland grew with every hour that followed the enactment and the carrying out of the Coercion Act. Mr. Forster struck boldly and blindly. He selected as his agents for the carrying out of the Coercion Act, the most violent of the kind of official that is always to be found. Everywhere in Ireland he had such agents for the carrying out of his policy as Major Bond, who had been dismissed from the Police Force in Birmingham, and Major Traill, whose removal from his regiment had been requested by his commanding officer. Worst of all, he had Clifford Lloyd, a man of action, and of the type who had something like a consuming hatred and even contempt for his own people. He bore down upon a meeting in Drogheda with a large body of police with fixed bayonets, and dispersed the meeting forcibly. After he had thus succeeded in accomplishing his purpose, he shouted to the people: "If you do not be off at once, I will have you shot down". For his conduct on this occasion he was denounced by Mr. Whitworth, brother of the then Member for Drogheda, as a "firebrand"; and the Member for Drogheda himself—and no man was a more bitter opponent of the Irish Party and the popular movement—declared in a debate his great surprise that the Government had employed Mr. Lloyd. "A more dangerous man", said Mr. Whitworth, "they could not send to the South of Ireland." Mr. Whitworth's brother, who was a magistrate in Drogheda, told him that if this man were sent to disturbed districts, there would be bloodshed.

One of Major Traill's exploits was to go to a police barrack on a Sunday, where some men were in custody, to hold a court there and then, with himself as sole magistrate, and to impose on the men sentences varying from eight days to one month with hard labour. When the case was brought before the superior Courts, the action of Major Traill was overruled. Baron Fitzgerald, the presiding Judge—a strong Conservative—declared that Major Traill had "sentenced three several men to imprisonment illegally". The defence made by Major Traill's counsel was that, being only a major in the Army, he "could not be expected to know the law accurately, as he was not a lawyer". But meantime the persons who had thus been illegally convicted had served the whole term of their imprisonment, and had taken their sleep on plank beds. Mr. Forster thought, when the matter was brought before him, that Major Traill had been "sufficiently penalized for the error he made by becoming the defendant in three actions".

Land Bill: Royal Assent, August 22, 1881

These excesses were aggravated by the fact that every single act of police tyranny, petty or large, found Mr.

Forster its staunch defender in the House of Commons. The landlords, at the same time, too, proceeded to justify the worst anticipations of the Land Leaguers. It had been over and over again pointed out that the effect of the Coercion Act, coming as it did on the threshold of the Land Bill, would be to inspire the landlords with the idea that the tenants, once more terrorized and broken, could be treated with the cruelty of old times. Large numbers of the tenants had not recovered from the reeling shock of 1879, had not paid their rent, and could not pay it; and even in the Land Bill that was coming there was no provision for them. The result was that evictions, which had been brought down when the Land League was completely triumphant, now made a sudden bound upwards. When the Coercion Act began to be applied, and the various local defenders of the tenants were rounded up and imprisoned by the Clifford Lloyds and the Traills, the evictions got a sudden rise from 1732 to 5262.

Finally, Mr. Forster gave further outrage even to English opinion by proclaiming the city of Dublin, although not a single political crime had been committed by any one of its three hundred thousand inhabitants. Mr. Forster was forced to confess that he proclaimed the city to prevent the meetings of the Land League, whose chief offices were in Dublin. He took advantage of the Coercion Act to arrest Mr. John Dillon.

Thus, while they were being driven to madness, the Irish Party found themselves compelled to reconsider their action. There was a strong opinion in favour of marking their fierce disapprobation of the outrages under Coercion by leaving the House of Commons for the time being; but wiser counsels prevailed, and the Irish members remained to encumber the path of Mr. Forster.

The terrible session of 1881 at last had come to an end,

but everybody knew it was not to give place to a recess characterized by the usual tranquillity when the fierce voices of controversy on the floor of the House of Commons are for the moment stilled. On the contrary, it was from the frying-pan into the fire. Enthusiastic meetings were held all over Ireland. The great political riddle of the moment was, what would be the attitude of the Irish members and their constituents to the new Land Act. There was grave difference of opinion among the people. There were abundant reasons to doubt the efficacy of the Act, and the men who were appointed by the Government to administer it were properly suspect of landlord sympathies. Even though they had desired to give the rack-rented peasants the largeness of relief demanded, it was still a question whether the peasantry as a whole should not adopt an attitude of suspicious detachment from the courts.

Many of the more extreme leaders argued that the tenantry should not touch the unclean thing, for they were full of wild confidence that anything which perpetuated rent and the landlord and the bailiff was only an additional obstacle in the path of that creation of a peasant proprietary which had now become the sole ideal of the land reformer.

The Convention in Dublin, September 15, 1881

A convention was held in Dublin, and went on for three days. Upwards of a thousand branches were represented; the tone of the speeches was triumphant, and the whole assembly breathed a spirit of exultation. The members of the extreme section formed no inconsiderable portion of the delegates. To this section enormous strength had been added by the use to which Mr. Forster had put his Coercion Acts. By this time great numbers of the men who had been most active in building up the mighty organization were in gaol. From their cells these men appealed to their colleagues not to give up the fruits of the victory for which they had consented to struggle and to suffer, and the advocates of extreme courses found the most telling argument in favour of their policy in the sufferings of Mr. Davitt and Father Sheehy, a bold Nationalist priest who had been put in gaol. The proposal of this section was that the tenantry should have nothing whatever to do with the Act; that they should continue the organization and the agitation, and go on to the bitter end, until landlordism was completely crushed, and the Government could have no choice but to accept the programme of the Land League and purchase peace by the expropriation of the landlords and the creation of a peasant proprietary. The weapon which this section held to be the means of bringing about the final consummation was a "No-Rent" manifesto; but to this course Mr. Parnell and the greater number of his colleagues were at this moment opposed.

They thought it possible at the same time to maintain the organization and to test the Land Court. This slogan of testing the Land Court was one of Parnell's greatest inspirations: he was careful to explain that he was not using, but "testing the Land Act", and the compromise was accepted. This policy, the good faith of which was afterwards questioned, represented Parnell's views sincerely. Means were taken to find test cases, and Mr. Healy and other men acquainted with the Act and with the Land Laws were sent on missions to investigate the favourable cases for such a test.

And then came another and, as it turned out, a disastrous new policy on the part of the Government. The exasperation against the Irish leaders, the insane idea to which Mr. Forster had over and over again given expression—that they did not represent the views or opinions of their people—was more or less forced, I assume, by his obstinate will on his colleagues. In rapid succession there came a series of disastrous coups, strong in appearance, futile in result.

Mr. Gladstone's Speech at Leeds, October 7, 1881

The first indication of this new policy on behalf of the Government was given by Mr. Gladstone, above all men, in a memorable speech he made at Leeds. He dressed up with his usual eloquence the thesis of Mr. Forster that Mr. Parnell represented not the majority but a minority of the Irish people. The fact that nearly a thousand men and women had been sent to gaol by Mr. Forster was in itself, to anybody accustomed to popular movements, a sure indication of the realities of Irish opinion. To this insane misapprehension of the situation Mr. Gladstone gave full adhesion. "The people of Ireland, we believe," said Mr. Gladstone, "desire, in conformity with the advice of the old patriots and their bishops and their best friends . . . to make a full trial of the Land Act; and if they do make a full trial of that Act, you may rely upon it, it is as certain as human contingencies can be, to give peace to the country. We shall rely on the good sense of the people, because we are determined that no force, or fear of ruin through force, shall as far as we are concerned, and as it is in our power to decide the question, prevent the Irish people having the full and free benefit of the Land Act."

And then came the ominous passage which prepared Ireland and England for the tremendous events that were immediately to follow: "When we have that short further experience to which I have referred, if it should then appear that there is still to be fought a final conflict in Ireland between law on the one side and sheer lawlessness on the other—if the law, now purged from defects, is still to be rejected and refused, the first condition of political society remains unfulfilled, and then, I say without hesitation, the resources of civilization against its enemies are not yet exhausted."

It should be added that, under the spell of Mr. Gladstone's eloquence and of the violent and blind resentment which the Irish leaders and the Land League had created, these words were received with a whirlwind of cheers. The memory of these cheers soon sounded vain and even grotesque in the progress of the struggle between Gladstone and Parnell.

Nobody could mistake the meaning of Gladstone's words. They meant that the Irish leaders were to be imprisoned. Parnell himself so interpreted the words of Mr. Gladstone. On October 9, two days after the Gladstone speech in Leeds, Parnell attended a meeting at Wexford. The reception given to him at this meeting is described by those who saw it as perhaps the most tremendous of the many receptions of almost frenzied enthusiasm which he received during that momentous year. Triumphal arches were erected in the streets; bands came from several parts of the county, and special trains brought thousands from the surrounding districts. Mr. Parnell's speech was in the same passionate tones as those of the speech to which it was a reply. Mr. Gladstone had complained that the want of all support to the efforts of the Cabinet from the landlords and other classes weakened the action of the Government, and finished up by saying that "the Government are expected to keep the peace with no moral force behind them".

"The Government", said Mr. Parnell, taking up this point, "has no moral force behind it in Ireland. The whole Irish people are against them. They have to depend for their support upon the interest of a very small minority of the people of this country, and therefore they have no moral force behind them; and Mr. Gladstone, in these few short words, admits that English government has failed in Ireland. . . . I say it is not in his power to trample on the aspirations and the rights of the Irish nation with no moral force behind him."

Parnell arrested, October 13, 1881

In another speech the next day Mr. Parnell used words which showed he had some presentiment of what was coming. "I am frequently disposed to think", he said, "that Ireland has not yet got through the troubled waters of affliction to be crossed before we reach the promised land of prosperity to Ireland. . . . There may be—probably there will be—more stringent coercion before us than we have yet experienced."

The next day (Tuesday) Parnell went to his home in Avondale, but he was back in Dublin on Wednesday evening, as he had promised to attend the Kildare County Convention of the Land League, which was to be held at Naas on Thursday. But on Wednesday a Cabinet Council had been held in England, and in the evening Mr. Forster had crossed to Ireland, authorized to arrest his chief opponent. Here is Mr. Parnell's own account of what actually occurred—

"Intending to proceed to Naas this morning, I ordered, before retiring to bed on Wednesday night, that I should be called at half-past eight o'clock. When the man came to my bedroom to awaken me, he told me that two gentlemen were waiting below who wanted to see me. I told him to ask their names and business. Having gone out, he came back in a few moments and said that one was the superintendent of police and the other was a policeman. I told him to say that I would be dressed in half an hour and would see them then. He went away, but came back again to tell me that he had been downstairs to see the gentlemen, and had told them I was not stopping at that hotel. He then said that I should get out through the back part of the house, and not allow them to catch me. I told him I would not do that, even if it were possible, because the police authorities would be sure to have every way most closely watched. He again went down, and this time showed the detectives up to my bedroom."

The following extract is from the *Freeman's Journal* of October 14, the day after Parnell's arrest:

"In case of any emergency a force of one hundred policemen was held in readiness in Foster Place. When Mr. Mallon, the detective, entered Mr. Parnell's bedroom, he handed him two documents without any explanation, and Mr. Parnell received them with perfect calmness; as he had had private advices from England regarding the Cabinet Council, he was well aware that the Government meditated some *coup d'état*.

"Superintendent Mallon was anxious lest a crowd should collect and interfere with the arrest, and requested Mr. Parnell to come away as quickly as possible. Mr. Parnell responded to his anxiety, and a cab was called, and the two detectives and the prisoner drove away. When the party reached the Bank of Ireland, five or six Metropolitan police, evidently by preconcerted arrangement, jumped upon two outside cars and drove in front of the party. On reaching the quays at the foot of Parliament Street, a number of horse police joined the procession at the rear. In this order the four vehicles drove to Kilmainham.

"This strange procession passed along the thoroughfares without creating any remarkable notice. The curiosity of a few people who stopped to look at it was probably aroused by the presence of 'the force' rather than by any knowledge that, after a short lull, the Coercion Act was again being applied to the *élite* of the League. . . . At half-past nine o'clock Mr. Parnell appeared in front of the dark portals of Kilmainham."

Interviewed by a reporter of the *Freeman's Journal* a few hours afterwards, Mr. Parnell closed the interview by one of those *mots* which marked important epochs in his career. "I shall take it", he said, "as an evidence that the people did not do their duty if I am speedily released."

17,000 *evicted in* 1881

Up and down the country, meantime, the police authorities were pursuing the other methods which are associated with unchecked authority and the efforts to override a people. The same war was made on boys as on women. A boy named Lee was brought before the magistrates for whistling; another boy was accused by another constable for the same offence, and, in addition, was charged with abusive language—the abusive language was whistling "Harvey Duff", a song which spoke in satirical terms of the police. A policeman in Waterford rushed into a shop where a woman was engaged in reading *United Ireland*, the Land League paper, threw her down, and, kneeling on her stomach, searched her. In Cappamore, County Limerick, a sub-constable attacked a girl twelve years of age because she was singing "Harvey Duff". He drew his bayonet and inflicted a wound.

The police made domiciliary visits by day and by night into the rooms alike of women and men. They broke into meetings; they stood outside doors and took the names of all persons entering into even the house of a priest to take steps for relieving the tenantry. Meantime Dublin Castle exhausted the resources of civil power in augmenting the rigour of the regime. Troops were supplied in abundance; horse, foot, and artillery took part in the work of eviction; and sometimes the bluejacket and the war-vessel were employed in the task of turning out the starving to die.

With the Government making the cause their own; with all the resources of the British Exchequer and the British naval and military forces at their back; with Mr. Forster to imprison every popular journalist and every popular orator; with Mr. Clifford Lloyd to make non-payment of rent a crime and the erection of huts for the outcast and the dying an act of intimidation, the landlords were not slow to turn the situation to their full advantage. For the first time in all their annals of power they had been confronted, defied, and beaten; they had been compelled, under the regime of the Land League, to surrender rights of immemorial date—to lower rack-rents, to stay evictions, to treat their tenants as fellow-beings and not as so many ciphers or serfs. The mighty organization which had made this revolutionary change was now, they thought, beaten and dead; they had now rights to reconquer, rents to exact, vengeance to feed.

They went to work with a will that recalled the spirit of the days which followed the Great Famine. The evictions for the first quarter of 1881 were 1732 persons; for the second quarter they had increased to 5562 persons; for the third quarter they were 6496, and for the last quarter 3851 persons. During the entire year of 1881, 17,641 persons had thus been deprived of their rights as tenants, and the greater proportion of them had been absolutely thrown on the roadside.

Nor did these evictions take place without scenes of

unnecessary cruelty or desperate encounter. In County Clare a man was killed by a body of police who were protecting a process-server; in April a policeman and two farmers were killed, in June a police charge killed a man, in October a man was killed at a Land League meeting by a bayonet-thrust from a policeman, and later on in that month an event occurred which produced widespread indignation. A body of police were sent to collect poor-rates due by a number of miserable tenants. Disputes arose as to how the struggle between the police and the people began, but the police fired into the people; several were wounded, and two women—a young girl and a feeble old woman of sixty-five years of age—were wounded and subsequently died. The coroner's jury brought in, in both cases, a verdict of "wilful murder" against the police.

Bloodshed in Dublin, October 1881

In Ireland the arrest of Parnell was accepted throughout the country as a national challenge. Indignation meetings were held, unless they were dispersed by the police or the soldiery, in every town and village in the country, and in most cases the shutters were put on the windows as was the custom in times of death and funerals. The country was swept by a passion of anger and grief, the more bitter because it had to be suppressed. Troops were poured into the country. Dublin was given over for two days to the police, and there occurred scenes of unnecessary violence. On the ground that there was danger of a riot in O'Connell (then Sackville) Street, it was taken possession of by large bodies of police; and when the crowd, attracted by this curious spectacle, began to jeer and groan, the police made charges, struck the people with their batons and clenched fists, and kicked those whom they felled.

The *Weekly Irish Times*, a Conservative organ in Dublin, of October 22, wrote:

"Their conduct was such as to appear almost incredible to all who had not been witness to it. . . . After every charge they made, men, amongst them respectable citizens, were left lying in the streets, blood pouring from the wounds they received on the head from the batons of the police, while others were covered with severe bruises from the kicks and blows of clenched fists, delivered with all the strength that powerful men could exert."

Later on this is what occurred, and it was perhaps an even worse scene—

"The police drew their batons, charging headlong into the people; the constables struck right and left, and men and women fell under their blows. No quarter was given. The roadway was strewn with the bodies of the people. . . . Women fled shrieking, and their cries rendered even more painful the scene of barbarity which was being enacted. All was confusion, and nought could be seen but the police mercilessly batoning the people. Some few of the people threw stones; but with this exception, no resistance was offered. Gentlemen and respectable working men, returning homewards from theatres or the houses of friends, fell victims to the attack; and as an instance of the conduct of the police it may be mentioned that, besides numerous others, more than a dozen students of Trinity College, and a militia officer—unoffending passers-by—were knocked down and kicked, and two telegraph messengers were barbarously assailed. When the people were felled, they were kicked on the ground; and when they again rose, they were knocked down by any constable who met them."

It was assuredly a strange proof of the idea that the Irish longed to be liberated from the tyranny of Parnell that the population had to be dragooned by overwhelming military and police forces into the tame acceptance of his imprisonment. The two nations, in fact, stood opposite each other—both unanimous. Not a voice in England was raised in defence of Mr. Parnell; not a voice in Ireland was raised in favour of Mr. Forster. Ireland and England confronted one another in universal and undisguised hatred. This was the strange pass to which Mr. Forster's statesmanship and his colleagues in a Liberal Government had brought the two countries.

Other Leaders arrested, October, 1881

The arrest of Parnell was followed by that of Mr. Dillon and Mr. O'Kelly. Mr. Sexton was ill in bed when a warrant came for his arrest, and he rose immediately and accompanied the police to Kilmainham. Warrants were also issued for the arrest of Mr. Healy, Mr. Arthur O'Connor, and Mr. Biggar. Mr. Healy was on his way to Ireland to give himself up, when he was met at Holyhead by an official of the League and advised to remain in England; Mr. Arthur O'Connor was also advised to escape arrest if he could, and so was Mr. Biggar. The realistic leader of the Irish movement was anxious that as many of his followers as possible should remain outside the gaols, so as to carry on the movement; and his followers, though reluctantly, accepted his mandate. In Dublin and throughout the country every person in any way connected with the League was arrested. It was evidently the resolve of the Government to destroy the organization by the removal of its most active members. Finally, the Land League was suppressed.

I myself, of course, would in all probability have been among the arrested, but I had already departed on my mission to America. I sent a cable offering to return, but Parnell did not want to waste any men, and he thought I was much more useful in America raising funds for the cause than in the idleness of a prison cell. There was no wireless in those days, and I did not learn of the arrests until I arrived on the shores of America—to find, of course, the Irish-American population more rabid than ever, and more generous in support of the movement at home.

CHAPTER XI

My sister arrested—My first mission to America—Patrick Ford and P. A. Collins—The oratory of Wendell Phillips—The "No Rent" manifesto—A clash at Chicago—Father Sheehy and the "English Pope"—I meet a famous Fenian—Parnell's mother and sisters—Anna stops Lord Spencer's horse—My father, my sister, and the landlord.

Women sent to Gaol, 1881

THE time had now come when the Government resolved to apply the Coercion regime even more stringently, when every restraint of prudence was cast aside, and Ireland was ruled with a rod of iron indeed. The pretences on which the Coercion Acts had been originally obtained from Parliament were completely forgotten. The Acts were obtained only for the purpose of putting down crime or the incitement to crime. They were now employed, openly and avowedly, for the purpose of compelling the payment of rent. The warrants of arrest contained the confession of this entire change of purpose.

The proceedings taken against women did perhaps more than anything else to expose the savage character of the regime now established, and to create the fiercest popular passion. A number of women had taken up the work of the organization as it fell from the hands of the men whom Mr. Forster had sent to gaol. Against several of these women the Chief Secretary ordered legal proceedings. The method of these proceedings was characteristic of a nature at once coarse, clumsy, and savage. In the reign of Edward III. a statute was passed against prostitutes and tramps; it was under a statute like this that young ladies, brought up delicately, were tried, and such of them as were convicted were condemned to sentences which cannot be described as lenient.

Mr. Clifford Lloyd pranced round the country with as large an escort as could have been required by the then Tsar passing through a Polish city. He arrested wholesale, trampled on the laws of the country, and carried out laws of his own suiting; he employed boldly and shamelessly every weapon of coercion for the purpose of extracting the rent. Thus the Coercion Act became simply one of the additional agencies of the rent office.

Huts were erected by the Ladies' Land League for the purpose of sheltering the evicted. Mr. Lloyd insisted that the huts were for the purpose of intimidation and not for shelter, and arrested and sent to gaol every person who was engaged in this work of relief. Against women he was at last allowed to have plenary powers. Women were, as a matter of fact, suffering far more severely than the men arrested under the Coercion Act; for the men arrested under the Act were allowed to have communication with each other for six hours out of every day, whereas the women sentenced by Mr. Clifford Lloyd were in solitude throughout the entire day. In the prisons in which they were placed, there were none but the degraded of their own sex. Mr. Lloyd sent two women to gaol for six months, and another for three; and other magistrates also sentenced women to six months' imprisonment. Among these women, I may incidentally mention, was a young sister of my own, Mary O'Connor, as she then was. I first heard of her arrest in a cablegram to the newspapers in San Francisco, where I was then delivering a series of speeches. I may as well insert here a brief account of my first mission to America.

My First Visit to America, 1881

This was one of six missions I conducted there for the purpose of replenishing our always scanty funds. I did not at first contemplate going there on that particular mission. I had been told of the very high fees that lecturers received there, and I thought a lecture tour might make some very immediate addition to the comparatively small income I was making by my pen. I told Parnell of this project. He had a very pleasant and tactful way in dealing with his followers. The stories that were told at the time of his death, and have been repeated frequently since, of his arrogance of language and of manner, are all false. One of the most popular of these stories is that when he was addressed as "Parnell" by one of his followers, he replied, "*Mr.* Parnell, if you please". Not only did Parnell never say that, but he was incapable of saying it.

As a matter of fact, he had a great dislike of personal conflict, even with his English opponents; he rarely if ever joined in such, and it was evident that these recriminations pained him. When it came afterwards to bitter political conflict between him and his former friends, he used very bad and sometimes rather dishonest language; but then he was with his back to the wall, and looking—though perhaps he did not realize it—into his own grave. But, taking him as a whole, my judgment of Parnell's personal character was that, in most respects, he was a very great gentleman.

When I mentioned this project of mine to Parnell, he asked very gently if I thought that I should thus lecture for myself when the Party stood in such need of financial help from the United States. He had to say no more. I immediately accepted his point of view and went to America as an unpaid missionary of the Party, and for seven months I spent practically every day in travelling and every night in speaking. How I survived such an ordeal I find it hard now to realize!

On October 5, 1881 (my 33rd birthday) I found myself on board the *City of Brussels*—a vessel afterwards lost in the Mersey—on my way to America for the first time, entering upon this new, unknown, hazardous enterprise of a lecture tour in the United States. I little anticipated how rich it would be in experience and how much it would cost me in labour.

I arrived in New York in the midst of a great Irish crisis at home. Parnell and several of his colleagues—Dillon, O'Kelly, and Sexton—had by this time been arrested and lodged in Kilmainham Gaol. Nothing could have been a better start for such a tour as mine, for it had set all America in a blaze.

These missions to other lands were repeated by myself and by others; they were necessary in order to gather the funds which we required to carry on our very active and very expensive movement at home. Mr. Dillon and Mr. Devlin afterwards went all through Australia; the late Mr. Swift MacNeill went to South Africa, and there obtained a very important addition to our funds by getting a subscription from Mr. Cecil Rhodes for ten thousand pounds. We of the old Irish Party did not spare ourselves, and, it may be said, walked all the streets of the English-speaking world to help the cause. And all did it without a penny piece of remuneration.

I got a foretaste of the kind of reception I was about to receive by the appearance of a steamer with green flags and an Irish band—a reception partly intended, I should say, for Mr. James Redpath, an Englishman who had taken up our cause warmly, and who both wrote and spoke brilliantly for it, and Mr. D. R. Locke (better known as "Petroleum V. Nasby"), a brilliant journalist with prosperous newspapers in the city of Toledo in the State of Ohio, and one of the great American humorists of the period, who, in the Civil War had written the most scathing though humorous articles on the Southern cause. He was a warm friend of Lincoln, who is alleged to have said that his articles were as fine a contribution as an army brigade to the triumph of the Northern cause.

I found a big and enthusiastic audience the day after my arrival and a corps of reporters ready to interview me, to describe my appearance and even my clothes; and, in short, I found myself with an America-wide notoriety within a few hours of my arrival.

It was then that I got a knowledge of the vast extent and power of our race in the United States, a fact then and for many years afterwards unrealized by statesmen at home—unrealized to the injury both of England and of Ireland.

An Irish-American Feud

The first person whom I thought it my duty to visit was Mr. Patrick Ford, then the editor of the *Irish World*. That newspaper at the time was in the full tide of its success. It had, I believe, admitted to its columns violent revolutionary articles, and it was the organ of the revolutionary party; but by this time it had given its full adhesion to the Parnell movement. One of the many ridiculous misconceptions of the situation by the English Press and English politicians was that Parnell was the slave of the revolutionary party in America. As a matter of fact, the revolutionary party, though it helped Parnell to start the movement, grew weaker as his constitutional methods justified themselves by the power we had shown in the House of Commons.

I found Mr. Ford in a house in Brooklyn. I remember

still how nervous I was as I sat in what then was common in America—a rocking-chair. Mr. Ford looked his part very well. He was a little man with a small grey beard and whiskers, but the remarkable feature in his face was the brilliant eyes that looked out from under heavy eyebrows. In a conversation with him I soon realized that the Irish forces in America, though powerful, were divided.

He and Mr. P. A. Collins, then a prominent citizen of Boston, and afterwards its Mayor and also for some years the Consul-General for America in London, were at daggers drawn, and had a pretty serious quarrel later on; and Collins in his wrath, and with a very keen sense of humour, described Mr. Ford as a cross between Marat and Danny Man—Danny Man being a hunchbacked villain in one of Boucicault's plays.

Mr. Ford had already a grievance against Collins. I had scarcely landed in New York when I found that Collins had made a series of engagements for me all through the towns of Massachusetts; this was taking my tour practically into his hands. It was a quarrel that I had to regard as serious, because, though Collins was the head of our organization, it was through the columns of the *Irish World* that we got the large subscriptions that were making our movement omnipotent in Ireland, subscriptions that reached the height of four thousand pounds sometimes in a single week. However, I had made my engagements with Collins, and, in spite of the objections of Mr. Ford, had to fulfil them.

My Tour of America, aet. 33

Thus it was that the very morning after I had made my first speech in New York I was on the way to Boston. My first meeting in Boston was enormous, and the platform was made momentous by the presence upon it of Wendell Phillips, then regarded as the foremost and most powerful orator of the United States. I remember him well—a tall figure, rather spare, clean-shaven, and grey. The remarkable thing about this man's oratory, which to a large extent helped Lincoln in the Civil War, was that the language was extremely simple and the delivery calm even to coldness.

He had, a year or two before, received Parnell in Boston, and had used a phrase which passed into history. "I want", he said, "to meet the man who has made John Bull stop and listen."

I remember another and a very different incident. There was a concert before I rose to make my speech; the chief singer was a very pretty Irish-American lady with an exquisite squint. When she was answering to an " encore" her deep curtsey brought her down into my lap, much to the amusement of my audience and much to my confusion.

I found American audiences in many respects quite different from those at home. In the House of Commons especially one can rarely make a speech without some pause created by a "hear, hear", and which by the way is translated into "cheers" by the descriptive chronicler. The audience in America never uses "hear, hear"; they as a rule sit apparently stolid and silent. On the rare occasions when they do become excited and want to approve the speaker, they clap their hands. I found this type of audience rather disconcerting, and I am sure my first speeches were rather a failure. Besides, I had not yet been fully trained in that self-possession which gradually comes to a speaker with long practice, and which enables him in the end to think aloud when on his feet.

I remember being in the presence of an audience of

some four or five thousand people in the Academy of Music, a magnificent hall in Philadelphia. The hall was constructed on the lines of a great theatre; tier succeeded tier of seats, until the last tier was almost under the roof. When I thought that I had to reach the ears and the minds of those people whom I could scarcely see, I had one of the worst fits of stage-fright in my career.

I also began to change my style of speech entirely. I found that the best method was to give my audience a connected narrative of the events in Ireland, of our purposes and of our hopes; and soon I made what to me was a great and almost disconcerting discovery.

The "No Rent" Manifesto

Mr. Parnell and his associates had issued the famous "No Rent" manifesto. Deputation after deputation came to see me before my meetings, with a leading lawyer or merchant or priest among them; and I found that, instead of setting America aflame, as was the expectation, I fancy, of the men in Kilmainham, it had created a good deal of anxiety and division of opinion. It was interpreted as more or less of an antagonistic declaration against all rent in all countries. Mr. Ford, who was an ardent adherent of Henry George and of nationalization of the land, and whose influence to a large extent had helped to elicit that declaration from Kilmainham, was of course ready to give the manifesto a wide and entire significance as a declaration against all property and land except under the control of the State.

This extreme opinion did not represent the views of all Irish-Americans, and I had to explain, as I was perfectly entitled to do, that the "No Rent" manifesto was simply a war declaration with special and avowed conditions—

namely, that the refusal of rent only applied to the period when the British Government, on the one side, were coercing Ireland; and the landlords, on the other side, were evicting the tenants in spite of their universal approach to bankruptcy owing to the failure of the potato crop. I generally sent the deputation away satisfied, and in all my speeches I devoted several minutes to explaining and justifying the refusal of rent under the then special conditions.

It was rather a relief than otherwise to me to find that the Irish-Americans had amongst them a large rational and conservative element who could not be rushed into revolutionary or confiscatory policies; in short, instead of vehement sentences, I substituted a narrative explaining and justifying our policy. This difference of tendencies among the race found its climax when I consented, with Mr. Healy and Father Sheehy, who by this time had joined me, to speak at a great national convention which was held on the 30th November and the 1st and 2nd December 1881. This was a very largely attended body—I fancy there were 900 to 1000 delegates, who had come from every part of the country. It was a striking demonstration of the power and width of the movement which Parnell had succeeded in creating in America.

I can remember no town which I visited in which there was not a branch of the then omnipotent Land League, with officers, periodical meetings, and regular subscriptions. I may make the casual remark that sometimes I found myself in communication with the secretary of a branch of the League of the name Mr. Johann Schmidt, or something like that, the explanation being that the bearer of the name, though he had a German father, had an Irish mother—one of the many clues to that very powerful influence which then and long afterwards men of Irish blood even without Irish names exercised in America. Marriages were, and probably are now, very common between the German and the Irish Catholics.

The Machinery of Politics

The clash between Patrick Ford and Collins came at Chicago, as well as a good many other things, the importance of which I was too ignorant of American conditions to realize and to which I shall have presently to refer. Whatever be the verdict upon the politicians and the policies of the United States, in one thing I found already they were supreme; and that was in what I may call the machinery of political movements. The moment a question arose, a committee was immediately appointed; this committee pursued its deliberations with its rules of order as strict as those of the House of Commons, and the machine came into existence as quick as a flash of lightning. The agenda and, above all, the resolutions were submitted to this committee and became at once the subject of a long, orderly, and good-tempered discussion; the speeches were businesslike, and were listened to in silence.

The Irish delegates were of course invited to these meetings in Chicago. I remember that once when I said "Hear, hear" or uttered some other mark of agreement with one of the speeches, I was rebuked by an American member of the committee as violating the method in which such discussions in committee should be conducted.

Of these resolutions the main discussion was on the question whether we should adopt on the land question the nationalization theories of Mr. Ford and the *Irish World*, or the policy of establishing a peasant proprietary with compensation to the landlords—the policy, as everybody now knows, which was ultimately adopted with the assent of all parties in the House of Commons.

Mr. Ford was represented in the committee by his sister and by a Labour leader named Mr. T. V. Powderly. The discussion went on through the hours of the evening and of the night, and finally our policy was adopted and that of Mr. Ford rejected. I was in absolute agreement with this result, but at the same time it made me extremely nervous, and I was afraid that it might lead to an unseemly and disastrous division of opinion in the public convention of the following day. I thought the best thing I could do was to face the situation immediately, and go and report the result to Mr. Ford and thereby disarm him. The fates played into my hands. I found Mr. Ford in bed with an infant in his arms.

I felt some compunction in bringing so contentious a subject to a man in this somewhat disabled position, but I had to go on. He expressed disappointment and disapproval, and said that any such policy as that of peasant proprietary was committing a fraud on the Irish nation. But he had to yield to the situation, and the protest at his behest the next day made, if I remember rightly, by Mr. Powderly was brief and tranquil.

Father Sheehy's Indiscretion

We had public meetings after the convention, and Mr. Healy, Father Sheehy, and I made speeches which were described by the papers as eloquent, and elicited considerable applause from the audiences. There was, however, one rather amusing incident. Father Eugene Sheehy was a courageous and self-sacrificing patriot; but he had violent opinions; he used vehement expressions—he spoke of Mr. Gladstone as a "white-haired, palsied old hypocrite", and he made speeches so violent that once at least he had to serve a sentence of imprisonment during the Coercion period. But what created the trouble in Chicago was this. In the course of a scathing analysis of English policy in Ireland, which he found universally tyrannical from the day that Strongbow landed in the twelfth century, he added the phrase, "sent by an English Pope". Nothing was said at the moment, but the next day I received visit after visit from the Catholic clergy who were present when the phrase was used, and who protested violently against it. I had to soothe them as best I could, and there was no public protest.

I have described these public proceedings of the convention, which were entirely satisfactory to me; but I was in happy ignorance that behind the public convention and in secret meetings, another and in some respects a more important convention was going on.

The full account of this subterranean work was given afterwards by Major Le Caron, who was the chief spy of Scotland Yard in America, and who will figure very prominently later on. Here the arrangements were made by which the control of the organization passed from the hands of what may be described as the constitutional supporters in full sympathy with our constitutional methods to the hands of the revolutionary party. We, of course, neither knew nor suspected anything of these movements; we were all young to America at the time. But Mr. Healy, who was a good deal more observant and sharper than I, said to me one day that he suspected what had happened, and that the gentlemen of the revolutionary organization had just led us quietly into a trap they had carefully prepared.

There was always this internal conflict going on between the revolutionary party and our friends of the constitutional party: the one put forward the demand that neither the separation idea—an Irish republic—nor the use of force should be condemned. Our friends believed in neither the one thing nor the other; but the revolutionary party was then so well organized that nearly always they managed to keep a majority of the officers in our organization.

A Celebrated Irish Trial

I remember one incident very distinctly, though it had nothing to do with this particular feature of the convention. When I was still a young reporter in Ireland the attention of the whole country was attracted by the trial of a young man named Lomasney. There was something extremely winning about the man's character. There had been an order issued by the leaders of the Fenians in the City of Cork, where he lived, that no Fenian should allow himself to be captured by the police without resort, if necessary, to his revolver to prevent his arrest. Lomasney had obeyed this order when a police constable tried to arrest him, and the constable, I believe, was killed.

Extraordinary scenes took place during his trial, so much so, that instead of being sentenced to death as he might have been, he was found guilty only of manslaughter, and the judge, Mr. O'Hagan (afterwards Lord Chancellor of Ireland) wept as he uttered the sentence.

In addition to his other qualities, one of the contradictions of the revolutionary spirit, Lomasney was an ardent Roman Catholic, and practised faithfully all the ordinances of his creed. For the time being he became one of Ireland's favourite heroes.

As I sat on the platform in Chicago I was approached by a small thin man, the leading expression of whose face was one of sweetness. He had some communication to make to me—I forget what, except that it was friendly and had nothing to do with revolution—and when I asked his name and he told me it was Lomasney, I almost jumped from my seat. This short, thin, gentle creature was the terrible revolutionary who had haunted the visions of all young Ireland in his time. I may here say that he came to England some years afterwards as an agent of the revolutionaries, went out in a boat with explosives for the purpose of blowing up London Bridge; but the explosives blew him up, and he was drowned in the Thames under the bridge he was attempting to destroy.

Parnell's Mother and Sisters

I settled down in a hotel in New York largely because Mrs. Parnell, the mother of my chief, resided there. She was then a still handsome woman of middle age, extremely like her son both in face and in figure. I found her a very strange being: she talked slowly and deliberately, but almost perpetually. She was then very well dressed. I saw her several months later; the good dress had disappeared, and she was in shabby clothes. She told me that she had become almost a pauper. There were various rumours—as to the truth of which I can say nothing—that she was an incessant gambler on the Stock Exchange, and that the change of her fortunes was due to losses in that pursuit.

There was no doubt about the strength of her Nationalist convictions, nor her desire to push so far as she could the political fortunes of the Party of which her son had become the leader. She used to accompany me to meeting after meeting while I was in the vicinity of New York. Her speeches, without any disrespect, appeared to me to be somewhat rigmarole. She could go on and on for an hour or more, pointlessly and indefatigably, but the immense respect felt for her personally, and for her son, always secured her an attentive, though a puzzled, audience.

One of my experiences was to walk behind her when we were returning from one of these meetings, and I was struck very much by the extraordinary resemblance between her figure and that of her son. There was the same immense width of hips; there was the same strange pallor and impassivity of face. Her eyes were not so brilliant as his, and I do not think they were quite of the same colour. Her eyes, if I remember rightly, were rather dark blue; his looked dark—as a matter of fact they were hazel, with those gleams of red which sometimes accompany the hazel eye. The best description I can give of the colour of Parnell's eye is red flint. In another respect the eyes of mother and son were different, because his were always bright and alert, and hers were dull and even more enigmatic than his.

She was an ardent Nationalist, even in the days of her youth. She had intense sympathy with the Fenians, who were then trying to make a revolution in Ireland; gave them, especially when they were on the run, the hospitality of her board and her bedrooms; and, though Parnell never really had even an approach to faith in revolutionary methods, he was thus brought by his own mother into intimate association with these extreme advocates of the rights of Ireland. She will recur in my pages later on. For the moment, I leave her in America, where, apart from a sojourn in Ireland, she spent many years of unbroken habitation.

There were other women in the Parnell household who doubtless also influenced the young mind of Parnell. Two of his sisters certainly were Nationalists and of rather a violent type. The first of these was Fanny. I never saw her, but I have been told that she was a beautiful girl, and she certainly had a brilliant and an ardent mind. One of her poems, "Post Mortem", written shortly before her own death and beginning "Shall mine eyes behold thy glory, O my country?" takes its place in the anthologies of Irish patriotic poetry, and probably is immortal. Her tragic fate was to be found dead one morning in Bordentown—the family mansion, which they had inherited from old Commodore Stewart—whether by accident or illness or self-destruction, nobody was ever able to tell.

The Ladies' Land League

The other sister, Anna Parnell, I did know very well. She was not in the least pretty, either in face or figure, though she bore a somewhat startling resemblance to her illustrious brother; she had great angularity of figure. Her manner and voice were even colder than his, though behind the frigidity of the language there was intense and passionate feeling and opinion. She was far more extreme both in thought and in method than her brother. When he and his colleagues later on were removed from all control of the Land League by their imprisonment in Kilmainham Gaol, she was partially responsible for the creation of the Ladies' Land League, and as such she was perhaps the most violent of the women zealots who controlled that somewhat revolutionary organization.

One of her exploits was to approach Lord Spencer, then Lord-Lieutenant of Ireland and carrying on a fierce war with the Land League, and, holding the bridle of his horse, address to him language of reproach and remonstrance. It should be added that one of the very first things Parnell did after his release from prison was to put an end to her political activities.

I may as well close her story by saying that, after the

death of her brother and the breakdown for the time being of the organization of the movement which he had created, she disappeared, and the leaders of our Party were informed that she was in something like a penniless condition. She was mainly concerned at the moment in obtaining the publication of a book of poems. We got the poems published, and sent her a sum which was supposed to be the profits—entirely imaginary—on the sale of the book. Then one day we heard that, going out for a bathe on a somewhat ugly morning at Ilfracombe, she had been caught by the waves and drowned.

At a later moment I will describe the endings of the other members of this very remarkable and most unfortunate family. For the present I conclude my allusions by saying that in the family history of Parnell there was more than one case of madness and of suicide. His brilliant grand-uncle Henry, to whom I have referred, hanged himself in his dressing-room in Cadogan Place, Chelsea. It was one of the abiding terrors of those quite close to Parnell in hours of crisis that his brain might also give way and his end might be like that of some of his ancestors. The truth is that Ireland was led—and consummately led—by a madman of genius, not an uncommon phenomenon in the history of other leaders and other countries.

My Sister arrested—My Father's Landlord

One morning, on taking up a paper in San Francisco, I saw a telegram announcing that Miss Mary O'Connor had been sentenced by a resident magistrate to six months' imprisonment for a speech she had made in reference to a local landlord, Thomas Naughton, or to his widow. Tom Naughton, as everybody called him, though he was a bad landlord, was not a bad fellow. He was, if I remember rightly, the illegitimate son of his predecessor in possession of the estate.

I remember him still: tall, extraordinarily handsome, though a prematurely rather obese young man. They used to say he could scarcely read or write. He certainly was illiterate, but he had plenty of good sense, and reticence enough to cover his defects. Everybody loved him, for he was a genial soul, and his good-nature beamed through his blue eyes. He was one of a type of landlord whose personal good-nature fought in vain against the iron necessities for ready money which the generations of idleness and practical separation from any part of a landlord's duties, except that of collecting rent, had imposed on the majority of the small landlords of Ireland.

His family had been spendthrifts, and he was a spendthrift. He was a splendid horseman; I can still see his figure speeding across the racecourse near my native town; and he looked a regular Centaur, the horse in a rapid gallop seeming to be almost a part of himself. He was a good judge of horses, especially of racehorses, and I remember how the whole town was thrilled by the news that his horse, called Thomastown—that was the name also of his estate—had won the Grand National.

In those days the Irish landlords of this type, as soon as they got possession of their heritage, made a trip to London or to Paris; but some of them had to be content with the glories and the less luxurious vices of Dublin, and many of them, after one single excursion of this kind, returned broken in fortune and broken in health. Among all these wild men, poor Thomas Naughton left Dublin with a reputation as the wildest of them all.

My father got the great idea, as so many Irishmen of the period did, that he could make a good living as a farmer. He came from a race of farmers, but he knew nothing about farming. I spent some years as a child off and on at his farmhouse; they are among some of the pleasantest memories of my life. One fine day my father found himself unable to pay his rent; and, in spite of the ten years or so he had given to the farm, with all his small capital, he had to be evicted, though his good-natured landlord handed him the notice almost with tears in his eyes. I think he was dead when the incident took place in which my sister took part; she was the last person in the world you would expect to figure in such a scene.

She was, like her father, small in stature, very gentle, and, like him also, very fearless, and she soon became one of the leaders of the hopelessly rack-rented tenants of Tom Naughton. He had disappeared by this time, and his closing years were, I believe, clouded by a paralysis which was the inevitable consequence of his disorderly life. His widow, who was a fine woman, tried to bring up their children to reign in his place. This was the state of things on which the Land League was to try its great weapons of refusal of rent and resistance to eviction. And this sister of mine became the leader of this movement. She was brought before the Resident Magistrate—who was also a friend of her father—and who, having to send her to gaol under the orders of the Government, of which every magistrate at that time was a servile and dependent creature, was said to have almost wept as he sentenced.

As soon as I heard what had happened I borrowed fifty pounds from an Irishman in San Francisco, and sent it home as some salve for the sorrow I knew must be there. I paid back this loan with the money I got by writing some articles for a San Francisco paper.

When the "Kilmainham Treaty" was concluded, the time had come for me to start on my voyage home to Ireland. Feelings of hopefulness, of triumph, and of peace came with that event, and I started on my voyage with the confident hope that the first person to meet me on the quayside at Queenstown would be my liberated sister. I will tell later how rudely my expectation was to be frustrated.

The Session of 1882 begins, February 7

The reader has now the causes which produced the fit of absolute frenzy which passed over Ireland during the winter of 1881 and the spring of 1882. The country stood at bay, with speech and writing and organization suppressed, with every day adding a new wrong and a new insult, with wholesale eviction, exile, and starvation once more confronting the nation as in the dread past. A wild and horrible wave of crime passed over the country; the days of 1880 might well have been looked back to as extraordinarily peaceful in comparison with the period which had now set in, and neither the Queen's Speech nor the Marquess of Hartington could any longer declare that there were but comparatively few murders.

In the year 1880 the number of murders was eight; there was no homicide, and there were twenty-five cases of firing at the person. In 1881 there were seventeen cases of murder; there were five homicides, and sixty-six cases of firing at the person; and in the first six months of 1882 there were fifteen murders and forty cases of firing at the person.

These were terrible and eloquent demonstrations of the failure of Mr. Forster's policy. This was clear practically to everybody in England, and one of the curious developments of the situation was a bold move on the part of some important Tories in the House of Commons to question the whole policy. The Tory Party, indeed, as they had done in discussing Gladstone's Land Bill in the first stages, and as many of the wiser members of the landlord party in the House of Lords also foresaw, preferred the policy—which happened to be that of the Land League, too—of peasant proprietary, however perilous, to the long, wearisome, and, to the landlords, rather disastrous process of fixing reduction of rents through the Land Courts.

Sir John Hay gave notice of the following motion:

"That the detention of large numbers of Her Majesty's subjects in solitary confinement, without cause assigned and without trial, is repugnant to the spirit of the Constitution; and that, to enable them to be brought to trial, jury trials should for a limited time (in Ireland), and in regard to crimes of a well-defined character, be replaced by some form of trial less liable to abuse."

And Mr. W. H. Smith gave notice of his intention

"To ask the First Lord of the Treasury if the Government will take into their consideration the urgent necessity for the introduction of a measure to extend the purchase clauses of the Land Act, and to make effectual provision for facilitating the transfer of the ownership of the land to tenants who are occupiers on terms which would be just and reasonable to the existing landlords."

If the leaders of the Land League required any justification of their policy, here it was. They had declared all along that Coercion would fail, and that peasant proprietary was the only final and practical settlement of the Irish Land question; and while they were in prison, and after their country had passed through the agony of a fierce and bloody strife, English Conservatives came forward to adopt their scheme.

Meantime, undoubtedly inside the Cabinet that section which had always been doubtful of the wisdom of Forster's policy were active. At this time, also, there came two new figures into the background of negotiations; one was Captain O'Shea, and the other Captain O'Shea's wife.

CHAPTER XII

Parnell and Mrs. O'Shea—Irish members' hatred of Captain O'Shea—An encounter in Vauxhall Bridge Road—How a birth was announced—Mrs. O'Shea as political emissary—Parnell jilted by an American girl—His release from gaol—The Phoenix Park murders.

Parnell and Captain O'Shea

I HAVE not noted up to the present any of the premonitory signs of the coming of that tragedy which was to kill Parnell and ruin Ireland for at least a quarter of a century of agonized expectancy. I have often asked myself when it was that I first suspected the possibility of this oncoming disaster. It was suggested in a recent notorious trial that the Irish members were cognizant of the whole story for years, that they discussed it, that it was well known in society, and that among the other persons who must have been cognizant of it was Mr. Gladstone.

This was an entire misconception of what really occurred. No man ever took more elaborate, or sometimes more childish, means of hiding the story of his passion than Parnell. Mrs. O'Shea lived in a house at Eltham, near to Mrs. Wood. Mrs. Wood was the widow of one of the Woods who played so large a part in the conflict between Caroline of Brunswick and George IV., and she inherited a vast fortune. Mrs. O'Shea was her favourite niece; though they did not occupy the same house, they practically lived together. It is an interesting little item in this story that the evenings of the poor old lady and Mrs. O'Shea were enlivened by a gentleman who read to them from the classic works of the period; the name of that gentleman was George Meredith.

I say with confidence that for years after the love story of Parnell and Mrs. O'Shea had begun there was not among the members of the Irish Party a breath, perhaps not even a suspicion, of the real state of affairs. So great was our sense of Parnell's overwhelming importance as the leader of our Party, and as the one man who could unify the fissiparous nature of our people, that anything which contemplated any injury to Parnell, or anybody who contributed in the slightest degree to such a result, would have been regarded as guilty of high treason to Ireland. What whisper there may have been among Englishmen I have no idea, for, as I have already said, at that time all communications between our Party and our English colleagues in the House of Commons was cut off by the absolute boycott—they of us, and we of them. I have not the smallest doubt that the matter may have been discussed among some Englishmen, but that could happen without reaching our ears. Men in public life—and, indeed, decent men in private life—feel themselves debarred from discussing mere scandalous stories. The air is always thick with such stories where politicians are concerned, but the one rule that a politician must apply to all such things before accepting and acting on them is, whether they have been subject to the inquisition of a public trial.

I could add that Captain O'Shea, for reasons I do not profess to be able to penetrate, took as much pains as Parnell to conceal the state of things between Parnell and his wife. People used to remark that the relations between Parnell and O'Shea were almost ostentatiously fraternal. O'Shea used constantly to cross from the Ministerial side of the House to our benches on the opposite side to speak with Parnell. This was made the more remarkable that it was happening years before the historic Galway election. O'Shea appeared quite free from suspicion as to the real state of things, but long before the relations between O'Shea and his wife were known, he had become an object of hatred and bitter suspicion among the members of our Party.

As I said in a recent trial, it was O'Shea the Whig, and not O'Shea the *mari complaisant,* that formed the chief ground of the almost frenzied hatred with which some members of our Party resented his return for Galway. Whenever O'Shea came across the House to Parnell, the attitude of Parnell to him was always that of an elder brother—indeed, the attitude of a brother advising or even reproving a younger brother. I remember one day hearing Parnell say to O'Shea, "I think it would be very foolish"—evidently discussing some action which O'Shea contemplated, and O'Shea seemed to submit to the advice.

Stories of Captain O'Shea

Here is a little incident which puzzled me at the time. I had left the House during a sitting one day, to pay a visit in Vauxhall Bridge Road; I was astonished to meet O'Shea walking by the side of a lady. Now I have made it a rule in my life to become blind when I pass an acquaintance, still more a friend, in company that may or may not be compromising, and that occasionally occurs; so I passed O'Shea by without any sign of recognition. And, so far as he could observe, I had not seen him. But within a few hours of this incident I was astonished to find O'Shea approaching me in the House of Commons, to which he had returned. He began eagerly to enter into an explanation as to the identity of the lady with whom he had been walking. He told me, but whether true or false I do not know, that the woman I had seen with him was a maid to a very important lady of the social world whom it was his duty to conciliate or to consult. I could not help thinking even at that time that his manner suggested that of a man—as the Americans say—covering his tracks.

There is another even more striking, and I think even more puzzling, incident which remains in my memory. One night Parnell and O'Shea came together to the little building at the corner of Essex Street, which was where the London offices of the *Freeman's Journal* were situated. Mr. J. M. Tuohy, the brilliant journalist, who recently died, was then in charge. Shrewd, observant, a little cynical, he had a very clear eye for everything that was going on in the Irish Party, both on the outside and the inside. He was the last man, however, to interpret wrongly, and he was incapable of inventing any event. From his own lips I heard this extraordinary story. When Parnell and O'Shea had communicated to him some statement as to the political situation which they desired should be conveyed to the Irish people through the columns of their own influential paper, Parnell took a piece of paper out of his pocket and, showing it to O'Shea, asked him whether he should also supply this information to the *Freeman's Journal*. O'Shea nodded an assent, and Parnell handed the document to Mr. Tuohy. It was indeed an astonishing document under the circumstances. It was an announcement in due and also rather curt form of the birth of a daughter to Mrs. O'Shea, the wife of Captain O'Shea, late of the 10th Hussars.

I hesitate to repeat a story from the lips of Mr. Labouchere. O'Shea had become an early friend of Labouchere. Labouchere, rich, a great journalist, great social leader, especially among a semi-Bohemian circle, as well as among a more sober people, used to give Sunday receptions during the summer in the beautiful grounds of Pope's Villa at Twickenham. O'Shea had a certain similarity of mind to that of Labouchere in his cynical outlook on men and things. He represented Labby as saying to him, as they stood at the door of the Villa looking down on the large company assembled on the beautiful lawns which led down to the Thames: "I think we have every rascal in London here". O'Shea added that Mrs. Labouchere was at that moment in an interesting condition, and that was supposed to account for the birth of a daughter some months afterwards. O'Shea said, "Labby alone could do it". Labby repeated to me a story O'Shea told him, as he alleged, about his relations with his wife. O'Shea for many years lived in rooms at Albert Mansions in Victoria Street, while Mrs. O'Shea lived at Eltham. The story of O'Shea to Labby was that Mrs. O'Shea used to pay him occasional visits at Albert Mansions and—I need not be more precise, but suggest the humiliating and shameful compromises which married women who have a lover sometimes have to submit to. At that I have to leave it.

Mr. Joseph Chamberlain, 1836–1914

There is something rather curious, all the same, in the fact that Mrs. O'Shea should have been used, as undoubtedly she was, as a go-between in important and secret political transactions. I remember as one of the many explanations of this curious state of things that one of the Liberal leaders with whom O'Shea kept in touch was Mr. Chamberlain. This was not remarkable, as Mr. Chamberlain was known to be very much out of sympathy with the policy of Mr. Forster, and probably he was one of the chief agents in procuring the downfall of that Minister.

O'Shea and he could very well hold intercourse, as, on the one hand, Chamberlain was against Coercion, and on the other, O'Shea was at that time anxious to keep in as well as he could with the Liberal Party. O'Shea played so questionable a part in the House of Commons, and was regarded with such dislike and contempt, that his countrymen underrated him, and, above all, underrated his ambitions. I believe he was pursued all through his Parliamentary career by the impossible dream of becoming Chief Secretary for Ireland. It would have been an extraordinary position for any Irish member who had been elected as a Home Ruler, and, although he was not without his cleverness, this position would have been impossible to him. But it was a constant vision of his, and accounts for many of the disasters in which he played so vital a part.

It was intelligible that under these circumstances he should constantly keep in touch with Mr. Chamberlain, who was at once a very important member of the existing Cabinet, and, what from the O'Shea point of view was much more important, was also consumed by a voracious ambition—which would in time involve his dethroning Mr. Gladstone from his domination of the Liberal Party.

There was undoubtedly a pretty constant and lengthy correspondence between O'Shea and Mr. Chamberlain. I would suggest it as rather a fault in Mr. Chamberlain, perhaps a peril to himself and his future prospects, that he had such a ready and very often such an indiscreet pen. Anyhow, the fact remains that, either through the relations between Mr. Chamberlain and Captain O'Shea or for some other reason, Mrs. O'Shea was employed more than once as a go-between in very delicate negotiations. I am afraid that she, and perhaps even Parnell, sometimes dallied with the idea of making these interventions one of the defences which might save them from the disastrous consequences of the discovery of their relations.

I do remember some mysterious suggestions—I forget whence they came—that if the case were ever allowed to go into court there would be some surprising revelations which might in some way compromise Mr. Gladstone. I am convinced to-day, as I was at the time, that Mr. Gladstone had, up to the time of the bringing of proceedings by O'Shea, no idea of the real state of things between Parnell and Mrs. O'Shea. He was not the type of man either to look for or to suspect illicit sexual relations. There was never a man I met who gave me the impression of being freer from any tendency towards sexual irregularity.

However, negotiations began to take place between Parnell and the Government. Parnell certainly had abundant reasons for desiring to end as soon as possible the disastrous state of things which Forster had brought about. Evictions were increasing; so were crimes. As Parnell himself put it, "Captain Moonlight" had taken his place as the guide of the Irish people.

Women in Parnell's Life

He may have desired release for himself. There never was a passion which seemed to have taken more full possession of a man than Parnell's passion for Mrs. O'Shea had taken of him, and by the time of his imprisonment in Kilmainham it had certainly reached one of its most violent moments. I have often asked myself, in thinking over the past, when it was that this passion had its first beginning; sometimes I put it down to a curious little scene that took place between him and me early in 1881, as I recollect it. We were sending off a telegram from the telegraph office then underneath the Westminster Palace

Hotel. I observed that Parnell was not in his usual composed temper. He tried to write; finding the pencil somewhat blunt, he threw it from him with an angry gesture and an angry face. I jumped to the conclusion that something unusual had disturbed his nerves—was it refusal or was it concession of the last surrender of the woman he loved? But this I must admit was an afterthought; I at the moment had no real suspicions.

I have already told another incident which first made me begin to think that there was a woman in Parnell's life. I knew from a previous story—of which I heard very vaguely at the time, but which I have since been able to trace more in detail—that there had been a violent love affair in his past. A third sister of his has added another story to those which we have heard. She was the member of the family who had its characteristic eccentricity more wildly and publicly developed than any of the others. I never saw her, but I have been told she used to drive about Dublin in the weirdest garments—flaring yellow, or some such outrageous colour. In her old age she quarrelled with some of her friends in England, packed up her boxes, crossed to Ireland, drove with her luggage to one of the Dublin workhouses, demanded admission, and died that night in a pauper's bed.

She contributed to the literature of Parnell's biographies a strange book. The character of the book will be guessed from the fact that she gave a considerable number of pages to a nude and candid story of her struggle against an infatuation for a man who was not her husband. One must take with caution anything that comes from her pen, and therefore the story may be true or false in which she describes how a youthful amour of Parnell at Cambridge University had a tragic result in the death of the young woman who was the object of Parnell's passion.

Charles Stewart Parnell

To face page 232

Anyhow, the other love affair is well established, and certainly much more creditable as well as more credible. In paying one of his visits to Paris, Parnell met a beautiful young woman—an American—who was turning the heads of all the young men of the period. Parnell fell violently in love with her, and, after many refusals, was accepted as her fiancé. I heard a good deal about the lady on my visits to the town of Providence, Rhode Island, to which she belonged, and from all I heard the passion of Parnell became quite intelligible, for she was a beautiful and attractive, and also, I think, a very uncertain type of her sex and of her nationality.

Parnell heard, to his dismay, that after her return to America she became engaged to another man. Without hesitation or delay he rushed over to America; but he rushed in vain, for she never became his wife. What a strange difference it might have made, not merely to Parnell, but to Ireland, if this devoted love had met with a true response! As a matter of fact, her refusal of Parnell brought her as well as him to tragedy. She married, I was told, a lawyer in Boston; the marriage proved unhappy, and I believe she returned to her native city and passed her last years there—perhaps in remorseful recollections of the man in whom not even the penetration of real love could have foreseen in his obscure youth the predestined greatness. Parnell, when he met her, was simply a small country gentleman whose name had never been heard outside his own property.

One night I was walking home with him and John Barry, a member of our Party. Parnell separated from us, and Barry repeated to me the somewhat strange conversation—strange, because Parnell was usually so reticent—which he had just had with Parnell. Parnell, turning to Barry, asked him if he had ever been jilted. Barry had had his own unfortunate experiences, but jilting did not happen to be one of them. I believe, if I remember rightly, that Parnell added that it was this jilting that had brought him into Irish politics.

Parnell's Lodgings in Bloomsbury

For the first years after he had entered Parliamentary life Parnell had no time left for women. He was living during these years in miserable lodgings in Keppel Street, near Russell Square; he had to work there during the day, and then, from four till four the next morning, he was in the House of Commons. He was busily engaged in the work of obstruction, which then he had to carry on with practically the sole assistance of Biggar. It was work the absorbing character of which, in my own case at a later epoch, I have already described. Anyhow, thus he was when one day there came the first scene in the tragedy that was to destroy and kill him.

Our authority for what took place is an autobiography by Mrs. O'Shea (or Mrs. Parnell as she was when the autobiography was written). Her statement is that, having invited Parnell to several dinners she was giving, she had received no reply, and that at last, determined to catch the elusive figure never seen by anybody in those days outside the House of Commons, she tracked the lion to his den, and sent in her card to Mr. Parnell at the House. He came out: so far as one can judge, it was a case of love at first sight. And so Parnell at last came to a dinner.

I heard from Justin M'Carthy a description of that dinner which differs slightly from Mrs. O'Shea's account. The dinner took place in what was then Thomas's Hotel, in Berkeley Square, and Mr. M'Carthy's version was that, as the party was waiting, and apparently in vain, for the appearance of Parnell, Mrs. O'Shea indulged herself in some witticisms at the expense of—I think it was she herself who invented the phrase—the "Uncrowned King", harping on the phrase again and again, always in a spirit of light mockery. Anyhow, so the thing began.

I dare say it had proceeded some distance when, on a visit to Parnell's house at Avondale, I first caught a strange inspiration. That visit I recall very vividly. Parnell was one of those magnetic personalities, at once so taciturn, so inscrutable, and at the same time so hypnotic, that everything about him, even the most trifling, took your attention, and perhaps set you guessing. I remember still his simple preparations for a lunch we were to take during our pilgrimage to Glendalough, one of the many historic places within a short distance of Avondale. With his own hand Parnell took a loaf of brown bread, cut it into slices, buttered them, and then wrapped them in a paper parcel: this was to be our lunch.

After we had visited St. Kevin's Bed (the precipitous stone couch to which the ascetic saint fled from the alluring eyes of the historic Kathleen, and whence he flung the maiden into the lake below), we had a little wait for our car. I was surprised to see the approach to angry passion with which Parnell rebuked our driver for his delay. Before the arrival of the car, Parnell took out from his pocket a very beautiful watch; large, of gold, it had all the latest devices in the shape of additional hands that pointed to the date of the month, and so on. My curiosity was excited, and I asked him where he got the lovely watch. There was a smile, I remember still, on his face, half abashed and half self-complacent. He confined himself to saying that it was a present. I said to myself: "That is a present from a woman, and a woman in love". I think now I was right, and that already the fatal passion had begun to consume him.

A Nationalist Defeat in Ulster

There was one other incident a little later which produced a profound impression on my mind. Parnell did not, as I have already said, rise to his supremacy and his omnipotence at a jump. In the Parliament of 1880–1885 he was in the difficult position—which, of course, was thrown at him by Forster and by others—of not representing in the House of Commons a majority even of the Home Rule representatives from Ireland. The number of his followers, which began at something like twenty, very gradually increased on the infrequent occasions when a by-election took place. In one case he had a real defeat. A vacancy had been created in the county of Tyrone; the Liberals put forward an excellent candidate, Tom Dickson, an Ulster man, always a strong defender of the rights of the tenants, and in himself estimable, kindly, popular.

In the strained relations which the passage of the Coercion Act had brought between us and the Liberal Ministry, we resolved to make war on the Liberal candidate, though he was opposed by one of our deadly enemies in an Orange leader, Colonel Knox, more hostile even than the English Tory to any concession to Irish nationality or the Irish tenant. To secure the defeat of the Liberal candidate we put forward a third candidate. We selected an Englishman, the Rev. Harold Rylett, a Unitarian clergyman who had a "cure" in the North of Ireland, and who was a member of our organization.

It was one of the most exciting elections I ever attended, largely because it was practically my first acquaintance with the North of Ireland since my visit as a young reporter in 1867; and to me, from the South, it was a surprise to find that in the Black North, as we called it, there was Nationalism more ardent, more fierce, than among the Nationalists of the South.

We had meeting after meeting. Parnell worked as hard as any of us; I made innumerable speeches. In spite of us, Dickson, the Liberal, was returned. It was immediately after that that Parnell and I went to Monaghan, a neighbouring county. It was when we were going to bed in a country hotel there, and had to occupy the same room, that I had the experience of seeing Parnell take a revolver out of his pocket and put it under his pillow.

I remember also another little incident which had its meaning. We travelled together either to or from Monaghan with a man who talked incessantly, and in a voice so low that neither of us could understand a word he said. I had been discussing with Parnell whether, when we were both in gaol, as we expected to be under the suspension of the Habeas Corpus Act, we should be deprived of the privilege of talking to our fellow-prisoners. Parnell, when the garrulous but unintelligible gentleman had disappeared, asked me, with his delightful smile, whether it would be any solace to imprisonment to have the benefit of the conversation of such a gentleman.

Travelling with him at the same time, I asked jokingly —I used to make many observations, I may say, in pure devilment, just to draw him out from his obstinate reticence—when something sounded like the impact of a stone against the window of the carriage, whether I should not publish an alarmist telegram about an attempt on our lives. Of course, I had no such intention; but the reply of Parnell was significant: "Mocking is catching"—one of the many instances of that strong vein of superstition that ran through his nature.

Earl of Kildare, then let the Earl of Kildare govern Ireland'. The King thought it was better that the Earl of Kildare should govern Ireland than that there should be an arrangement between the Earl of Kildare and his representative. In like manner, if all England cannot govern the Hon. Member for Cork, then let us acknowledge that he is the greatest power in Ireland to-day."

Parnell had fought and he had beaten all the mighty resources, from soldiers to gaols, of the Government, and he stood supreme, more unchallenged than ever, in his control of the Irish people. His release had been accompanied by everything that could mark the end of the struggle between him and the Government. One of the reasons of the capitulation on the part of the Government was the existence of the Bill dealing with the question of arrears in rent, which had been drawn up by the hand of Mr. Maurice Healy and on the lines suggested by Parnell. Parnell had been very much worried by this problem of arrears, which remained outstanding even after the passage of the Land Act. To some of the existing tenants even the Land Act had not given any relief, because they were too overladen with unpaid and unpayable arrears of rent to enter the courts.

One of the many testimonies to the justification of Parnell came from the pages of *The Times,* which had been one of the most persistent and effective of Parnell's enemies. The extract is from a leading article of March 17, 1882:

"The recurrence of St. Patrick's Day, with its traditional celebration, its old toasts and its old memories, reminds us that the Irishman of history and of tale is nowhere to be found. . . . The Irishman is becoming like the Englishman—that is, the Englishman of the dull, morose, self-satisfied sort, the man who sees everything and everybody from his own point of view, and pursues his object with a dogged indifference to all reasons, interests, feelings, and beliefs that may happen to clash with it. The Irishman, like the Englishman, is now righteous in his own eyes, and his righteousness is to hold money and land, and have the use of it as long as he can. . . . He has actually become a citizen of the world, and a very cute fellow. He has played his cards well, and is making a golden harvest. He has beaten a legion of landlords, lawyers, and encumbrances of all sorts out of the field, driving them into workhouses. He has baffled the greatest of legislatures, and outflanked the largest of British armies in getting what he thinks his due. Had all this wonderful advance been made at the cost of some other country, England would have been the first to offer chaplets, testimonials, and ovations to the band of patriots who had achieved it. As the sufferers in a material sense are chiefly of English extraction, we cannot help a little soreness. Yet reason compels us to admit that the Irish have dared and done as they never did before. They are welcome to that praise. But they have lost, and it is a loss we all feel. Paddy has got his wish—he is changed into a landowner."

The Phoenix Park Murders, May 6, 1882

Everybody knows now how this roseate dream was turned into the blackness of night by the assassination of Lord Frederick Cavendish and Mr. Burke in the Phoenix Park. No element that even the intervening genius of ill-luck and accident in human affairs could devise was wanting to make more tragic this terrible tragedy. Lord Frederick Cavendish had succeeded Mr. Forster with the mission of undoing the evil work of his predecessor, of restoring peace and goodwill where there had been war and hatred. The gentleness of his character, his straightforwardness, his courage, his simplicity, made him the ideal instrument for such a policy of reconciliation. He had none of the harsh and narrow prejudice of his elder brother, though physically the resemblance between the two, as I have already noted, was considerable—the same beard, the same stammer, the same unaccountable and painful wail in the middle of a sentence. But, on the other hand, he had palpably greater gentleness than his brother, and was sweeter-tempered. He was married to a woman of ideal beauty of character; her conduct during the tragic crisis will remain one of the most beautiful pages in the history of Englishwomen. And, to add to the mischievous trickiness of fortune, his death to a certain extent was accidental. The men who murdered him did not want to murder him—did not know who he was when they murdered him.

And again, a further element of poignancy, he was murdered because, like the splendid fellow he was, he came to the rescue of Burke, and it was in trying to save Burke's life that he lost his own.

I was not either in London or near it at the time of the great tragedy, and I can only speak from hearsay of what occurred. Parnell had got back to the Westminster Palace Hotel, and was doubtless full of confidence in the future. Davitt was actually on the train bringing him back from the convict prison to liberty, to hope, and to London. The news was conveyed to Parnell as soon as it was known. Justin M'Carthy, who was very soon closeted with his Chief, told me that Parnell bore himself with extraordinary courage. Naturally he might very well regard his life as in danger passing through the streets of a London seething with natural rage and fury against this terrible outrage.

One of the first things the Irish leaders found themselves compelled to do, was to issue a proclamation which not only denounced the crime, but even expressed a hope that the criminals would be discovered and brought to justice. Parnell also, in the despair created by this wreckage of all his hopes, made the offer to Mr. Gladstone, very much commented upon afterwards, to resign the leadership of the Irish Party so as to free Mr. Gladstone, in conducting his new Irish policy, from the embarrassment that had been created by this dreadful interlude.

As a matter of fact, the authors of the crime were almost immediately known. In that respect Dublin Castle justified itself, and under Mr. Forster's Coercion Act these men were arrested and lodged in Kilmainham. There was no doubt, I believe, in Dublin, as to who had done the deed. A prominent colleague in my Party said in private conversation that the men who had committed the murder were at that moment in Kilmainham Gaol. But no evidence could be found that would justify their being put on trial; and a very short time afterwards, James Carey, the central figure in the tragedy, was not only walking the streets of Dublin, but, as a member of the Corporation of Dublin, appearing at the festive gatherings in the Mansion House.

My Return to Ireland, May 1882

I promised to tell my readers how the Phoenix Park tragedy reacted on myself. I was on the ocean, returning from my first trip to America. My sister had been in gaol, as I have already told, but under the terms of the Kilmainham Treaty I expected that she would be released and would be the first person to greet me on the quayside at Queenstown.

There was no wireless telegraphy in those days, and the Phoenix Park assassinations had taken place whilst we were in mid-ocean. There was a very nice naval officer in the same berth as I was, and we became great friends. Just, however, as we were approaching the quay, after the pilot had come on board, this naval officer came down to me with a very sombre expression on his face. The pilot had brought him the news of the assassinations, and soon after he came with some of the ghastly details of the stabbing to death of Mr. Burke and Lord Frederick Cavendish.

I need not say how ghastly was this news, in contrast with what I had so confidently and hopefully expected to hear on my return to my native country, after the absence of seven months. I remember how I looked at the smooth waters leading to Queenstown Harbour, and wished heartily that I were beneath them and free from this tragic disaster, in which I saw the cause of my Party and my country overwhelmed by an act of suicidal madness.

I could do nothing but leave the boat and take the earliest train I could to Mullingar, in which town was the gaol where my sister was lodged. I found her quite collected and not in the least miserable; her main theme was the almost cowardly grief, as it so appeared to her, with which her townspeople had followed her arrest and her progress to gaol.

Next day I started back for London. I did so with a certain amount of apprehension, and the possibility before my mind that vengeance might be taken on my innocent and grievously shocked self by the English people, who would be incensed and provoked by the horrible crime.

To my astonishment, my reception was not only not hostile, but utterly friendly. This was another example of that wonderful self-control and love of fair play, to which I have already drawn attention, among the English people at very provocative moments in the Irish troubles. Even the engine-driver got off his engine at Chester and assured me that no one thought of accusing my colleagues or myself of any participation in this dreadful trouble. I got no hatred, but everywhere sympathy.

CHAPTER XIII

The young Balfour—Mr. Forster turns on his old colleagues—My angry taunt to John Bright—The Phoenix Park approver—Carey's duplicity—A discovery of knives—Mallon the detective and two jarveys—Informer's attempt to involve the Land League—Five executions—A swift vendetta—Informer shot at sea.

THE situation in the House of Commons that followed the Phoenix Park assassinations was very mixed. Bitter passion, which one would have thought would be stilled in face of this gigantic event, broke out worse than ever. The "Kilmainham Treaty" appeared to the Conservative Opposition a splendid weapon to use against the Government; there was something, of course, inviting in bringing out the contrast between a Coercionist Government which had imprisoned Parnell and his colleagues, and which had by speech as well as by action sought to identify the Irish leaders with encouragement of the disorder that was then devastating the country, and these same gentlemen entering into confidential and friendly communication; and on this theme Tory speaker after speaker dwelt.

Mr. Balfour in 1882, *aet.* 34

I remember one of the fiercest speeches on this theme was uttered by Mr. Balfour, then a slim, rather shy, rather unconfident young member. It required the Parliamentary courage which he always possessed to stand up against the mighty Gladstone, then in the zenith of his inexhaustible powers of rhetoric—even passionate rhetoric.

I still remember the pause—it looked like a shrinking

from the odious word—which Mr. Balfour made before he applied to the transaction the words "an infamy"—a terrible word, it need scarcely be said, which stung Gladstone to the quick. Gladstone got up in a tearing passion—so far as anything can be called passion in a man who, when he was on his legs, had always a cool bearing and at least an appearance of inner composure. He lashed at his young assailant. Some of his hits evoked the frantic cheering of his friends, but to me they appeared at the moment rhetorical rather than effective. For instance, Mr. Balfour had made his attack under cover of a motion for adjournment, that somewhat innocuous method of getting an excuse for a speech; and Gladstone, with eyes flaming, with scorn in his tones, having described the terrific indictment by Mr. Balfour—which was really an indictment of the good faith of the Government, and, to use Mr. Balfour's own words, the attributing to it of so terrible a thing as infamy—said that Mr. Balfour was satisfied in presenting such an indictment with the miserable expedient of a motion for adjournment.

Around the "Kilmainham Treaty" there raged day after day tempest after tempest, attack after attack. A time was to come a year later when these attacks got a horrible addition to their effectiveness from the discovery and indictment of the Phœnix Park assassins; but even at the moment things looked so black, there was such universal suspicion in the air, there was such a natural horror at any communication, especially of a friendly character, with a man who had been so much denounced as Parnell, that the weapon was undoubtedly very effective; and no man appreciated this fact more than Mr. Forster.

He had left, of course, the Treasury Bench on his resignation of office as Chief Secretary for Ireland; but he took up another seat which was dramatically suitable for the part he was playing; he sat on the second bench above the gangway—that is to say, immediately at the back of Mr. Gladstone. It was a point of vantage, the strategic importance of which he fully realized, for there was no point in the Parliamentary game that he did not realize and play to its utmost possibility. It was as if—I think I used the words at the time—the envious Casca had placed himself at the point from which he could most certainly and most effectively stab the great Caesar in the back.

Mr. Forster assails the Government, May 15, 1882

Mr. Forster struck the first blow, and one of the most effective, in the scene in which Captain O'Shea played a most important, and by no means a successful, part. The chief charge of the Opposition was that letters had been exchanged indirectly between Parnell and the Government. Captain O'Shea stood forward as the chief repository of this correspondence, and was called upon to produce the letter of Parnell. Mr. Forster had dealt the first of these deadly stabs by reading a memorandum which he had written of a conversation with Captain O'Shea. This memorandum had supplied some terrible weapons to the now excited and somewhat triumphant Opposition. It contained the suggestion that Captain O'Shea had undertaken "that the conspiracy which has been used to get up boycotting and outrages will now be used to put them down". Captain O'Shea objected that he did not use the word "conspiracy", saying "organization is, I believe, the word I used".

This apparently fatal admission of connivance, if not of absolute connection, between Parnell and the organizers of the disorders and murders was followed by even a deadlier thrust. It was by exposing the request that a man who was in flight should be brought back to Ireland to help in putting down the murder organization. He was, said Mr. Forster, "a released suspect against whom we have for some time had a fresh warrant, and who, under disguises, has hitherto eluded the police, coming backwards and forwards from Egan to the outrage-mongers in the West".

I will here interject that the name was not then mentioned; the man's name, however, was P. J. Sheridan. He was destined to play a most important, and even sinister, part in later events, but for the moment he was suspected of being the man who, passing through Ireland periodically, disguised as a priest, suggested and organized some of the sanguinary crimes that were then the horror of the world. Mr. Forster signified that his sense of the proposal, that he should employ a man suspected of murder to put down murders, was too horrible. "I did not feel myself", he said, "sufficiently master of the situation to let him see what I thought of this confidence, but again told him that I could not do more at present than tell others what he had told me."

It will be seen what deadly ammunition Forster supplied to the enemies of the Government, and of Parnell; and, above all, what support his speech gave to the plea of the Opposition that Gladstone and his colleagues were now willing to shake hands with murderers, and that Parnell was supporting their cause for the purpose of making the deal which came to be known as the "Kilmainham Treaty".

A good deal of discussion took place afterwards on Mr. Forster's conduct in thus revealing to the House of Commons a memorandum presented by him to his colleagues in the Cabinet. There was, I think, a general feeling, except among the heated partisans on the other side, that Mr. Forster was rather playing a questionable game, obeying his passions, and, above all, his passion for vengeance against Mr. Gladstone and his former colleagues by revealing a confidential memorandum.

Mr. Gladstone denies a Deal

Mr. Forster aimed another, and perhaps even a more sinister, blow at his old friends. After various challenges, Captain O'Shea got up to read the letter, often referred to, which he had written. Mr. Forster ostentatiously handed a copy of the letter to Captain O'Shea. Captain O'Shea refused to take it, and then read his own copy; but immediately after he had read it, Mr. Forster, with his skilful instinct for striking with apparent innocence an ugly blow, asked Captain O'Shea to read another sentence, which apparently Captain O'Shea had omitted. It was a disastrous sentence which contained the words: "That with the Government's readiness to bring in the Arrears Bill, and order the release of the prisoners, they might be able to co-operate with the Liberal Party". The terrible import of these words was that they seemed to imply that which Mr. Gladstone had always denied, and Mr. Forster had always suggested, that there was a deal between the Government and Parnell. Such a deal between the Government and the political supporters of Parnell was the very gravamen of the whole case of the Opposition, and, in their view, justified such an expression as "infamy" by Mr. Balfour on the "Kilmainham Treaty".

Mr. Gladstone was able to show that in a letter of his he had refused to accept this offer, and desired that it be expunged from the whole transaction. But Mr. Forster had already done the very evil damage to the reputation of the Government which was to remain, and of which a year later he was to make vehement use in the most powerful speech of his career.

Meantime the chaos remained in the House of Commons, and, instead of there being that co-operation between the Irish members and the Liberal Party which had been foreshadowed, they were drawn up in most uncompromising opposition to each other.

Everything got into the way of everything else: Coercion into the way of Conciliation, long debates on the Closure in the way of Coercion. There was a menacing quarrel between the House of Lords and the House of Commons. I should be only repeating the description of the same scenes that took place in the session of 1881 in recording what took place with regard to the new Coercion Bill. Sir William Harcourt was in charge of this Bill. There was then no member of the Ministerial party who had such a genius—always excepting Mr. Forster—for exasperating the Irish Party as Sir William Harcourt. If I were to try and sum up in one adjective his demeanour on this occasion, I would employ the word "mantling". He was "mantling all over": his immense height, his haughty expression, his large, well-shaped nose, his double chin, his resounding voice—all might be summed up in that one adjective. By this time he has passed into history; there has been a most complete biography of him prepared by his son, and written by the able pen of Mr. A. G. Gardiner.

My own feelings towards Sir William Harcourt changed in time very much from what they were at that particular moment. He was one of the most difficult of men, and actually an impossible colleague during the greater part of his life; and he paid the penalty of losing the Premiership by the dread inspired in all his colleagues of being under so impossible a chief. At this time, too, he was in a somewhat morbid state of mind; as Home Secretary, he was haunted almost every hour of his life by the designs attributed to the Irish-Americans, for it was then that their dynamite explosions and wholesale murder schemes were being hatched. He felt in dread of assassination every hour of the day, and perhaps his fears were not altogether ill-founded; but there was a general assumption that his physical courage—no one could doubt his political courage—was not in proportion to his splendid physique. His arrogance in debate often led him unto language of perhaps unnecessary provocation. Thus, for several months, his very rising to speak was the signal to the Opposition to prepare for a heated debate on the new Coercion Bill.

Sixteen Members suspended, July 1, 1882

Whenever any of the Irish members dropped some menacing observation, Sir William was on his feet denouncing him in strong language. There were prolonged sittings, sometimes extending from the afternoon of one day, through the night, to another day. There was one scene in particular that created a great deal of excitement and some uneasiness afterwards. The Irish members had been carrying on their campaign for several days and nights in succession, when Dr. Lyon Playfair, the Chairman of Committee and Deputy Speaker, drew out from his pocket a paper, and reading from it, he astonished everybody, including perhaps the Ministry and the supporters of the Ministry, by the following words:

"I think the time has come when it is absolutely necessary to stop the persistent and wilful obstruction of the business of the Committee that has been going on, and I severally name to the Committee as having so engaged in this course of obstruction the following members: Mr. Biggar, Mr. Callan, Dr. Commins, Mr. Dillon, Mr. Healy, Mr. Leamy, Mr. Justin M'Carthy, Mr. Marum, Mr. Metge,

Mr. T. P. O'Connor, Mr. O'Donnell, Mr. Parnell, Mr. Richard Power, Mr. Redmond, Mr. Sexton, and Mr. Sullivan."

This was really further than the Speaker had gone in his famous *coup d'état* of 1881, and there were many misgivings and doubts. Mr. O'Donnell stated that he had been absent all night. Mr. Marum was stopped when trying to say that he had not been in the House of Commons many hours. I myself was walking up and down the Terrace in the morning light when, to my surprise, I was told that I had been suspended. Mr. Dillon's case was even more eccentric: he had gone home to his lodgings to take his sleep, and on coming back, in blissful ignorance of what had taken place, was as calmly as usual walking through the doors of the House of Commons, when the attendant informed him that he could no longer enter, as he had been suspended.

There were motions after motions, debates after debates, but of course what Dr. Lyon Playfair had done remained irrevocable, and nothing happened afterwards—all we could do was to accept the accomplished fact.

Dr. Lyon Playfair was the last man in the world from whom one would have expected such a violent proceeding, but at this time he was old and not very strong. A tiny little man with full cheeks and great big glasses, he looked far more what he was, a man of science, than a politician, and he was quite unfitted for these stormy times. This unexpected outburst on his part was rather the result of weakness trying to look strong than strength. He was really quite an impossible Chairman; he had all that calmness of mind so essential to a man of science, but he had not any absorbing interest in Parliament to qualify him to fill the place he occupied.

The only two great Parliamentary Chairmen of that

period were Mr. Raikes, who had held that position under Lord Beaconsfield, and Mr. Lionel Courtney, who came at a later date.

John Bright in Limerick, 1868

There is another episode in this session I must notice, for it had very considerable results on the future relations between the Irish Party and one of the most powerful men in the House of Commons, Mr. John Bright. I am afraid I still retain a little of the bitterness which the great tribune had created in my mind at this particular epoch in his career. This bitterness was a good deal accounted for by the difference between Mr. Bright's earlier and then later attitudes. For two generations at least Mr. Bright had been the foremost among English statesmen to have both a knowledge of Ireland and some idea of her position and her needs. I will here mention a personal episode—it will illustrate his position during this earlier part of his political life. I was then a young reporter, a poor thing who wrote bad shorthand and then was unable to read it. Everyone acquainted with shorthand well knows that the art of writing it is different from that of reading it. Charles Dickens tells his own experience of this by describing how, by learning the one, he found himself ignorant of the other, and had to start all over again.

I still remember as if it were yesterday, although it is nearly sixty years ago, that remarkable moment of my life. Mr. Bright had come to Ireland on a visit to his great friend George Peabody, and he took advantage of the excellent salmon-fishing which the American magnate rented yearly near Limerick. The Liberals of the city, in their turn, took advantage of his presence to give a lunch in his honour, and I had been sent by my newspaper to report it.

The appearance of John Bright was my first surprise.

I had seen many caricatures of him in *Punch*, and many denunciations of him. It will surprise people of this generation to learn that for a considerable part of his career Mr. Bright was regarded with about the same hatred and contempt as Mr. A. J. Cook in our own day. In *Punch* John Bright never appeared except as a prize-fighter, and a very stout one too, with gloves on his hands and a single eyeglass in his eye. I never saw Mr. Bright wearing an eyeglass; I don't think he ever did. And, if he had a reasonable girth of waist, he was certainly not the obese creature of the caricatures that *Punch's* artists made him out to be. Nor had he a pugilistic expression on his face; on the other hand, though he was at bottom a benign character, he was a severe man, often a bitter man, and there was terrible bitterness in the small mouth.

Apart altogether from his hostile relations with us, and the resentment which that caused in our breasts, he was sincerely loathed by all the Tories in the House, and he did his best to merit that hostility. He would not spare them: they were never right; they had always been the enemies of the people's rights; all through their historic career they had always been on the wrong side—and all this was spoken with an absolute certitude, and an almost arrogant expression on his face, and in a language and with a voice that poured vinegar into the wounds. He certainly was a good hater!

But my next surprise was his manner of speech. I had fully expected from these anticipations I had received to find a thundering and bellowing voice, and even violent language. Judge of my surprise when I found this awful man speaking in a soft and rather a low voice; but what a voice! I do not know that there was any voice I ever heard so beautiful, and I also observed that the voice had almost something of a nasal sound—which at that time, and for a long time afterwards, I regarded as characteristic of the Nonconformist pulpit.

John Bright, 1811–1889

This speech, which I heard at Limerick, and tried vainly to report accurately, was delivered in 1868, two years before even the first creation of the Home Rule movement, and was practically a Home Rule speech. It certainly was one of the first moments I can recall in which my own mind became convinced of the justice and necessity of Home Rule. I have already revealed the fact that in my education both at school and at college I had read scarcely a single page of the history of my own country. I was absorbed in the history of Greece and Rome; intellectually, I stood apart from all the thoughts and conditions of my own country. Around me there was the tragedy of the cruel evictions and the dreadful emigrations reaching sometimes to a quarter of a million a year. If I had listened to my inner ear, I might have come to hear the wail of sadness from all these broken homes and broken hearts; but innocently my eyes were blinded, and my ears deaf, and my convictions unformed. And then I heard this great man, and not a man of my own race, utter the phrase: "I believe what every Englishman believes—that what one Act of Parliament has passed, another Act can repeal". It was a terrific awakening. For more than half a century the Repeal of the Act of Union had been the policy of Irish leaders and of Irish members. It was almost as if Bright had taken on himself the mantle and the policy of Daniel O'Connell.

Everyone who understood the methods of Mr. Bright always felt that the most characteristic thing about him was his magnificent composure, and the sense of the resolute and perhaps impenetrable mind and character—

at once stern and lofty—behind the words he used. In oratory, I must insist that the temperament of the orator counts as much in effectiveness as even his intellectual gifts.

I went out after the speech to see Mr. Bright going away with Mr. Peabody in his carriage, and again as I looked at the profile I was surprised, perhaps even a little shocked, by that terrible severity of his expression and especially of the tight-lipped mouth.

I was one of those who, many years afterwards, had to reply to Mr. Bright's attacks on my party. I made a speech in which I recounted the incidents I have just described, and up to that point I think my tone was fair and my speech was listened to; but in my last words I slipped into the observation, which I have ever since regretted, that "a mean and vain old age had followed the splendid manhood".

The Liberal Party shouted at me in violent anger, and not without justification. From that time I never exchanged another word with Mr. Bright. Indeed, the sad part of this collision between him and us was that it broke so many of his old Irish friendships. Mr. Justin M'Carthy had been the editor of the old Radical *Star* of the 'sixties—not the *Star* I afterwards founded, which is still existing, but the organ of Cobden and Bright. Mr. Bright used to go constantly to the office, and he and Mr. M'Carthy used to be in almost eager and always friendly conversation. It was to Mr. M'Carthy that Mr. Bright made the announcement that perhaps in the next Administration which Mr. Gladstone was soon to create he would be a member of the Cabinet. For years he and Mr. M'Carthy had ceased to recognize each other.

In spite of the terrible strain of the long and truculent sittings, the effort to grapple with Irish obstruction compelled the Ministry to have an autumn session. By this time all chance of united action between the Government and the Opposition was destroyed. If there had been any possibility of any such joint action, Lord Randolph Churchill would have put an end to it. More and more he got into antagonism with Sir Stafford Northcote and more and more he took an independent position. Anyhow, the Conservative Party by this time had come to the conclusion that the closure as proposed by the Government would play into the hands of those Radicals (Mr. Labouchere in a speech pleaded guilty to the suspicion) who wanted drastic legislation, and an opportunity of pushing it through with greater celerity than in the old House of Commons with the old rules. There were endless discussions, endless adjournments, generally an alliance of the Parnellites and the Conservatives against the new rules, and especially against the rule of closure. In that autumn session there was also established what has since proved to be one of the most useful pieces of machinery in the House of Commons—namely, the Grand Committees.

James Carey turns Queen's Evidence, February 13, 1883

These prolonged sittings produced their toll. Mr. Gladstone was compelled to go for some months to the South of France, and Sir Stafford Northcote had also to take a long vacation. Ireland, in fact, was wearing everybody down. Parliament was not prorogued until December 2, and in the session which began on February 15, 1883, Ireland might have been expected to give something like a respite from the devastating obsession it had exercised on the time, energy, and health of the House of Commons. Parnell was still pressing for some more remedial legislation; there had been a number of terrible crimes, and there had been fierce reprisals and wholesale arrests under the newest

Coercion Act. But still Ireland was not as prominent at the beginning of this as it had been at the beginning of previous sessions, and it looked as if the policy of the new Chief Secretary, Mr.—afterwards Sir—George Otto Trevelyan, who succeeded Lord Frederick Cavendish, and Lord Spencer (the new Lord-Lieutenant in place of Lord Cowper), would remain without producing any more Ministerial crises.

And then suddenly, as in the case of the Phoenix Park murder, there burst upon the House unexpectedly a new event which once more revived the old passions and the old controversies. The Government had at last got evidence which enabled them to put James Carey and the other Phoenix Park assassins on their trial; and there was reason to believe—as turned out subsequently—that at last they had evidence which would bring the verdict of conviction.

One afternoon the evening papers of London came out with the startling announcement that James Carey was giving evidence against his former associates. Everybody could see the tragic and tremendous portent of such a development; it must mean convictions and hangings. There was an immediate flight of men who were either implicated or might think themselves in danger of being implicated in the revelations. The trial stirred up again the violent hatreds caused by the assassinations that threatened to cripple and discredit the Irish Party, though their entire innocence of the transaction—more damaging to them than to anybody else—could clearly be proved.

No life story is more extraordinary or self-contradictory than that of Carey, the religious hypocrite, from his proud leadership in the Assassination Club to his betrayal of his comrades and dupes, and onward to his own assassination, the news of which was received with exultation in Ireland. Carey withstood for months the temptation of the Government reward of £10,000 and a free pardon for information that would lead to conviction.

When first arrested he conducted himself very jauntily, and he confidently declared that he would become even with his gaolers, and that he would bring an action for damages against the authorities for arresting him on a false charge. Up to a point the prisoners put up a bold front; they scoffed at statements by the Crown witnesses, and their attitude in general was that of jaunty scorn. But they underestimated the resources and cleverness of the detective Mallon. He had to wait for months before landing his catch; scruples, if he were susceptible to any, were to be set aside; every sign was to be watched for in the prisoners that would indicate nervousness among any of them. Carey appears to have been given away by the involuntary lack of control of his sympathetic nervous system under the influence of fear.

Mallon plays for his Man

Now Mallon played for his man. The shutter in the door of Carey's cell was left partly open, as if by accident, and Carey saw Mallon go into the next cell; there was whispering, the banging of a door, the sound of coughing now and then, voices, voices. The next incident in Carey's watch of untold terror was the opening of the other cell door, more whispering, words, words, and the emergence of Mallon, apparently very pleased with himself, and arranging sheets of foolscap in his hands. Carey passed a night of terror; was not his fellow-prisoner, Dan Curley, in the next cell? The warder, who pretended to be Carey's friend, played upon his prisoner's terrors, and told him when he brought his breakfast that there was "black treachery" afoot. The warder would say no more; he seemed in terror for himself, as if there were a very cataclysm of informing about them, and that the walls were listening. It was not long until Carey saw Mallon go into the cell, and later in that awful day Mallon was accompanied there by George Bolton, the Crown Prosecutor, with the dreaded sheets of paper in his hand.

Carey sent for Mallon, who did not show any eagerness or surprise, and, in fact, kept up the pretence that Carey had made up his mind too late—that the Crown had now all the evidence they wanted independent of his proffered aid. This drove Carey into deeper panic; certain knives had been found hidden on his premises. He waived all question of terms; he would tell everything. As a fact, Curley had previously been removed without Carey's knowledge from the next cell, and all the business of Mallon and Bolton, the foolscap and the whispering and the warder's fears, were a piece of consummate acting staged in the gloomy corridors of Kilmainham for the purpose of striking terror to Carey's heart. And the result was that Carey told all.

The degradation of the ex-bricklayer aspirant to the office of Lord Mayor of Dublin was complete. On the morning when he came forth publicly as the betrayer of his comrades and followers, he had to be prepared for his ordeal in the witness-box by several glasses of brandy, so that he was in an excited condition when he took his place in the box. When a shout of execration went up from the prisoners, he turned to Curley, and taunted him: "Ha, Dan, I got there before you".

Carey in 1883, *aet.* 38

James Carey differed from other informers in that he was the originator of the very organization which conducted the murders; he was the first member in Dublin, and was one of the "big four" who made decisions and handed on commands to the rank and file. Conceive, then, the sensation among the prisoners when they realized that he was missing from their group in the dock during one of those police-court sittings in Dublin in February 1883. Then they heard the cry, "Bring up James Carey". And there he was in the witness-box, James Carey, their chief, determined in cold blood to save his skin at the expense of their lives. There was no hope when he would tell all, for he knew all, being himself the pulse of the conspiracy, the man who drove the others on to their desperate courses. No wonder that as he stood there prepared to take the oath the prisoners began to hiss at him.

Born in Dublin in 1845, Carey was the son of a bricklayer from Celbridge, county Kildare, and was himself a bricklayer for eighteen years. He then set up as a builder for himself, and at this time, while on the one hand he was taking a prominent part in revolutionary organizations with the object of establishing an Irish republic, he was enriching himself by the unpatriotic trade of taking over slum property from his former employer and sub-letting it by the room to poor people. A man of ambition, he had come to be recognized as the spokesman of his trade in Dublin. He had been elected a councillor of the Dublin Corporation only a few months before the murders, and was even spoken of as a future Lord Mayor. He had appealed to the electors, not on political grounds, but as one who would "see fair-play for the working-man". He was an active member of an association for the support of Irish manufactured goods. In outward show he was a most exemplary man, being an officer of a religious confraternity and a frequent communicant.

At the time of his arrest he was building a mortuary

chapel in one of the Dublin workhouses, and this work was continued by his brother Peter, until he too was arrested.

And now to go back to the murders of May 6, 1882.

The only clue to the perpetrators was black-edged cards found in the letter-boxes of the Dublin newspapers on the evening of the crime. These cards bore the words: "This deed was done by the Irish Invincibles".

The Government proclaimed a reward of £10,000 for the discovery of the murderers, and even offered £1000 for "hearsay evidence". Here, no doubt, there were plenty of applicants. Two jaunting-cars had been seen loitering about the scene of the crime, and there was talk of a car driven furiously that Saturday afternoon from the Chapelizod gate of the Park with four men aboard "laughing and talking like mad".

Accordingly, four thousand jarveys were examined by the police on their movements during that fatal Saturday. All were able successfully to account for their actions, including, indeed, had the authorities known, the two actual drivers concerned in the crime—Myles Kavanagh and James Fitzharris, who was known by the nickname of Skin-the-Goat. Shortly afterwards James Carey; Dan Curley, a carpenter; James Mullett, a publican; Edward McCaffrey, a shopkeeper; and two brothers named Hanlon, were lodged in Kilmainham Gaol, on suspicion of being connected with the conspiracy, and underwent searching examinations. But nothing could be got from them, and after having been detained for some months they were released.

The Invincibles did not lie low for long. Pat Delaney was arrested when drawing a revolver on Judge Lawson as the latter was about to enter the Kildare Street Club. The Judge was so unpopular with the people that he had a bodyguard of seven, and, as he drew the revolver, Delaney betrayed his intention to one of them in mistake for one of his own gang. Delaney was arrested on the spot. Next a man named Field, who was foreman of the jury that condemned Francis Hynes, a Land League prisoner, was shot at on the steps of his house. Delaney, under rigorous examination, admitted that he knew some of the men whom the police were trying to connect with the assassinations.

Phoenix Park Trials, January 13, 1883

Suspects were now brought to Dublin Castle, and they underwent a rigorous examination for hour after hour at the hands of a special magistrate, Mr. Adye Curran. They seem to have stood the ordeal loyally enough towards one another, for when twenty-six prisoners were put in the dock on January 13, 1883, charged with the Phoenix Park murders, they appeared remarkably confident and jocular. The press immediately directed attention to Carey as the only man of any public prominence among the prisoners. It was said that he smoked cigars and wore kid gloves on the journeys between prison and courthouse. It was he, too, who advised his fellow-prisoners to change their positions in the dock from time to time, in order to test the identification by witnesses more keenly.

The "rot" began among the prisoners when one of them, Farrell, turned Queen's evidence; he was not greatly in the "know", he was not in the inner gang, but he gave witness to Carey's connection with the Fenians. Then a frail old man, a tenant of Carey's, was brought forward as a witness. There was a loft over the room occupied by this tenant, and he had watched Carey mounting there on a ladder with a parcel. After Carey's arrest he investigated, and in the loft between the ceiling and the slates he discovered a rifle and two large knives. These in his own cupidity he further hid, so that some days afterwards when Carey's brother, wife, and son went to the loft and searched for a long time they could not discover this incriminating property. After their visit the tenant, Fitzsimon, went to the police. The knives, which were a foot long and an inch broad, were described by doctors as surgeons' amputation knives.

The prisoners were badly shaken when Myles Kavanagh, the jarvey, turned Queen's Evidence, and told how he had driven four of them to the scene of the crime, had seen Fitzharris, the other jarvey, drive up with "Mr. Carey", and then he described the details of the crime. It was said that the detective Mallon had brought Kavanagh "over" by a ruse. There was an old feud between Kavanagh and the other jarvey, Fitzharris. One morning Kavanagh was brought down to the prison yard, where he found his horse and car. Mallon bade him drive round for identification, and then turning away engaged in earnest conversation with Fitzharris. Presently Kavanagh was told to get down from his car and Fitzharris was directed in turn to drive, while the detective, smiling with an air of deep satisfaction, wrote in his notebook, as it seemed to the alarmed imagination of the terrified jarvey, apparently important facts supplied to him by Fitzharris. "Skin-the-Goat" had merely been engaging in a battle of wits with the detective; as a fact, Fitzharris gave nobody away; although then an ageing man he served the better part of twenty years for his part in the conspiracy, and lived on until the other day in Dublin with a little job under the Dublin Corporation.

Readers of James Joyce's *Ulysses* will remember a discussion as to whether a coffee-stall keeper is "Skin-the-

Goat" during a halt at O'Connell Bridge on the night of the inimitable Daedalus's rake's progress in Dublin.

Carey in the Witness-box, February 1883

Carey was one of the strangest mentalities in the annals of crime—this virtuous communicant and sodality man who became the leader of an assassination club, took charge of the knives and pointed out the victim, withstood for months the temptation of colossal reward, and in the end swore away unequivocally the lives of the men whom he had drawn after him into his nefarious murder gang. But from the mire of his degradation he still kept up a certain ostentation of patriotic virtue. "I became a member of the Assassination Committee", he said, "when the country was in a bad state, when coercion was in full force, when the popular leaders were in prison, when any man might be thrown into prison at a moment's notice and kept there without trial. But for that the Committee would not have had so many recruits." Again, expressing his dislike of Lord Spencer's Irish regime, Carey declared smugly: "I would not like to meet him in the next world".

Thus for a time at least, while swearing men on to the gallows, he kept up a show of denunciation of the very things to which he had sold himself. He declared that the knives which had been found were not the actual bloody instruments of the deed: the blades of those had been broken up and the handles burnt. And then he added with his unpleasant, clownish attempt at witticism: "I thought bad of destroying the knives; I wanted to send them to the Dublin Exhibition".

Once he went over he was without compunction; and among those whom he sent to the gallows was Dan Curley, who was the godfather of Carey's youngest child, then two months old. Carey confessed that he had been a member of the directory of the Irish Revolutionary Brotherhood—that is, the Fenians—from 1861 to 1878. They used to hold courts-martial. "Up to 1879 we tried informers only", he declared.

"Informers?" asked counsel for the prisoners scornfully, as if he were not sure that he had heard aright.

Carey had been treasurer of the Fenians, but seemed to have left the organization before he engaged in the deadlier enterprise of the Invincibles. There was some assertion during his cross-examination that he had not been able to account for certain Fenian funds, and had been expelled, but this he denied.

He described how, in 1881, a "Mr. Walsh", who was said to live in the North of England, came to him with the purpose of introducing the Society of Irish Invincibles to Dublin. Its object was "to remove all tyrants". There were to be four principals, and Carey consented to be one of them. Subsequently Walsh introduced the other three—James Mullett, Edward McCaffrey, and Dan Curley. Each brought in one or two others, and these again brought more, but there were not to be more than forty members. Carey described the many attempts the Invincibles had made to "get" Forster, but he always appeared to travel at unexpected times or somebody neglected to give the signal. There was some very sensational evidence of how Forster walked down a street where a gang of men were waiting to kill him, and yet by a miracle of misunderstanding he came out alive; and again, the gunner looked into a carriage at Kingstown and saw the Chief Secretary's wife and daughter, but Forster had decided not to accompany them at the last moment. The Invincibles were desperadoes, and capable of any criminal folly, but it is not unlikely that Carey was seeking to bid high for his own immunity by endeavouring to relate the activities of the Invincibles to the politics of the time. Thus his cool statement that they had discussed the mysterious funds behind the organization, and that some of them said the money was likely coming from the Land League. I need not point out, in these calmer days, the absurdity of an open organization like the Land League allying itself with a desperate underground assassination club. But the fact was that our opponents at the time would believe almost anything that might incriminate us. It was on such blind credulity that Pigott the forger played.

Informer's Story of the Crime

Carey kept up a bluff of injured purity in his evidence. He declared that he did not "come in" until his life had been sworn away by Kavanagh, which was true enough. He asserted that he had turned Queen's evidence "to save innocent lives". The hypocrisy of some of his answers and the inelegant essays at flippancy and smartness exasperated even the Crown Counsel. For the ruffian told how he had himself suggested that the murders should be committed with knives, so that the deed might be done without noise. And it was he who sat on a seat beside a gardener from the Viceregal Lodge, who had been brought there to identify Burke, the Under-Secretary, for none of the assassins knew the appearance of their intended victim.

And it was Carey who gave the signal for the deed, and he told how he said to Brady: "Mind, the man in the grey suit".

This was part of the false cleverness of Carey; he sought to show that he had warned them to kill Burke only. But the prisoners' counsel had much to say about the propriety of the witness who, self-confessed, had egged his assassins on to kill "the man in the grey suit". Carey also confessed that the Invincibles usually met at his house or at a club-room for which he paid the rent. He told of the visits of a mysterious gentleman called "Number One", who told them they could have £1000 if necessary, and arranged "tyrants" on the rota for "removal"; and there was also a man disguised in priest's clothes whom they called Father Murphy, but was believed to be P. J. Sheridan from America.

One fact Carey told of "Skin-the-Goat", who drove him to and from the scene of the murders, was that the jarvey had a trick of driving horses of different colours in order to confuse identities, a white horse on the day of the crime, a brown horse thereafter. It was true, Carey said, that none of the prisoners knew who Lord Frederick Cavendish was on that Saturday afternoon. Carey said he asked Brady why he had killed the second man, and Brady explained that Lord Frederick had struck at him with his umbrella and called him a scoundrel, which made him lose his temper.

Five Executions and a Vendetta

Joe Brady, Dan Curley, Timothy Kelly, Michael Fagan, and Tom Caffrey were found guilty, sentenced to death, and sent to the gallows. Pat Delaney, who cried out that "all his misfortunes in life were due to that man (Carey)" —Carey had initiated him into the Invincibles—was induced to plead guilty, and had the capital sentence reduced to ten years' penal servitude. James Mullett received the same sentence, while the hunchback, Joe Mullett, Lawrence Hanlon, and Skin-the-Goat were sent to penal servitude for life. Kavanagh the informer, haunted by the recollection of his treachery, and by the fear of

whose office it is to watch the living dead, was told that the prison gardener was digging a grave for Brady, who was to be hanged in the morning. Whereupon Kelly, who was Brady's bosom friend, wept for hours, but regaining his composure, he lifted up his fine tenor voice and sang Brady's favourite song, which was Balfe's "Memories of the Past", so that his friend during his last hours of life might hear and be cheered. And again that night Kelly controlled his tears and lifted up his voice in those corridors of doom, singing a homely Catholic hymn: "Mother most pure, Star of the Sea!", which entreats the Virgin to pray for the sinner. Of such extraordinary contrasts was the whole story of this ghastly drama made up.

CHAPTER XIV

Excitement in the House—Mr. Forster's onslaught on Parnell—I defend the leader—Parnell taunts Forster—"Little better than an informer" —A memory from Mrs. Humphry Ward.

THE immediate effect of the Phoenix Park trials was the renewal of the warfare waged so persistently and so skilfully by Mr. Forster against Mr. Gladstone, and, of course, against Parnell. The House, which might have thought they were rid of the dreadful subject, found themselves once more back at the "Kilmainham Treaty"; and again and still again the Conservative leaders, and especially the Fourth Party, endeavoured to proclaim the alleged understanding and co-operation between Parnell and the Ministry.

Side by side with this there was a dead set made against Mr. Chamberlain. He was credited with being one of the influences which broke down the policy and the official life of Mr. Forster; and against him attacks were made in some respects almost as bitter as those against Parnell.

Mr. Gorst attacks Mr. Chamberlain, February 20, 1883

The first move in the now renewed and even more bitter campaign over the so-called Kilmainham Treaty was made by Mr. Gorst. There could have been no better choice for leading such an assault. In his cold, clear, apparently passionless way—though every word subtly breathed passion—he made his indictment, and, above all, his indictment of Mr. Chamberlain. I can still remember the bitter passage in which he drew an analogy between Mr. Chamberlain and "Number One"—that terrible and sinister figure who remained anonymous for many years, and whose identity is still a matter of controversy. "Number One" appeared and reappeared, as has been seen, in the mouths of some of the witnesses in the murder trials, and apparently was the originator, the inspirer, and the guide of the deadly conspiracy. He obtained greater prominence, deadlier importance, more ruthlessness, from the mystery by which he was surrounded. It will therefore be understood what deadly effect these words had when uttered in this clear, cold voice of Gorst.

The language did not directly call Mr. Chamberlain an assassin, but the closeness of the comparison on which Mr. Gorst insisted between the assassin creator of the Invincible Society and Mr. Chamberlain was enough almost to suggest that the English Cabinet Minister was as great a criminal as the Irish conspirator. It is over forty years since I heard these sentences, but they still ring as clear and as deadly to my inner ear, and I can make no better comparison of their effect than with the words with which a Judge precedes his sentence of death on the murderer in the dock. There were other speeches of a similar character, but though there might have been more passion and fury in the other speeches from the leaders of the Opposition, Gorst's indictment always remains with me as far and away more deadly than any of the rest.

These incidents were, however, but the raising of the curtain on what was to prove the central scene of the tragic drama now being enacted on the floor of the House; but they had created the atmosphere, which was electric, eager, vindictive, that Mr. Forster required. All the old hatred and suspicion of Parnell and his party had been revived from the temporary grave in which they had been buried after what was called the Kilmainham Treaty and the release of Parnell.

Mr. Forster denounces Parnell, February 22, 1883

Never in the whole course of his Parliamentary career did Mr. Forster rise more dexterously, more effectively, with deadlier blows, than in this indictment he proceeded to utter against the Irish leader. He had evidently thought out every word and every count of his indictment. By way of leading up to the deadlier blows which he was about to deal, he began in a light and almost an airy vein; he tried to put himself right with his fellow-Liberals—who naturally saw in the Tory onslaught an attack on their leader and on their party—by expressing some opposition to the motion that had been proposed by the Fourth Party, a somewhat innocuous and meaningless motion. Having thus liberated himself from any possible charge of lack of fealty to his old leader or to his party, Mr. Forster proceeded to his attack on Parnell. He came fully documented, and every document was brought out at the exact and most telling moment: probably Mr. Arnold-Forster, his adopted son and his relative, had devoted his great secretarial gifts to the collocation of this documentary evidence. Every violent speech by every man closely or distantly connected with the Land League—most of them quite insignificant persons—was quoted.

United Ireland was also quoted—a great newspaper which had been founded by Mr. William O'Brien, recently returned to Parliament, one of the most brilliant journalists of his time, and destined to play a very large part in the Irish conflict for several years afterwards. But the paper had fallen from his control; he was in gaol; his paper had been suppressed; it had to be produced furtively, sometimes in Paris, sometimes in Liverpool, and always was brought into Ireland against the vigilant and ubiquitous efforts of the Government to exclude it. At the moment when it was being quoted as a weapon against Mr. Parnell, Mr. O'Brien was in gaol. My recollection is that the paper had fallen almost entirely under the control of the chief of the female figures in the revolution who formed what was the Ladies' Land League, which had as its dominating personality Anna Parnell; and, as is usually the case, the woman revolutionary was much more violent than the male.

Among the most effective counts in Mr. Forster's indictment was his quotation of a heading—"Incidents of the Campaign". It was a dreadful title, for the so-called incidents of the campaign were every violent act, including even murder, as a demonstration of the unconquered spirit under Coercion of the Irish people. As Mr. Forster read out paragraph after paragraph that appeared under this heading, the blood of the House ran cold. Having thus built up so laboriously and so skilfully the counts of his indictment, Mr. Forster summed it all up in these terrible words:

"It has been often enough stated and shown by statistics that murders followed the meetings and the action of the Land League. Will the Hon. Member [Mr. Parnell] deny and disprove that statement? I will repeat again what the charge is which I make against him. Probably a more serious charge was never made by any Member of the House of Commons against another Member. It is not that he himself directly planned or perpetrated outrages or murders, but that he either connived at them or, when warned by facts and statements, he determined to remain in ignorance, that he took no trouble to test the truth of whether these outrages had been committed or not, but that he was willing to gain the advantage of them."

Such was the indictment. It would be difficult to exaggerate its tremendous effect on the House in the temper to which it had been driven by the revelations in the trial of the Phoenix Park assassins, and in the renewal of all the hatred and dread with which Parnell had been invested, and the bitterness of feeling against Mr. Chamberlain, and all the other deadly passions that had once more affected the Parliamentary and public atmosphere.

Parnell under the Onslaught, February 22, 1883

The Irish members as a rule listened in silence, but once or twice there was an outburst. In reply to one of the sentences of Mr. Forster, Parnell shouted out, "It's a lie!"; simultaneously there came the same words, "It's a lie!" from Mr. James O'Kelly. O'Kelly, though he was for many years a Member of Parliament, was the least Parliamentary of men; he had been trained in his youth as a soldier in the Foreign Legion of the French Army. While with that body he had gone under Bazaine to Mexico; and he had escaped imprisonment, and perhaps execution, by building a temporary and rough boat, on which he travelled in solitude and in great danger over many miles of broad and dangerous river from Mexico to the United States, after the execution of Maximilian. He had the appearance of a French soldier; he had fine, bright, defiant eyes; he had twisted eyebrows that added to the martial and almost ferocious look, and he had a violent temper.

I once chaffingly said that I would publish a volume of his Parliamentary speeches; they would all consist of the one sentence, "It's a lie"—a sentence which he used on frequent occasions, and which on frequent occasions ended in his expulsion from the House. On this occasion his angry exclamation produced the usual expulsion; except for that,

Mr. Forster's speech was made in almost deadly silence, interrupted occasionally by the ferocious cheers of the now triumphant Opposition.

I have heard various descriptions of how Parnell took this terrible attack. O'Connor Power—who, as I have more than once said, always disliked and underrated Parnell—said to me afterwards that Parnell, when he had the opportunity of an effective reply, sat and shivered in his seat. I sat next Parnell during this speech, and saw no such sign of any great mental disturbance. I met him a few moments afterwards, and I saw on his face a rather deprecatory smile, which used to come to him often in moments of embarrassment; but it was not more than that. He certainly showed no signs of terror.

But, with all his great gifts, he was not the man to meet properly such an occasion; he had not the readiness of speech—especially the readiness of invective and of retort—which belonged to some members of his party. O'Connor Power, though a very inferior man to Parnell, would probably have delivered an effective reply, which was beyond Parnell.

And then came one of the most trying hours in my whole Parliamentary career. Parnell asked me to speak instead of himself. What I have said will make the reader realize the difficulty of my task. I had, fortunately, a couple of hours to think over what I had to say. I remember very well going down to the lower smoke-room to write out some notes, and at once my head began to burst with a violent headache. An extraordinary thing happened. I made up my mind that the proper line of defence was to bring the war into the enemy's camp—the enemy's camp meant at the moment the Liberal Government: the attack by Forster, as has been seen, was made as much on them as on Parnell. Taking up the criticisms of the Tories and of the Fourth Party against the alleged offences of the Government, their vacillations, their change of policy, their sacrifice of Forster, I brought back the debate to an attack on them from the attack on Parnell.

My Defence of Parnell, February 22, 1883

With the passions among them, and the natural party desire to use all weapons possible against the Government, the Tories listened to my indictment with loud approval; they laughed and they cheered. A distinguished Member of Parliament, I am told, said that, on his return to the House some hours after the attack on Parnell, he was astounded to find the whole Opposition laughing with and cheering an Irish member. He had gone home, he said, under the impression of Forster's tremendous indictment of Parnell, with a kind of sinister anticipation of something terrible happening—of Parnell, so to speak, being sent to Tyburn to be summarily hanged; and then he came back and saw one of Parnell's colleagues thus so enthusiastically received by the Tory Opposition! I put that speech down, with another I delivered some years afterwards, as one of the few Parliamentary successes of my long House of Commons career.

After I sat down, it looked as if the debate was about to close, and to close without any attempt by Parnell to answer the indictment that had been made against him. Lord Hartington, who, of course, hated Parnell as much as any of the Tories, did not make any attempt to rise; nor did Sir Stafford Northcote; and the eager and hostile House, determined to put Parnell on the rack, began to shout angrily his name. Parnell was still very reluctant to answer; he even said he thought he might leave the debate where T. P. had taken it. But the House was not to be denied its triumphant crucifixion of the Irish leader, and in the end Parnell was forced to his feet to move the adjournment of the debate, which involved the consequence of his having to open it the next day.

And the next day he opened it. I have often wondered since what is the true impression one should form of that speech; as a House of Commons performance it was most pitiful. I do not believe that the greatest of orators in Parnell's position could have done much more, considering the terrible tide of passion against which he was swimming. He left much of what Forster said against him unanswered, though he did give some hard blows to Forster in return.

Parnell replies to Forster, February 23, 1883

He looked upon Mr. Forster, he said, as little better than an informer, without the informer's excuse that he wished to save his life. "Out of a number of speeches—many hundreds and perhaps thousands—delivered during the land movement by other people, and not by me, upon which to found an accusation against me for what has been said and done by others . . . upon this occasion also, he has displayed the same remarkable ignorance as to matters of fact in connection with Irish affairs as he displayed during his tenure of office as Chief Secretary for Ireland."

"Why was he [Mr. Forster] deposed?" he went on—"he, the right hon. gentleman who had acquired experience in the administration of Ireland—who, according to his own account, knew everything, although he was almost invariably wrong. It would have been far better, if you were going to pass an Act of this kind, and to administer it as you are going to administer it—up to the hilt—to have had it administered by the seasoned politician who is now in disgrace. Call him back to his post; send him to help Lord Spencer in the congenial work of the gallows in Ireland. Send him to look after the secret inquisitions of Dublin Castle. Send him to levy the payment of blood money. Send him to raise the taxes which an unfortunate and starving peasantry have to pay for crimes not committed by them. All that would be congenial work for him." He passed by most of the charges Forster made against him, except that he made the necessary correction of his responsibility for that terrible episode of the "incidents of the campaign".

Thinking over the speech and re-reading it, I am not quite sure that my first impression was correct. The tone that Parnell adopted was probably the best for his own people; he knew well that the more those they considered their English enemies—and Forster was considered the worst of them—attacked him, the dearer he would become to them. He did not affect the scorn he had for these attacks—he felt it in his heart of hearts; and it was a sure and just calculation that these attacks by Englishmen did him no real harm. But he had to a certain extent the air of at least a partially defeated man. It may have been his natural disappointment that twice the revolutionary wing had snatched glorious victory from his hands. His heart also, perhaps, had begun to be corroded by the ever-present terror of the exposure of the mad love by which he was consumed. For years he knew he was standing on the brink of a disastrous precipice. Anyhow, so the episode ended.

The following passage in a book by Mrs. Humphry Ward (*A Writer's Recollections*) will add a few interesting particulars on this famous duel between Forster (her uncle) and Parnell.

"I happened (said Mrs. Humphry Ward) to be in the

House the following day to hear Parnell's reply. I remember my uncle's taking me down with him to the House, and begging a seat for me in Mrs. Brand's gallery. The figure of Parnell—the speech, nonchalant, terse, defiant, without a single grace of any kind—his hands in the pockets of his coat—and the tense silence of the crowded House, remain vividly with me. Afterwards my uncle came upstairs for me, and we descended towards Palace Yard through various side passages. Suddenly a door, communicating with the House itself, opened in front of us, and Parnell came out. My uncle pressed my arm, and we held back while Parnell passed by, sombrely absorbed, without betraying by the smallest movement or gesture any recognition of my uncle's identity."

It is eminently characteristic of the House of Commons that this tragic scene—the memory of which still pains me—was forgotten in a few days' time, and, except as a Parliamentary exhibition of a great hatred, the episode had little or no effect on the future proceedings of the House of Commons.

CHAPTER XV

The duty of a journalist—Reporting for an Orange journal—My shorthand "Vicar of Wakefield"—Dean Magee's 220 words a minute—Talks with John Morley—A disappointed politician—Joseph Cowen—His disagreement with Gladstone—The Newcastle rivals.

THE tremendous attack by Mr. Forster on Parnell took place on February 22. A short time afterwards—March 16—there was another attack by Mr. Forster; this was on the South African policy of the Government. It showed something of the growing bitterness of the relations between the two men that, immediately after Mr. Forster had spoken, Gladstone got up to describe him as "a man of peace" who, "notwithstanding, in the most unequivocal terms, has taught us to-day the doctrine of war". It also shows that extraordinary power of the House of soon forgetting even great scenes in the onrush of other interests, that on March 14—that is to say, three weeks after Mr. Forster pronounced his tremendous indictment against him—Parnell was quietly moving a new Land Bill, and he was able to make out so good a case that he had sixty-three members in his lobby against 250 of the united Liberal and Conservative vote. His supporters came not only from all the Irish Liberal Members, but also a good many English Radicals; and ultimately most of his proposals were adopted by the Government and became law.

The Explosives Act, April 9, 1883

But again the quiet course of Irish Land Reform, which Parnell was thus advancing steadily, was threatened by an outburst of the revolutionaries. An attempt was made to blow up by dynamite the Local Government Board and *The Times* office; and the police force had to be increased, the principal public buildings placed under military control, and Cabinet Ministers were accompanied in their goings to and fro by detectives and constables. These outrages, and the prospect of others to follow, led to a very strong measure which Sir William Harcourt moved, and passed through all its stages in the House of Commons in an hour and a half.

It was a curious coincidence that on the very day when this almost unprecedented method of steeplechase legislation was carried through, the new system of Grand Committees was introduced.

I have already dealt sufficiently with the Bradlaugh difficulty, which obtruded itself at all sorts of times in the various sessions of Parliament, whatever the other business might be. It was in the debate on the Affirmation Bill, brought in by the Government to settle the question, that Mr. Gladstone made far and away the finest speech that had been delivered during the many debates on that question.

Egypt came up again with greater urgency, in consequence of the bombardment of Alexandria and the other military measures which had followed; and the ranks of the non-interventionists by this time had received a very powerful recruit by the election of Mr. John Morley as Member for Newcastle-on-Tyne.

I had known Mr. Morley pretty intimately since 1880, when, as I have already said, I had been given by him the heavy but interesting duty of writing—anonymously—the daily chronicle of Parliamentary life for the *Pall Mall Gazette*. Our relations had been of the friendliest; I do not think there were ever more than a few sentences extracted or modified in the articles I wrote; and the reader will understand that, with the active and sometimes vehement part I was then taking in the stormy discussions of the times, it was always a little difficult for me to observe an impartial tone, especially when writing for a Liberal paper, for I was then a fierce opponent of both the Liberal Party and the Liberal Ministry.

And here, perhaps, as an old journalist, I may make a slight interruption of my narrative to give my conception of what the duty of the journalist is, and how far his training enables him to fulfil that duty. Unless he is purely a leader-writer, and therefore to a large extent a party advocate and a partisan, his duty, as I conceive it, is to be objective and candid. I always deprecate the style of journalism, more popular in older days than now, of dragging into the chronicle of events the narrowness, the bitterness, sometimes the want of candour which are incident to partisan warfare. A journalist becomes, in my opinion, not merely untrustworthy, but dull and uninteresting, who makes all swans of his geese, and all geese of the swans of other people.

How I learnt Shorthand

It was to a certain extent the ridiculous habit in Liberal journals of the period to describe every speech of a Liberal spokesman as brilliant, and every speech of a Conservative as dull and unsuccessful. I learned the spirit of detachment as a chronicler in my earliest days in journalism. My first three years, as I have already said, were spent as a reporter on a strong Tory and Orange journal in Dublin, and the first meetings I had to attend and record were meetings of the ultra-Tories at a time when their passions had been lashed to fury in the debates over the Irish Church Bill. I had to listen almost nightly to denunciations in no sparing terms of the Church in which I had been brought up by its most devoted adherents; but, either by temperament or with an overwhelming sense of my professional duties, I succeeded almost without effort in listening to these diatribes with perfect equanimity, and in recording them with such accuracy as I could then command.

With such accuracy, I say, as I could command: for I have to make here the humiliating confession that my record as a mere reporter, especially as a shorthand writer, was exceedingly bad. I had learned shorthand in the usual way of those who live in a small country town and far away from the cities where tuition can be obtained. I was then a student at Galway College, and working pretty hard. I got up at six o'clock every morning, and worked at my classics or French and German for an hour; at seven o'clock I called my brother, six years younger than myself. Between him and me there was an intense affection; one of the sorrows of my later life was his recent death in America. For an hour or an hour and a half every morning he read to me, and I took down in shorthand as well as I could what he read. The number of pages I thus wrote seems extraordinary to me now. I think he dictated to me all Robertson's long and somewhat dreary history of Charles V.; I am not sure that I did not write in this way the whole of *The Vicar of Wakefield*. I carried on this practice for a year or so, and at the end of that time I had a fair knowledge of shorthand: though, as I have said, I knew that contrast, familiar to all shorthand learners, and graphically described by Charles Dickens in his account of his own study of shorthand, of finding that the process of writing was only one of the necessities of shorthand learning: that there was a second process—that of reading what you had written—and that the second process was, if anything a little more difficult than the first.

Reporting Archbishop Magee

One of the very first engagements I was sent to after I had been employed as a reporter was a meeting of shareholders in an Irish railway company. The first thing I discovered was the use by the speakers at this meeting of words I had never heard before. I won't say they were as strange to me as Greek—because at that time I could read Greek quite fluently—but as if they were in some strange unknown tongue. The word "debenture" frequently occurred—I had never heard the word debenture before; the antiquated learning in which I had been brought up would regard such a word probably as beneath the contempt of the scholar. There was a speaker—a very able one, I still remember—who used the, to me, strange phrase, "Money is now cheap". Money cheap!—an astonishing assertion which created all the more impression upon my young and ignorant mind from its being delivered in suave tones by a handsome Jewish gentleman. I need not say I made a hash of my report, and was well nigh in despair.

But I had a worse and even more humiliating experience. I was sent with another reporter to a meeting of the Trinity College Historical Society—an ancient and distinguished body, with traditions of Edmund Burke, Robert Emmet, and Thomas Moore. The inaugural meeting of that body was, and I believe still is, one of the great social as well as intellectual events of Dublin life. There is an address by the Auditor, who is the chief officer of the current year. That, however, is of less note than the speeches which follow of the distinguished men who have already attained to great position in their various walks of life. The chief spokesman on this occasion was a man who had already attained in the Irish Church the high position of Dean of Cork and of the Chapel Royal, who was afterwards to attain even a greater distinction in England, first as Bishop of Peterborough and then as Archbishop of York, and as certainly the finest debater the Episcopal Bench had for a century given to the House of Lords.

I shall never forget that speech or that man. People used to speak of him as the ugliest man of his time; he was small, rather yellow-complexioned, with somewhat protruding lips, and rather a Jewish nose. But the eyes were really the most remarkable feature of the face. They were very dark, they were very brilliant, they were very deep-set. As you looked at him sometimes, you might think of him as a man with a monkey-face; at other times those wonderful eyes, especially when he was speaking, gave to the face that beauty which must always emanate from a man of great intelligence.

He was not only the most eloquent but the most fluent speaker of his time. Using the language of the shorthand writer, I may say that, while the ordinary speaker is put down as speaking at 120 words a minute, Dean Magee, as he then was, spoke at 220 words a minute. He was the despair of all shorthand writers, and it was only the great experts who could make an approach to reporting him correctly.

My colleague at this meeting was an old and also a very wily reporter, with a genius for shirking and innumerable methods of shifting on to others the difficult jobs. He proposed to me, as a concession to my inexperience, that he should take the first hour of the meeting, and I the second. The cunning rascal knew that the first hour or so would be occupied by the Auditor's address, that the Auditor's address was in print before him, and that all he had to do was just to draw his pencil through the pages of this document, leaving enough in for his paper.

When the Auditor's address was over, there came the speech of Dean Magee. First, I was trammelled by my intense interest in his brilliant rhetoric and his sardonic wit; but, secondly, and still more, was I embarrassed by the lightning rate at which he spoke. I dare say it would amuse me if I could go back to the newspaper in which appeared my clumsy and ineffective attempt to give some idea of this speech. I am sure it must have been pretty terrible.

John Morley, 1839–1923

It will be understood from these experiences that I found very little difficulty in writing a fairly impartial account of the Parliamentary debates for the *Pall Mall Gazette*. Anyhow, I succeeded in this respect so far that I kept the job for a year and a half, and might have kept it probably for many years more if it had not been for two events. The first was that I undertook my first mission to America to raise money for the Irish Party, and that kept me away until some months after the beginning of the next session of Parliament. The second was the disappearance of Mr. Morley from the editorship of the *Pall Mall* and the succession of Mr. W. T. Stead to the editorial chair.

I proposed to Mr. Stead on my return to England to renew my old work, but he refused the suggestion, giving as his reason, which was characteristic of the man's mind as a journalist, that he did not want anything like a fixed programme of articles in his paper. He wanted variety every day.

The first time I remember having a conversation with Mr. Morley after his election to the House of Commons was one day when I saw him in the tea-room reading a newspaper through a pair of spectacles. I had always regarded him as far too young for any such confession of age, and expressed my surprise. He replied by asking me to realize that he was forty-nine years of age—several years more than I gave him credit for. At no time of his life, indeed, did Morley give any impression of his real age; except for his somewhat feeble walk and a certain wistfulness in his expression, he looked young up to the day of his death. One of the reasons of this was his extraordinary retention of his youthful figure; there never was a superfluous ounce of flesh upon that firmly knit, rather symmetrical figure of his. He used to complain that he was one of the men who had a troublesome liver, and he had a curious habit of keeping his hand pretty constantly across his mouth—which I interpreted as indicating that his digestive troubles interfered with his breath. But, for a man with his thin physique and with apparently this weakness of digestion, he could do things that would make a robuster physique hopelessly bankrupt in a few years. He was always a perfectly temperate man; I never saw the smallest approach in him to the want of control either of his mind or of his legs—which, if I am to tell the truth, is not what I can say of many of the most distinguished figures in my time. But Morley had not only no affinity with the ascetic, but something like scorn; he loved good cooking; he loved good wine; at dinner he rarely drank anything but champagne—a wine which, perhaps from personal reasons, I regard as one of the deadliest of drinks. When I made that confession to him he told me that for a good many years of his life champagne had no more effect upon him than water.

This love of good food, good liquor, and good company might suggest a man of a joyous temperament. It would be an entirely false view of Morley's character. His philosophy, on the whole, I should describe as ultimately pessimistic. He had, as everybody knows, in early years entirely liberated himself from the orthodox doctrines in which he had been brought up in a strongly Nonconformist provincial family; he was a convinced materialist with an entire absence of all faith in an existence beyond the grave. I asked him within a short time—I think only a few weeks—of his death if he had modified his religious opinions—as men very often do in the near presence of coming death. He made no spoken reply, but pursed his lips and shook his head.

Conversations with John Morley

I am inclined to think that, though he had a devoted wife—at one time very beautiful, always very gracious, never suggesting any distinct intelligence—she was not the companion to give the infectious joy, or at least the pleasant tranquillity, that the wives of literary men and politicians are often able to impart to their husbands of a different temperament. The result was—to me at least—that whenever I paid a visit to the home of Mr. Morley, I had a horrible feeling that gloom encompassed it from the very door, that even in the hall I could feel the dank odour of a sad interior. Whenever I spoke to him, if I saw any chance of getting into disaccord, I had one invariable remedy: if I uttered some words of that despondent view of current events and experiences which, as I have already avowed, is my natural tendency, I always found an immediate response.

Once, after a big meeting where he had delivered a much-applauded speech, I said, perhaps with some impish or gloomy impulse, something about death. "Well, I am ready", he said. This was quite thirty years before his death, and it was said as we walked with his wife, the cheers still ringing in our ears, through the tumultuous life in the glaring light of Piccadilly Circus.

I once discussed with him the eternal question whether men of letters did not make a mistake in entering into political life; and justifying his conduct in doing so, I made the somewhat tactless observation that before he had become a politician he had said practically all he had to say. He gave a wry smile, as was natural, and, after a pause, said that he had had for some years the idea of writing a History of the French Revolution. Then I made a second tactless observation, though I think a profoundly true one—that neither he nor any other Englishman, above all any Englishman brought up in the Protestant faith, could write a true history of the French Revolution; it was only an Irishman that could do so; it was he alone who realized what was the system against which France had risen in revolt.

On still another occasion, after expressing some flattering opinions as to what I might have done with either my pen or my tongue, with the same frankness he asked me the pointed question whether I did not regard myself as having had a squandered life. I replied promptly I did; and so I do; but immediately we got into complete *rapport* again when I said: "Are not most men's lives squandered?" On that somewhat pessimistic view of human adventure we at once came to common ground.

He was a failure in the House of Commons; somehow or other he did not know how to catch its ear; he lost control even of his voice there; sometimes he whispered; then, after a pause, he shouted; he nearly always came with a manuscript and recited from that; and there are few orators, especially in the House of Commons, to whom a manuscript is not ultimately fatal. He always spoke, after he had made a speech, with despairing contempt of what he had done; and yet the paradox was that Morley could be, in the right surroundings and on the right occasion, a most effective speaker. I have heard him over and over again on the platform, and I would put him down as one of the greatest platform speakers of his time. His speech was always well ordered; it was very well delivered; he had rather a powerful voice. In all his speeches there came passages of glowing and poetic eloquence, and when he felt very strongly there was almost an angry roar of scornful indignation: he held his audience in his grip from the first moment to the last, and he could rouse them to bursts of enthusiasm. What, then, is the explanation of his failure in the House of Commons?

Morley in the Commons, 1882–1908

It was partly because he entered it too late. The House of Commons has to be learned and to be mastered, and that can only be done by years of training and years of study, and these years can only be completed by men who have started in their early manhood. There are, no doubt, conspicuous exceptions to this rule. Sir Henry Fowler (afterwards Lord Wolverhampton) made a good speech when he addressed the House from the first; but Henry Fowler had had long training in local bodies—and any training in any kind of deliberative body is better than none. On the other hand, the training of a man of letters is in many respects the least suited for a man about to be a Member of the House of Commons. There is a tremendous difference between fighting for principles in the disembodied shadows of the study and in their embodiment in living flesh and blood in the House of Commons.

Walking one afternoon with Morley in the division lobbies around the House—to which reach the echoes, somewhat faint usually, of the speeches being delivered in the House—he made to me the remark that the hollowness and the hypocrisy characteristic of so much of the mere party debating of the House never sounded to his ears more hollow and more hypocritical than when he listened to their echoes in the division lobbies. And then he summed up his feeling in one of the great ineptitudes which I have noted in my memory uttered by the lips of really distinguished men. I will always give the first place to the famous *mots* of Lord MacDonnell. I remember how he threatened to introduce two rules in the new local body he and Mr. Bryce and the Government of the day proposed to give to Ireland—first that no Member should be allowed to rise from his seat, and, secondly, that no member should be allowed to speak, except from a manuscript. But Mr. Morley's ineptitude reached almost as great a height. He was describing to me the many things in the Chamber that antagonized him. "I hate", he said, "the air of contention." It would be hard to beat in misapprehension this suggestion that a deliberative body of many parties and of many opinions should be liberated from contention.

This inner conflict between the man of letters and the man of politics in Morley pursued and paralysed him all through his life. Jean Jacques Rousseau has described the haunting weakness of the literary genius whose visions are able to transform the mind of man, to bring as an accompaniment to their soft cadences the roar of contention and the swish of the guillotine. Morley had always, even from his early years, the haunting hope of eminence. It is recorded in the most recent biography of him that when he was leaving Blackburn for the first time it was noticed that nearly all his worldly goods were books. "He seemed a little anxious, but said bravely, 'I am going to the City, and I hope I shall do well'." From the moment he entered the House of Commons he intended to be a great man;

he even dallied with the thought of being Prime Minister. This opinion of mine with regard to him was not destroyed, but rather confirmed, when he mentioned, with a laugh against himself, that a lady had once in his presence spoken of him as a future Prime Minister of England.

John Morley: An Estimate

Honestly, I think he would have made rather a bad Prime Minister; he was lacking in the force and the decision which would be required from the chief of so difficult a combination, with such powerful characters and intellects in constant contact and, therefore, in frequent conflict. I remember, when he was talking about his work as Secretary for India, he mentioned among its many hardships that of always having to take decisions. He was not a man who wanted to take decisions; but one can never tell whether conditions might not have arisen which would have forced him into the Premiership in spite of any of his rivals. He had not the personal unpopularity of Sir William Harcourt, and he had a seat in the House of Commons, while Lord Rosebery was in the exile of the House of Lords. He was an older and more powerful Liberal leader than Mr. Asquith, and he had a far bigger position in the Party than Campbell-Bannerman. And Campbell-Bannerman suddenly emerged from obscurity into the full blaze of the Premiership and the Leadership of the Liberal Party. But Morley groaned internally instead of striking out for his own hand.

In another respect also he was a great contradiction. He had a gentle and almost deprecatory manner in conversation; with all his strong opinions, he gave them, as a rule, gentle utterance; he was impressionable enough sometimes to be moved by opinions entirely opposite to his own. He had not that alacrity of mind and boldness of self-assertion which enable a Dr. Johnson to be a tyrant in debate. But he was not free from violent outbursts of rage, and once when poor harmless Osborne Morgan took up some position on something Welsh remotely connected with the once-burning question of Church Disestablishment in that country hostile to the attitude of Mr. Gladstone, Morley flew at him—an outburst before which the gentle and loose-limbed Welshman quailed.

There was plenty of *saeva indignatio* in Morley. Whenever he allowed himself to depart from what apparently was his calm frigidity of utterance and of temper in debate, he really became fine and impressive. The greatest, perhaps, of his House of Commons speeches was the outburst in which he denounced the folly and the cruelty of the Boer War. If he could have had the tenacity, the promptitude, and the courage to let himself go like this, his history in the House of Commons might have been different.

I have been endeavouring in these lines to draw a clear picture of a remarkable man, and I may seem to disparage and to lessen him; if I do so it is unwittingly. My business is to present these figures in the political life I have seen from so close at hand, in their habits as they lived, in their frailties as well as in their strength. And this compels me to add to the points I have already noticed many things with regard to the splendid virtues of this very humane man. In action he was sometimes wanting in courage and in promptitude, but he never shrank from taking any risk on what he considered a matter of basic principle. He used to laugh at the epithet of "Honest John", but he fully deserved it; with all his little weaknesses and his small and human vanities, he was emphatically a noble figure. He hated cruelty, he was humane, he was consistent. He might see the faults of the poor, but in heart and soul he was always with them.

When I was talking to him once about the tragedies that lay behind the brilliant surface of aristocratic society, and suggested what material these things might give to a dramatist or novelist of genius, Morley almost impatiently replied that he took no interest in their rotten joys or their rotten sorrows; he was more interested in the poor wage-earner, who had to keep wife and children on scanty and uncertain resources. To sum him up; he failed, so far as he did fail, because he was a philosopher and not a bruiser.

Joseph Cowen, 1831–1899

Morley brings me to Joseph Cowen. Joseph Cowen's was one of the Parliamentary careers that might have ended in greatness. I used to say to him playfully that he ought to be the first democratic Prime Minister of England, and if his many qualities had not been embarrassed by his many defects and mistakes, this was a possibility. I remember seeing him for the first time from the Press Gallery in the Parliament of 1874. He stood out as rather a strange figure. In those days the House of Commons was a much more conventional assembly than it is to-day—every member wore a black frock-coat and a tall hat. But here was this man, looking for all the world like a very provincial Nonconformist clergyman, with his somewhat ill-shapen suit of black and his soft black hat. It was not from poverty, for he was a very rich man. He inherited from his father a very fine brick-works, and he had invested some of his money in the *Newcastle Chronicle*, which was for a long time not only the most influential but the most prosperous newspaper in the thriving city in which it circulated. He had, like so many Northumbrians, a great burr in his accent—sometimes really his words were scarcely intelligible to the Southerner. Nobody had taken much notice of him when first he entered the House of Commons, but one evening he got up—it was on the Disraeli proposal to confer the title of Empress of India on the Queen—and delivered a speech which held the House spellbound, and established his position as one of the orators of the House for ever afterwards. He was one of those strange people you find in so many Englishmen: a fanatical enthusiast, willing to risk everything—even life—in a revolutionary cause. You saw these possibilities in his beautiful dark eyes, soft and tender and visionary. In his early days he belonged to the generation that worked for the liberation and unification of Italy. He became, if not a friend, at least an associate of Mazzini, and he himself has recorded how he carried bombs, which were part of the propaganda of the great Italian revolutionary and his followers.

The Italian national cause was one which made its immediate appeal to him, and from an early age he was one of the chief of its English adherents. There is a considerable Irish population in Newcastle, whose affection and confidence he enjoyed. With his newspaper, his wealth, his brilliant powers of oratory, and his defence of liberty everywhere, he became the most commanding political force in that constituency.

Relations of Gladstone and Cowen

Something went wrong—I don't know what it was. Some people said it was a snub—I am sure unintentional—which he imagined he had received from Gladstone. I certainly heard him rudely and grossly insulted by John Bright, who, as I have already indicated, was not a very gentle controversialist. Estrangement also came because of a difference of opinion between Cowen and Gladstone over the Eastern Question. Cowen belonged to that race of old Radicals who regarded with justifiable horror the Tsarist regime in Russia, and dreaded the effect of Russian influence on all the aspiring nationalities of Eastern Europe. When Gladstone began his tremendous campaign in defence of the rights of the Christians in Turkey and their liberation, he had to count with Cowen. Differences of opinion between men of the same party are always more liable than others to widen as time goes on, and for some years nobody could count on a uniform support of either Gladstone or Gladstone's policy by Cowen.

Cowen supported Morley—not with much enthusiasm, I am afraid—in his first candidature for Newcastle; but the difference of temperament and of outlook between the two men, their position as more or less rivals for the affections of the Newcastle population, and a thousand-and-one things set them adrift from each other. Once during a division I had a curious, interesting little glimpse of the character of Morley, with his intense sensitiveness and also a certain suspiciousness. I happened to walk side by side with Joseph Cowen, who always remained a close friend of mine, and in going out saw Morley a few yards off looking with some suspicion in his face. He spoke to me a few moments afterwards with something like disapproval, or at least warning, as to such intercourse with Cowen.

Cowen always commanded the ear of the House of Commons, and his speeches undoubtedly sounded very well; yet I always thought they lost a little of their effectiveness by the fact that they had evidently been carefully dictated and committed to manuscript—though he never carried a manuscript—before he rose to address the House. This habit had grown upon him by the fact, I think I am correct in saying, that he dictated a London letter to his newspaper nearly every night during the Parliamentary session. I repeat the warning I have given over and over again to students of oratory, that the spoken essay is very rarely successful in the House of Commons. I have given some instances already; others will occur to me as I proceed.

To a certain extent, Egypt, which I now approach, brought the two men together, though they expressed their opinions in differences of words and of actions. Morley, though sometimes courageous in his condemnation of the policy of the Gladstone Government, at the same time tried to reconcile this position with his strong sense of party loyalty to both the Ministry and its chief. Cowen belonged to the Radical section which made relentless war on the Government and its policy.

CHAPTER XVI

Armed intervention in Egypt—W. T. Stead, crusading journalist—A moral espionage—General Gordon's daring—His magic cane—The mission to Khartoum—Mr. Chamberlain rends Lord Randolph—A rift in the Fourth Party—Mr. Balfour's handkerchief—Sir Charles Dilke's republican hour—The Queen offended.

Bombardment of Alexandria, July 11, 1882

I HAVE read again the long account of the Egyptian imbroglio which ultimately, more than anything else, brought the Gladstone Government to its doom. It would be outside the purpose of pages like mine to go into the full details of this long, involved, and, to a certain extent, out-of-date controversy. It is evident that from the start Mr. Gladstone was doubtful about the whole policy of intervention in Egypt, and had to be dragged through by the pressure of his colleagues and by those unforeseen catastrophes which lie in wait on every Government and embarrass nearly every great political decision.

I remember the day when he came into the House of Commons looking very flushed, very excited, very disturbed, and when, after he had got up to speak, one could see the signs of great embarrassment and grave anxiety in his somewhat halting words. It was one of the occasions on which he had found it impossible to come to any accord as to the policy in Egypt between France and England. It was this disaccord, and the rise of what was then considered the rebel militarist movement under the leadership of Arabi Pasha, that precipitated Gladstone and his colleagues into the first and, as it proved after, the fatal step of armed intervention in Egypt. Arabi had established the supremacy of the soldiers over the Khedive and the civil authorities in Egypt. There was a distinct threat to the lives and property, as well as the political position, of the English at Alexandria particularly, and things were precipitated there by the massacre of about two hundred Europeans and by the preparation as for a siege around Alexandria. The Government resolved that the necessary protection against this menace was the bombardment of Alexandria, a bombardment which had the suspicious beginning of the disappearance and disapproval of the French fleet.

Arabi defeated at Tel-el-Kebir, September 13, 1882

The next step led to the expedition under General Wolseley and the victorious battle of Tel-el-Kebir, and these things led to the outbreak of a passionate and, as I think now and as most people think, blind and insensate Jingoism. This fever spread to a large number of the English people; from them it spread to the Houses of Parliament, and for some years there were violent and passionate debates. And then came the most fatal step of all. To anybody with the mind of an Anatole France there could be no more interesting or instructive episode in confirmation of his theory of the incurable folly of mankind than the story of the Gordon mission to Khartoum.

I think I am correct in saying that but for W. T. Stead there would have been no Gordon mission. Let me try to give something like a portrait of Stead. He was honest and histrionic, pugnacious and sensitive, narrow and intolerant in religion, what in America they would call a Fundamentalist; in temperament half-crusader, and not altogether without a touch of the mountebank. Stead looked what he was.

He was fairly slight, but with suppleness and spring in all his movements, with a beard all round his face, rough features, and of a certain commonness of expression, increased by shabby and ill-cut tweed suits; but the eyes—large, blue, and brilliant—revealed the ardent and restless soul beneath. He looked as if he might have been a Revivalist preacher who dragged multitudes of people in adoration and loyalty behind him. It was, perhaps, a little unfortunate for him and for his country that he found his congregations in the readers of his papers. He deserved to have many readers; he was a truly great journalist; no man could make up a case so thoroughly and ardently, no man could state a case more vehemently and more convincingly. If he had been in another age and belonged to another creed, he might have been Peter the Hermit.

We always remained good friends, and I have retained some respect and some affection for him; but I expressed my opinion, which he received with the good-humour that nothing could exasperate, that he was too good a fanatic to be a real journalist, and too real a journalist to be a good fanatic. He belonged by training and by conviction to the straitest sect of the straitest Nonconformists; he had their passion for sexual morality. Except that he was quite honest, I would put him in the same category as Mr. Sinclair Lewis has depicted in *Elmer Gantry*. For a time sex became indeed an obsession. He sought everywhere for the violater of the strict sexual code. If he had been allowed to go on, he might have established something like a domestic espionage over the homes and habits of the men and women who sinned against his code.

It was he who drove Dilke first almost to madness and then to ruin; he ruined a poor devil called Hughes Hallett; he was one of the chief agents in ruining Parnell, and incidentally ruining the hopes and chances of Ireland for a quarter of a century. I still remember the almost sickening shudder which I felt when one day I paid Stead a visit at the *Pall Mall Gazette*, of which he was then the editor, and he said to me broadly and in almost a casual way: "The question I am now considering is whether I should ruin the Irish Party by exposing the *liaison* between Parnell and Mrs. O'Shea". Speaking still in that same tone as of almost a commonplace occurrence, he told me that he had actually sent for Captain O'Shea and put the question to him whether it was true or not that his wife was the mistress of Parnell.

General Gordon, 1833–1885

Gordon was just the kind of man who would make an immediate appeal to the enthusiastic admiration of Stead. He also was a Fundamentalist: there was something both comic and pathetic in reading Gordon's attempts to fix the geography of the Garden of Eden and other sacred spots. There was scarcely ever a man in human history who deserved more to be called a hero, and as a hero made such a direct appeal to popular affection and popular admiration.

He was absolutely without fear, and without regard to self. Some of the stories recorded of him are almost incredible. He rushed off to the Crimea when he was still little more than a boy. His daring, especially at Balaclava, was so conspicuous that he received almost every decoration that Great Britain or Turkey or France could bestow. It was also significant of his future that he developed a strong aptitude for obtaining personal knowledge of the movements of the enemy. He had an extraordinary record in China. First he took part with the British forces and the French combined; he was present at the capture of Peking, and had a hand in every expedition; but it was not until

1862 that his hypnotic power over men, his reckless though unconscious bravery, pointed him out even to the Chinese themselves as a man above men to deal with the then formidable Taiping rebellion. This rebellion had been going on for years, and it looked as if it never could end; but the Chinese realized the miraculous powers of this foreigner. They knew he could do with a few men what a lesser man could not do with ten thousand. The force they gave him to subdue this terrible and widespread rebellion consisted of three or four thousand Chinese, with about one hundred and fifty Europeans as officers—men of all nationalities, and often of doubtful characters. He fought thirty-three engagements in two years, and at the end of two years the rebellion was stamped out. He carried towns, heavily garrisoned, by assault. He captured Taitsan, although it had a garrison of ten thousand men, and it took him two days to do it. He showed tact and forbearance, qualities which were not always part of his character, by enlisting the captured rebels; and when he had to dismiss some of the undesirables, whom he had first been obliged to take, he replaced them with non-commissioned officers from the rebel ranks.

He captured Quinsan, the arsenal of the Taipings; he put down with a strong hand every attempt at mutiny in his heterogeneous army. In one case he quelled a mutiny at once by shooting the ringleader on the spot. In all these assaults on apparently impregnable positions and on armies much larger than his own, Gordon was the chief factor in gaining the victory. He was always in the front of the storming parties; he carried no weapon but a little cane. His reckless bravery and the small cane aroused something like superstitious worship, and he was regarded as a man whose life and whose victory were safeguarded by some divine power. The story is characteristic of him that when he had conquered the rebels and when he found out that their leaders, whom he had promised to spare, were murdered treacherously by the orders of Li Hung Chang, Gordon went carefully through every house in the search for Li Hung Chang, with the determination to execute him by his own hand. That, anyhow, is the legend.

End of the Taiping War, May 1864

He refused orders and big grants of money; the ten thousand taels of silver that were presented to him on account of the capture of Soo-chow are now on exhibition in the manuscript department of the British Museum. Gordon was now in partial retirement, but the resurrection of the Taipings brought him back. After he had extracted an apology from Li Hung Chang for the murder of Taiping agents, he started on a fresh campaign. He took town after town; when he was wounded he carried on the fight until he had to be carried to a boat. He broke the rebellion, and again he refused all pecuniary reward, writing home: "I shall leave China as poor as when I entered". But he was made a Mandarin of the First Class, with the highest title of military rank in the Chinese Service.

When he returned home he was stationed at Gravesend, commanding Royal Engineers. He gave all his leisure time to the poor and sick of the neighbourhood, spending all his money upon them, and often denying himself to have the more for them. He had special interest in the poor boys, took many of them into his own house, started them in life, and followed with interest their careers ever afterwards.

And then he went to Egypt designated by his character and attainments for the high position of Governor of the Equatorial Provinces of Central Africa. He was offered a salary of £10,000 a year, but he declined to take more than £2000. He made fierce war on the slave trade, and on all the people who were interested in it. The most important of the slave dealers was Suleiman, son of Zebehr, who was really the chief profiteer. Suleiman had settled down at Dara, and he had with him a garrison of 6000 armed men. Gordon did a thing that would be regarded as incredible if not well authenticated. He covered eighty-five miles on a camel, entered Dara without a sword, without an escort of any kind, absolutely alone; and the rebel camp, led by brutal, merciless men, were so dominated by this solitary, fearless creature that they surrendered.

On another occasion he made a journey of eight days on horseback to the wilds of Africa, dismissed Raouf Pasha, a powerful Egyptian authority, and then he had to take in hand renewed risings and movements by the slave dealers.

I must note that after his temporary retirement he paid a flying visit to Ireland. I do not know what he was expected to report, but the slavery and the poverty which he saw around him, and above all the miserable dwellings of the rack-rented and enslaved peasants, smote him to the heart.

Hicks Pasha's Army destroyed, November 1, 1883

Such was the man whom the Government, mainly, as I have said, on the shrieking imprecations of Stead, sent to deal with the tremendous and impossible situation in the Sudan, a situation mainly created by the rise and the extraordinary progress of the Mahdi—the new false prophet whom Mohammedans have at several epochs in their history been ready to follow. Everything about the choice of Gordon seems to us now grotesquely stupid; but it must, in modification of this judgment, be stated that the hands of the Government were forced by untoward incidents that, as has been seen in this narrative, so often have thwarted their best intentions and changed their reasoned-out conclusions.

Hicks Pasha, a brave officer, taking the initiative, was encouraged by the Cairo Government to attempt the reconquest of the Sudan. His whole force was cut to pieces, and what little was left of Egyptian authority was practically at the feet of the Mahdi. There still remained the question of extricating the Egyptian garrisons. This was a policy as to which the Ministry, and especially Mr. Gladstone, had grave misgivings; but there had swept over England one of those waves of popular emotion and of national pride that forced the hands of the Government. As Morley well sums it up in his *Life of Gladstone*:

"Unfortunately the ready clamour of headlong philanthropists, political party men, and the men who think England humiliated if she ever lets slip an excuse for drawing her sword, drove the Cabinet on to the rocks."

"When", goes on Morley, "the decision of the Cabinet was taken to send troops to Suakin, Mr. Gladstone stood alone in objecting."

And Morley's comment is:

"Many thousands of savages were slaughtered under humanitarian pressure, not a few English lives were sacrificed, much treasure flowed, and yet Sinkat fell, and Tokar fell, and our labours in the Eastern Sudan were practically fruitless."

Gordon's Mission to the Sudan, January 18, 1884

"In England", goes on Morley, who lived through the time and took a part in some of its most potent movements, "excitement of the unsound sort that is independent of knowledge, consideration, or deliberation; independent of any weighing of the actual facts and any forecast of latent possibilities, grew more and more vociferous."

The Government could not be deaf to this popular cyclone. Ministers, as Morley says, "quailed".

"Twice", he goes on, "they inquired of their agent in Egypt whether General Gordon might not be of use, and twice they received an adverse reply, mainly on the ground that the presence in authority of a Christian officer was a dubious mode of confronting a sweeping outbreak of Moslem fanaticism, and would inevitably alienate tribes that were still not caught by the Mahdi."

But a third application at last prevailed, and Sir Evelyn Baring, Nubar Pasha (the Egyptian Minister), Sir Evelyn Wood, and Colonel Watson, who knew Gordon well, agreed that Gordon would be the best man if he would pledge himself to carry out the policy of withdrawing from the Sudan as quickly as possible.

Meantime, Stead was placing himself at the head of the wild and blind clamour of the public, and shouting out the name of Gordon from the house-tops. Perhaps all these things will account for the extraordinary scene that follows.

"On January 18" (1884), writes Morley, "Lord Hartington (then Secretary of State for War), Lord Granville, Lord Northbrook, and Sir Charles Dilke met at the War Office in Pall Mall. The summons was sudden. Lord Wolseley brought Gordon and left him in the ante-room. After a conversation with the Ministers, he came out and said to Gordon, 'The Government are determined to evacuate the Sudan, for they will not guarantee the future government. Will you go and do it?' *I said*, 'Yes.' *He said*, 'Go in.' *I went in and saw them. They said*, 'Did Wolseley tell you our orders?' *I said*, 'Yes.' *I said*, 'You will not guarantee future government of the Sudan, and you wish me to go up and evacuate now?' *They said*, 'Yes', *and it was over, and I left at* 8 *p.m. for Calais*.' This graphic story does not pretend to be a full version of all that passed, though it puts the essential point unmistakably enough. Lord Granville seems to have drawn Gordon's special attention to the measures to be taken for the security of the Egyptian garrisons still holding positions in the Sudan, and to the best mode of evacuating the interior. On the other hand, according to a very authentic account that I have seen, Gordon on this occasion stated that the danger at Khartoum was exaggerated, and that he would be able to bring away the garrisons without difficulty."

"Thus", says Morley, "in that conclave of sober statesmen a tragedy began." But misgiving followed immediately on the sanctioning of the resolve. "The next day", says Morley, "one of the four Ministers met another: 'We were proud of ourselves yesterday—are you sure we did not commit a gigantic folly?' "

Gladstone telegraphed his assent to the decision; the Cabinet met four days later, Gladstone among them, and the decision was approved.

"There was hardly a choice," says Morley, somewhat sardonically, "for by that time Gordon was at Brindisi."

Gordon arrives at Khartoum, February 18, 1884

And then Morley makes this striking analysis of Gordon's character:

"Gordon, as Mr. Gladstone said, was a hero of heroes. He was a soldier of infinite personal courage and daring; of striking military energy, initiative, and resource; a high, pure, and single character, dwelling much in the region of the unseen. But, as all who knew him admit, and as his own records testify, notwithstanding an undercurrent of shrewd common sense he was the creature, almost the sport, of impulse: his impressions and purposes changed with the speed of lightning; anger often mastered him; he went very often by intuitions and inspirations rather than by cool inference from carefully surveyed fact; with many variations of mood he mixed, as we often see in people less famous, an invincible faith in his own rapid prepossessions while they lasted. Everybody now discerns that to despatch a soldier of this temperament on a piece of business that was not only difficult and dangerous, as Sir E. Baring said, but profoundly obscure, and needing vigilant sanity and self-control, was little better than to call in a wizard with his magic. Mr. Gladstone always professed perplexity in understanding why the violent end of the gallant Cavagnari in Afghanistan stirred the world so little in comparison with the fate of Gordon. The answer is that Gordon seized the imagination of England, and seized it on its higher side. His religion was eccentric, but it was religion; the Bible was the rock on which he founded himself, both old dispensation and new; he was known to hate forms, ceremonies, and all the 'solemn plausibilities'; his speech was sharp, pithy, rapid, and ironic; above all, he knew the ways of war and would not bare the sword for naught. All this was material enough to make a popular ideal, and this is what Gordon in an ever-increasing degree became, to the immense inconvenience of the statesmen, otherwise so sensible and wary, who had now improvidently let the genie forth from the jar."

What might be expected followed. Gordon forgot his instructions, changed his plans from day to day. His instructions were to leave Khartoum as quickly as possible, and merely to rescue the garrisons. Suddenly he settled himself down at Khartoum, and this involved a tremendous increase of the frenzied popular demand that their hero should be rescued. It ended in the Government having to send, with many delays and much difficulty as to the choice of routes, a costly expedition to reach and rescue Gordon at Khartoum.

Death of Gordon, January 26, 1885

It arrived too late; and in the meantime, amid these terrible perplexities, Gladstone had to face the possibility of a great war with Russia over a collision between Russian soldiers and Afghans at Panjdeh, and for several days it looked as if war were inevitable. Gladstone was able to settle this, but in the meantime the party passions which had lashed the multitude to such fury were carried to the House of Commons. The Tories, partly in the grip of the passions of Jingoism and partly encouraged by the many vacillations and hesitations of the Government, took every opportunity of making violent speeches and proposing hostile motions. I remember still the evening when, standing in front of my hotel in O'Connell Street, Dublin, I saw on the bill of the evening edition of the *Freeman's Journal* the words "Death of Gordon". I said to myself there and then: "This is the death of the Government, too"—and I proved to be right.

I give another glimpse into the character of Gordon, from the pen of Mr. Lytton Strachey:

"The Holy Book was not his [Gordon's] only solace. For now, under the parching African sun, we catch glimpses, for the first time, of Gordon's hand stretching out towards stimulants of a more material quality. For months together, we are told, he would drink nothing but pure water; and then . . . water that was not so pure. In his fits of melancholy, he would shut himself up in his tent for days at a time, with a hatchet and a flag placed at the door to indicate that he was not to be disturbed for any reason whatever; until at last the cloud would lift, the signals would be removed, and the Governor would reappear, brisk and cheerful. During one of these retirements, there was grave danger of a native attack upon the camp. Colonel Long, the Chief of Staff, ventured, after some hesitation, to ignore the flag and hatchet, and to enter the forbidden tent. He found Gordon seated at a table, upon which were an open Bible and an open bottle of brandy. Long explained the circumstances, but could obtain no answer beyond the abrupt words, 'You are commander of the camp', and was obliged to retire, nonplussed, to deal with the situation as best he could. On the following morning, Gordon, cleanly shaven, and in the full-dress uniform of the Royal Engineers, entered Long's hut with his usual tripping step, exclaiming: 'Old fellow, now don't be angry with me. I was very low last night. Let's have a good breakfast—a little b. and s. Do you feel up to it?'"

These events, both in Egypt and in the country here, had their repercussions at once in the House of Commons. Mr. Gladstone still displayed his extraordinary brilliance and predominance as a Parliamentary debater—there was scarcely a serious debate for months in which he did not make a brilliant speech reducing his opponents to silence and despair, always excepting Lord Randolph Churchill, whom nothing could either intimidate or abash—but he could not prevent terrible fissures in his ranks. He had on the one side the Radicals, who were opposed to the intervention of the country in the Egyptian imbroglio; but equally resolute on the other side were a series of Whigs still left in their places in spite of the reduction of the franchise. Many of them, county magnates, looked with no great favour on the new Franchise Bill giving the agricultural labourers the vote for the first time. A good many of them, like Mr. Goschen and Mr. Forster, were more Jingo than Liberal, and pushing Gladstone onwards, while the Radicals were trying to drag him back. There were also differences within the Cabinet itself.

I had to be one of the fiercest assailants of Mr. Gladstone at the time, and I had no love for him. The most successful speech I ever made in the House of Commons was one in reply to one of his great apologies in defence of his Egyptian policy; but now, looking back at the thing and understanding Gladstone better than I did in the distorted imagination of party passion, I fully sympathise with the judgment pronounced by Lord Morley on this period of his career:

"A Minister of unalterable patience, unruffled self-command; inexhaustible in resource, catching at every straw from the resource of others; indefatigable in bringing men of divergent opinions within friendly reach of one another; of tireless ingenuity in minimizing differences and convincing recalcitrants that what they took for a yawning gulf was in fact no more than a narrow trench that any decent political gymnast ought to be ashamed not to be able to vault over."

Mr. Joseph Chamberlain, from 1880 *to* 1885

I do not know enough of the inside history of Gladstone's Cabinet at the time to realize quite the special part that was played in its dissensions by Mr. Chamberlain and Sir Charles Dilke; but on the whole I am sure they were not helpful to their own Chief. I postpone any discussion of Mr. Chamberlain until I come to the final clash between him and Mr. Gladstone over Home Rule.

Of all the men in the Ministry of Mr. Gladstone I would certainly have pronounced Dilke as the most successful. It is a mistake to suppose that Mr. Chamberlain attained to his great Parliamentary position all of a sudden. He never made a speech in the House of Commons from 1880 to 1885 that excited any special admiration. He was clear; he struck hard; he had that admirable command of a good voice and a perfect delivery which he was always to display; but on the whole he was so overshadowed by Mr. Gladstone, and he got so little occasion for the exhibition of his most brilliant gifts, that I should be inclined to describe his career from 1880 to 1885 as rather a diminution than an augmentation of the great authority he exercised in the ranks of the party outside, and especially in Birmingham. The only oratorical Parliamentary triumph of his I remember in that old Parliament was a reply which he made to Lord Randolph Churchill's attack on him with regard to the somewhat ugly riots in Aston which took place when Lord Randolph—already contemplating a descent on the solid Chamberlain square in Birmingham—had his meeting violently broken up.

There was an ugly riot, and there was abundant reason to suppose that it was organized by the followers of Mr. Chamberlain; but Lord Randolph had not made up his case well, or his opponent had made up his so much better, that Mr. Chamberlain achieved an immense triumph in the reply to the formidable indictment. His defence was long, but every bit of it was brilliant, and it had so captivated the House that he was permitted to have a recess—the House was too hungry to go on—and he was allowed to resume his reply. Any biographer of Mr. Chamberlain must date the beginning of his great Parliamentary position from that particular speech.

The best proof of its success was the appearance of Lord Randolph Churchill. I still remember him, with his body doubled up, with his face downcast, and sitting not only dejected, but alone—without Gorst, without Drummond Wolff, even without Mr. Balfour. Never did I see a man looking more crushed, more deserted. At the moment I think there was a temporary schism in the small camp of the Fourth Party. This is the place to introduce an extraordinary experience I had recently with—as he himself described our relations—an old friend and an old Parliamentary enemy. Meeting Lord Balfour while I was contemplating writing these memoirs, I told him that I would call on him without doubt for some information with regard to the great Parliamentary incidents in which we had both taken part. Lord Balfour had various ups and downs in this Parliament; his antagonism to Sir Stafford Northcote now and then reached a point so scandalous as to arouse against him the opinions of the majority of the staid Tories. He aggravated his offence once or twice by attacks on Sir Stafford not only by a different line of action in the House of Commons, but by a public indictment. Of the four members who constituted the Fourth Party two were always to be accounted as steadfast—Mr. Gorst and Sir Henry Drummond Wolff—but Mr. Balfour (as he then was) was always an uncertain quantity.

I believe he himself has denied that he ever was really a member of the Fourth Party. Anyhow, his close relationship to Lord Salisbury—practically the head of the Tory Party—his much more equable and less reckless temperament than that of Lord Randolph, the hopes he could very well entertain of reaching a high official position when his party came into power—all these things subjected him to influences which had no control over Lord Randolph.

Mr. Balfour leaves the Fourth Party

One day there was very palpable evidence of the scission between Mr. Balfour and his reckless associate. The members of the Fourth Party, as I have already told, used to sit together on the front bench below the gangway on the Opposition side of the House, a choice of seats which, as also I have told, marked certain phases of thought, an independence of leaders—rather different from the somewhat blind allegiance of the ranks that sat above the gangway and immediately behind the Tory leaders.

But on this particular afternoon Mr. Balfour was discovered to have left Alsatia and gone back to respectability by taking his place among the obscurer and more disciplined members of the Tory Party above the gangway.

The rumours which had announced the approach of this scission were not confirmed until, at the end of question time, the tall, slim form of Mr. Balfour was seen to rise from the third bench above the gangway. He took out the handkerchief which he wore in his front coat pocket—"As I do now", said Lord Balfour at the time of our conversation a couple of years ago—a gesture he constantly made, and which at the time, in the very inexact and scornful manner in which he was then regarded, rather added to that niminy-piminy appearance which his enemies and even his friends regarded as characteristic of him. To the House of that period, and for some time afterwards, the thought of Mr. Balfour always suggested a recollection of the "Howell and James" type of young men who were the most prominent figures in Gilbert and Sullivan's satire on what were called the æsthetes of that period. . . . When Mr. Balfour, with the handkerchief in his hand and the deprecatory air then characteristic of him, and with a rather limp bearing and a limp voice, stood up to ask his question, the great scission in the small party was hailed as at last realized, and there were peals upon peals of laughter and cheers before poor Mr. Balfour was able to ask his question.

When I was conversing with Lord Balfour on this and other incidents, he made to me the astonishing reply that he had forgotten all about most of the things that had taken place in the House of Commons, and when I tested him on this particular and, as I thought noteworthy, incident, he replied that he could not recall it. By and by I shall recur, of course, to Mr. Balfour's brilliant and chequered career in the House of Commons, but for the moment and in the Egyptian imbroglio he does not much count. A more appropriate figure to bring in now is Sir Charles Dilke.

Sir Charles Dilke, 1843–1911

In contrast with Mr. Chamberlain and Mr. Balfour, Dilke's position in the House had been enormously improved during the course of these Parliamentary years. Never was there a man in British politics who was more truly, fundamentally, incessantly, untiringly a politician than Dilke. Heir to a considerable fortune, restless, energetic, after his fashion thoroughly patriotic, he had trained himself for political life as had no man of his time. He was an incessant globe-trotter from his youth upwards: he was still little more than a youngster when he undertook a long journey through the outlying portions of the Empire, and his observations found expression in a book called *Greater Britain*, which was regarded at the time as one of the first real attempts to give an insight into the conditions and prospects of our Empire in the Antipodes.

There was scarcely a year, especially when he was free from office, in which he did not extend these globe-trotting expeditions, with a mind profoundly interested in everything he saw; observant always, packing away in a memory that was as retentive as a rat-trap all the information he thus gained. If you talked to him about France, you would find there was no statesman of that country with whom he was not on terms of personal familiarity; a familiarity increased by the fact that he took a comfortable house in the rural regions near Toulon, in the South of France—a house that played some part in the gossip of the evil days of personal attack, of which more will have to be said by and by. If you talked to him about India, he would tell you of the size and appearance of a rather remote city like Peshawar, enlarging on its political problems and speculating on its future. He had visited the United States on his first all-round-the-world tour. On a second trip he visited China and Japan.

He was a man of prodigious industry. He took care of his physical condition by having a fencing match nearly every morning of his life. It was revealed afterwards that Gladstone never dreamed of including either him or Chamberlain in his Cabinet of 1880. The alliance of Dilke and Chamberlain at the moment was both politically and personally close, and, indeed, very loyal on the one side and the other. Dilke annoyed Gladstone by refusing to take office unless Chamberlain was appointed to a Cabinet position; and Dilke himself was satisfied with the position of Under-Secretary to the Foreign Office, and outside the Cabinet. It seemed as if, in this self-denying act, Dilke was sacrificing his own future to that of Chamberlain; but, as a matter of fact, he chose the office which was best suited to bring out his abilities and to advance his position.

Dilke as Foreign Under-Secretary, 1880–1882

Never in my time was there so effective a Foreign Under-Secretary. He had not the splendour of Lord Curzon, who occupied the same position many years afterwards; on the contrary, he was studiously prosaic; his answers were terse; with an appearance of candour, he avoided all the weak or the perilous points in the position of foreign affairs. These qualities in a Minister, with their absence of anything but the simplest, most prosaic, most cautious language, were not an obstacle, but an aid, to creating the tremendous reputation Dilke was building up. He was an official just after the English heart: the very absence of the more dazzling qualities in rhetoric which belonged to his colleagues and his rivals and his opponents rather added to that feeling of perfect safety which is always held to be the ideal quality of British statesmanship, especially in anything connected with the terrible delicacy and embarrassments of foreign affairs.

If one were asked at that time to prophesy who was the predestined and irresistible leader of the Liberal Party of the future, most Parliamentary prophets would have immediately mentioned Dilke.

I have not yet come to the moment when I shall have to describe the tragic disaster in which this splendid career ended; I deal only now with what Dilke proved to be when he had behind him the tremendous background of a great Minister dealing with a great department. Dilke could speak with extraordinary fluency; but it was a fluency—except when making a mere official statement—undistinguished and unimpressive. No man could pour out a greater tide of intimate and detailed knowledge; but it was a defect of his oratory as well as of his mind that he had apparently no sense of proportion, that he mingled the smallest detail with the biggest fact, that his delivery was in the same way as monotonous as his appraisal of facts. In private conversation I found him just the same. He talked almost incessantly; always with this exhibition of encyclopædic knowledge, but always in the same unimpressive manner; so that really, without disrespect, one might say that he chattered rather than conversed. He always suggested the suspicion that he was never quite candid.

The face—fairly handsome, with regular features, and a pleasant beard, which seemed to suit it—relapsed usually into a kind of impassivity that suggested a man who was vigilant and secretive. The eyes were especially noticeable, and not altogether pleasant; they looked as if they had too much white, and there was also a certain furtiveness in them. When you asked him a question, he answered you usually with that featureless fluency which was in his public speech; and really I often felt, when I consulted him, just as puzzled as to what he really thought or knew as before I had spoken to him.

He had also, I think, one fundamental line of thought which, in spite of his Radicalism, separated him from Mr. Gladstone and from the bulk even of the Radical section to which he belonged. He was at bottom a Jingo. By the date to which I have now reached, he had got rid of some of the disrepute into which he had fallen when, in his pre-Ministerial days, he had proclaimed himself practically a Republican, and had delivered speeches, sometimes at considerable personal risk, which criticized in a very severe way the subsidies given by Parliament to the Queen. He had to be guarded by police in halls in various parts of the country in which he attempted to initiate this campaign.

He and Mr. Auberon Herbert—a somewhat eccentric type of Liberal—were shouted down in the House of Commons when they tried to raise the discussion of the expenses of the monarchy. Mr. Gladstone passionately replied; and when the division came, Sir Wilfrid Lawson and one other member alone supported Dilke's motion, for which he and Herbert had to act as tellers. The Queen was very much offended, and it required all Mr. Gladstone's tact and strength of will to get her assent to Dilke's inclusion in the Government.

Dilke in the Cabinet, 1882–1885

When the upset of the Government came, with the resignation of Forster from the Chief Secretaryship, Dilke could have had his place in the Cabinet, but declined. Soon after, however, there was another shuffle of the Ministerial cards, and he became President of the Local Government Board, and a Member of the Cabinet. He told me himself, a short time after his appointment to this office, that he hated it; his heart was really in foreign affairs; but he brought to his new office the same indefatigable industry which he had shown in the old. Just as, when Foreign Secretary, he always answered tersely, to the point, and tactfully, so he answered with regard to this Department. Later on I shall have to say something about his action in a very momentous business; namely, the reduction of the franchise in the counties, and the still more difficult task of settling the principles of the redistribution of seats.

In the counsels of the party with regard to Egypt, Dilke, as has been seen, was one of the men who sent Gordon to Khartoum, and all through I am inclined to believe he was not in entire sympathy with Gladstone's misgivings of the Egyptian policy. His point of view, as I have said, was essentially Jingo; he was rather disposed to push than to recede from intervention in the internal affairs of Egypt. For the moment I leave him.

CHAPTER XVII

Lord Spencer in Ireland—The Maamtrasna murders—The "Dirty Trick" Debate—Whips in a panic—Morley's blow to the Government—A narrow division—Sir W. Harcourt's historic phrase—Shaky Ministry —The Franchise Bill—Redistribution—A comedy of Mr. Forster—Mr. Gladstone in 1885—Campbell-Bannerman.

Lord Spencer appointed Lord-Lieutenant, April 28, 1882

IN the midst of these violent convulsions, continuous party attacks, and heated divisions, Ireland still obstinately obtruded itself. Even at the end of a debate reaching to the small hours of the morning, the House, after it had already listened to violent diatribes against the Egyptian policy of the Government, had to sit listening to equally violent diatribes against the policy of the same Government in Ireland. Things there, indeed, continued to be in a bad way, and though externally there was less disorder, there was a terrible picture of force on the one side and bloody reprisals on the other. Lord Spencer, as Cabinet Minister, had really the chief responsibility for the regime which followed that of Forster. The Coercion Act which Lord Spencer administered was in some respects a less clumsy instrument than that which had been placed at the disposal of Mr. Forster. He had means of secret examination, of jury-packing and of quick justice, with judges in full sympathy with his ideas and determined as much as he was, both for their personal and family interest and for their political opinions, to be quite ruthless in enforcing the almost unlimited powers of dragooning the country under the latest regime. Many of the criminals were tracked down successfully; many of them were convicted; and yet it was a ghastly tale at the end of it all.

I cannot better sum up what the regime of Lord Spencer in Ireland involved than in these two figures: the country was once more half-conquered, but nothing was advanced; and the other half of the conquest was not any nearer.

The attitude of Ireland towards this regime was what might have been expected. "There lay Ireland", sums up Mr. Morley, "squalid, dismal, sullen, dull, despondent, sunk deep in hostile intent." The Government and their supporters might well believe that Lord Spencer had confronted terrible dangers, and had mastered a terrible situation with consummate success, and to stand by Spencer seemed not only necessary, but a noble purpose. In spite of his being associated with such terrible events, Lord Spencer personally could not help making an appeal, even to those who hated him. I saw him once or twice by accident, riding through the streets of Dublin at the time of his historic Viceroyalty. I did not know him then, though I came to know him very well afterwards, but even then I saw in the sad, almost deprecatory expression, a glimpse of not merely the anxieties, but all the sadness that accompanied his terrible task. He went through the streets of Dublin just as a Russian Governor might go through the streets of Warsaw after a bloody victory over a Polish rebellion, surrounded on all sides by a bodyguard of cavalry, the clank of whose armour echoed through the streets, and in the middle of them this man with the great red beard, the honest and candid face, the heavy-lidded, anxious, sorrowful eyes—the husband of a beautiful but childless wife.

But to the Irish people, with all this long tale of executions, he seemed no better than the English hangman sent to put down the national aspirations of Ireland. The men who died on the scaffold were known to have done their terrible deeds, not under the impulse of personal greed or hatred, but as a blow in defending the liberties of their country. Some of them were known to be young men who, in ordinary life and until the dread hour of doing their deed came upon them, were gentle, disinterested, courageous, and high-minded. They were brave soldiers lost in a terrible and unequal battle. The methods by which they were convicted, too, were notoriously those of sanguinary dictatorship, whose violence and irresponsibility were increased by the hypocritical pretences of constitutional government and fair trial. However terrible the crimes that Lord Spencer had to deal with—and some of them were very terrible—the scene on the scaffold tended to obliterate their horror, except against the Government that was responsible for such a regime.

The Maamtrasna Murders, August 17, 1882

All this great tide of national hatred, of national longing for revenge, was increased by rumours which, whether well or ill founded, obtained ready credulity among the exasperated and now helpless people. There were legends current which asseverated, and seemed in some cases almost to prove, that the executed men were the innocent victims of judicial murder. Francis Hines, a Clare youth of respectable parentage and of a very attractive personality, was held to be innocent. There was one terrible murder at Maamtrasna which spread horror even amid the Irish population themselves.

The scene of these murders was what is known as the Joyces' country in Connemara, because nearly everybody there is named Joyce. Early in 1882 an old bailiff named Huddy and his grandson were sent into the Joyces' country to collect rents, and were never again seen alive. Lough Mask was dragged, and their bodies were found tied up in sacks. In the following August a party of disguised men entered the house of a family named Joyce, consisting of a man, his wife, mother, two sons, and a daughter, and massacred them all, with the exception of one son, who was severely wounded. It appears that the Joyces knew something of the murder of the Huddys, and the murderers feared that they might betray them. In time the besotted miscreants who had been guilty of this dreadful and almost inconceivable murder were brought to trial, and several of them were hanged. It might well have been that the punishment for a murder so ghastly, unconnected with the agitation then proceeding in Ireland, unconnected with the movement for national liberty, would have been received, if not with approval, certainly without any great outburst of indignation by the general body of the Irish people: but here came in that new feature which helped to spread the horror and hatred of the Spencer regime—namely, a doubt as to the guilt of some of the executed men, and of one in particular. For months afterwards the story of Miles Joyce was on every Irish lip. Mr. Timothy Harrington, the secretary of a Nationalist organization called the National League, who was an effective and industrious propagandist, examined thoroughly into the case and published letter after letter in defence of the plea that Miles Joyce was innocent. He backed this up, again with the assent of his countrymen, by a description of the horrible details which accompanied the execution.

Thus it was that never at any period, not even in that of Mr. Forster, was Ireland more violently hostile to the

Government. All their sentiments, indeed all their interests for the time being, were submerged by this passionate hatred, and that was accompanied by aiming at the one supreme purpose of the Irish Party—to break down the Government which was held responsible for all these things.

Thus, then, the unhappy Government, confronted by the unsurmountable difficulties and the inevitable mistakes and mishaps in their Egyptian policy, were every day of the session also confronted by this party of resolute and able men who followed Parnell, by every single motion, by every speech, by every vote that might embarrass and break down the Government. The vindictiveness which is one of the features of Irish character had taken the place of calculation, of political balancing of ultimate consequences. It might ruin or it might help them that the Gladstone Ministry should fall, but the Irish members and the Irish people were determined that they should fall. This will be the key to their attitude and to the things which immediately followed.

Saturday Debate on Egypt, March 15, 1884

All the debates on Egypt gave them one opportunity after another of "feeding fat" their full revenge. I have already described how the forces behind Mr. Gladstone were hopelessly divided, and how on occasion one might hope that a dexterously drafted vote of censure on them might well send a large number of their supporters into the opposite lobby; and this is just what happened. I left Morley a few pages ago, and now I have to describe a moving scene in which he took a leading part, and almost, though unwillingly and with misgiving, gave to the shaky Government the last deadly blow.

On March 15, 1884, the Government had to resort to a Saturday sitting. This sitting did not promise the tempestuous and dramatic scene which was to follow. The House started at an early hour, and, as I wrote at the time, the House is like a ballet-girl, it does not look very well by day. It has a yellow and a bilious complexion. It rubs its eyes frequently, as though it had got up too early and did not at all like the process; and the elaborately painted windows, excluding the sun, add to the melancholy of the picture by clothing it in that chiaroscuro which, in anything but the wide sweep of a cathedral, is the most dolorous of all lights. The result is that there is always something ghastly and unreal about an early sitting of any kind. On those benches, breathing stertorously, like one that has a heavy dream, it is insane to pour out any eloquent appeal to passion. To any stirring reference to principle the House listens with open-eyed astonishment, and at best rewards even its most favoured orator with a faint and shamefaced murmur—as like to the robust heartiness of the post-prandial or midnight cheer as the drone of a lotus-eater to the natural voice of the vigorous and pushing realist of actual life. This is the reason why it was hard to get members to come down to a Wednesday sitting (in those days Wednesday, not Friday, was the day for the short sitting), and why there was always a difficulty in getting a House together on that day. But, bad as the Wednesday sitting was, it was usual and inevitable, and so was endured with groaning toleration. But a Saturday sitting was a dread portent, which was never believed in till it arrived, and was generally regarded as a sort of Parliamentary bogey, held up by Ministers in order to frighten members into hurrying up with the voting of money.

I was present, of course, at this Saturday sitting, and I

felt that this was going to be a day of dullness, that there would not be even a ripple of passion throughout the whole day, and that members would drone through the hours with the obstinate but hideous determination of men who were resolved to go through with a dull and hateful task.

And yet that Saturday sitting was the most interesting and important of the whole session, and that sleepy and dreary House for several hours was as fiercely and passionately excited as I have ever seen it. It is hard to say how much this result was due to accident or deliberate design; but I strongly believed at the time that the Tories had arranged the business, though in the clumsy and ineffective way which marked all their proceedings. "Why was it", I asked a leading and clever Tory, "that you had not a better muster of your men?" "Because", he said, with bitterness, "we are the worst-whipped Party in the world."

The beginnings of the debate corresponded to my anticipations. Ashmead-Bartlett was a frequent but not a welcome speaker. He was a leader of Jingoism, besides, and his subject was a plea that suggested the annexation of Egypt. As nobody on either side of the House was in favour of annexation, such a speech had no significance whatever, and was not listened to by anybody.

The "Dirty Trick" Debate

It was when Mr. Labouchere rose that the movement which was really dangerous to the Government began. Mr. Labouchere's motion was insidiously directed towards gaining votes on both sides of the House. It declared that there was no valid reason for the recent bloodshed: thus it could be voted for alike by the peace-at-any-price Radical and the Tory who contended that none of this bloodshed would have been necessary if the Government had been sufficiently prompt in taking energetic measures. This was made soon apparent by the fact that Mr. Labouchere's motion was supported by Mr. Richards, an amiable enthusiast who, in season and out of season, advocated a policy of universal peace.

It was one of the circumstances which at the same time added to the Ministerial difficulties that a Cabinet Council was being held at the very moment when this debate was going forward and threatened the very existence of the Government. The result was that Lord Edmond Fitzmaurice was the only person left to defend the Government, and he, though unquestionably an able man, had a very maladroit manner and enjoyed no authority as a speaker. The Under-Secretary, when he did speak, rather made the position of the Government worse, and the tide was now full against the Government.

Such a moment was especially suitable to Mr. Cowen. Sitting beside them, and yet in constant opposition to them, Mr. Cowen was a terrible thorn in the side of the Ministry. He had, as I have said, a marvellous gift of oratory, and therefore he was just the man at such a moment to change the wavering position of the Government into a *sauve qui peut*. His speech was a splendid piece of rhetoric, and produced a visibly depressing effect among the Ministerialists, who now began to have the downcast air of men advancing to certain slaughter.

By this time the Ministers had been made acquainted with the critical state of affairs, and Sir Charles Dilke put in an appearance. He delivered a most significant speech, which helped to accentuate the importance of the hour, for he used some words which clearly threatened a Dissolution, and therefore seemed to point more clearly to the possibility of a Government defeat, with all the serious consequences which a Government defeat would involve.

Another and equally serious portent of the hour was the arrival of Lord Hartington, hot-foot after Sir Charles Dilke, showing that the occasion was deemed so critical that the Cabinet had been broken up abruptly, so that the Ministerialists might have the advantage both of the votes and the speeches of their leaders. In the lobby there was even more significant proof of the gravity of the occasion. The Whips were to be seen in frantic consultation; the telegraph office was blocked with urgent and despairing wires, troops of messengers were being sent all over London, to house and club and known resorts, to hurry up the scattered stragglers on both sides.

Mr. Morley's Revolt

At the exit door of the lobby, where stand the Whips, like watchdogs, to prevent the departure of any of their supporters, there might have been seen on that day the portly form of Sir William Harcourt, Mr. Chamberlain, and a couple of under-secretaries, engaged in the humble and anxious drudgery of counting votes. This was the strongest proof of how dangerous the position of the Government had become. By this time the weak-kneed and thick-and-thin supporters began to show the seriousness of their alarm by raising the cry that a vote against the Government might mean their overthrow, and the substitution for them of Lord Salisbury and Sir Stafford Northcote. That was the way it was put. Of course, the real meaning was that there might be a General Election, and that a good many gentlemen might not be so sure of coming back again, especially if the reason of their going out was a vote against the Government of Mr. Gladstone.

The vehement cheers with which these views were received showed how thoroughly frightened the Ministerialists were, and how welcome even small mercies proved. But again the full danger of the situation was revealed when Mr. Morley rose to declare, with the nervousness of a new speaker, but with all the force of strong conviction, that he was more inclined to vote against the Government if they had made up their minds to abandon their principles and adopt a Jingo policy in Egypt.

I remember Mr. Morley as he rose to make this portentous and damaging speech. He was pale, and uttered his words with difficulty; you could see that nervousness had dried his mouth and his lips. He described the coming division as one that was very important to the Government, and, he added, "very important to me". But he went on to criticize the Government. The contrast between his appearance and evident trepidation, and his resolute vindication of the policy in which he believed, brought curiously to my mind the famous story of how the Duke of Wellington, seeing one of his soldiers, pallid and terror-stricken, still walk resolutely on to the attack, commented that this was the really brave man who could overcome his inner terrors.

The battle went on for hours, amid an excitement that increased with every moment, and that finally began to reach something like the frenzy of hysteria. Meantime the House itself changed its appearance; the benches filled, showing that the vigorous whip was beginning to tell. It was at such a moment that one had an opportunity of seeing what a potent factor in the destinies of the British Empire the Irish Parliamentary vote had become. The wildest and most bigoted Tory asked, in a voice trembling with affectionate interest, how many the Irish Party was able to muster for a division. Alas! Mr. Sheil—the cool, shrewd, and energetic Irish Whip—had not as favourable a report to make as it would rejoice his heart to give. Turn the calculation how he would, he could not make the number of his roll get beyond fifteen. After a while his heart was rejoiced by a message from Mr. Parnell that he had succeeded in getting a promise from a member whose vote was considered doubtful that he would go with his Party even though it involved going against the Government. This, Mr. Sheil calculated, raised the Irish vote to sixteen—which was, I believe, the number of Irish votes ultimately cast against the Government.

Close Division on Egypt

At last the hour for the division came. Both sides were silent enough, as is nearly always the case when a really serious piece of business is on hand—suspense ties, not loosens, the tongue. There were 111 Ministerial votes against Mr. Labouchere's motion, and 94 supporters, giving the Government a majority of only 17. When these numbers were announced, the pent-up emotion and the relieved fears of the Liberals were the first things to find expression, and there burst from the benches as loud and, I thought, as prolonged a cheer as I had ever heard. The Tories, after a slight pause, answered back the Ministerialists with cheers as loud and fierce as their own, the object being to mark the perilous narrowness of the Liberal victory.

Immediately after the division there occurred the most exciting incident of the wildly exciting day. Sir Michael Hicks-Beach got up, and in his most solemn tones called attention to the use of the phrase by Sir William Harcourt, "This dirty trick has not succeeded". Scarcely had Hicks-Beach uttered the words than there came an extraordinary demonstration from the Ministerialists. They raised a cheer so loud and prolonged that even the noisy demonstration by which the result of the division had been received could no more be compared to it than summer's breeze to winter's hurricane. This was a strange revelation of the depth and ferocity of feeling which had been evoked. Hicks-Beach stood at the table unable to make even an attempt at headway against the mighty storm. At last he was allowed to proceed, and asked the Speaker to rule Sir William Harcourt out of order.

An equally significant manifestation took place when the Home Secretary got up. For one brief moment in his life Sir William Harcourt could feel that he was popular. He had given one of those fierce and fitting battle-cries which conveniently epitomize the passion of a party, and he was met with an outburst of wild welcome and fierce devotion. He declined, with something a little like swagger, to withdraw his language—as the Speaker had ruled that he could not interfere with words used in private conversation—and was about to leave the House triumphantly, but the Attorney-General pulled him back, and he made in the end a clumsy and half-hearted apology.

Then there came a short conversation, in which each side accused the other of breach of faith, and the Speaker was visibly disturbed by the fierce appeals from the now uncontrollably excited Liberals to call all their opponents to order. Lord Randolph Churchill was howled at until, finally, the Speaker had to intervene. Notwithstanding, the leader of the Fourth Party was able to go on for a while longer, labouring heavily. In the end, however, he was brought to silence, and then Mr. Arthur O'Connor rushed upon the scene. Here, apparently, was the opportunity of the rabid Ministerialists. When Mr. O'Connor came into slight collision with the Speaker, a hoarse and fierce shout of "Name him" arose, and the Irish member narrowly escaped making a British holiday.

Government Majority of Fourteen, February 28, 1885

This narrow division, of course, only blooded the Tory Opposition, now very much again under the control of Lord Randolph Churchill. In 1885 the war was still continued, and there came another narrow majority. This followed the fall of Khartoum and the death of Gordon. Again the Government were deserted by many of their friends; amongst the most eager opponents were Goschen and Forster and other members of the Whig section, who were all for a forward policy. Mr. Goschen went the length of saying that if the Government flinched from the policy of smashing the Mahdi at Khartoum, he would vote against them.

Morley's *Life of Gladstone* gives an admirable description of the course of this debate. Having first mentioned Goschen's threat, Morley goes on:

"A Radical below the gangway upon this went to the Party Whip and declared, with equal resolution, that if the Government insisted on the policy, then it would be for him and others to vote against them. Sir William Harcourt, in a speech of great power, satisfied the gentleman below the gangway, and only a small handful of the Party went into the lobby with the Opposition and the Irish. The division was taken at four in the morning (Feb. 28), and the result was that the Government, which had come in with morning radiance five years ago, was worn down to an attenuated majority of fourteen."

This was another deadly blow at the already crumbling Government, but Mr. Gladstone refused to acknowledge it. "When the numbers were declared, Mr. Gladstone", says Mr. Morley, "said to a colleague on the bench, '*That will do*'." Mr. Morley goes on—

"Whether this Delphic utterance meant that the size of the majority would justify resignation or retention, the colleague was not sure. When the Cabinet met at a more mellowed hour in the day, the question between going out of office and staying in was fully discussed. Mere considerations of ease all pointed one way, for if they held on, they would seem to be dependent on Tory support; trouble was brewing with Russia, and the Seats Bill would not be through in a hurry. On the other hand, fourteen was majority enough to swear by: the Party would be surprised by resignation and discouraged, and retirement would wear the look of a false position. In fact, Mr. Gladstone, in spite of his incessant sighs for a hermit's calm, was always for fighting out every position to the last trench. I can think of no exception, and even when the time came, ten years later, he thought his successors pusillanimous for retiring on a small scratch defeat on cordite. So now he acted on the principle that with courage Cabinets may weather almost any storm. No actual vote was taken, but the numbers for and against retirement were equal, until Mr. Gladstone spoke. He thought that they should try to go on, at least until the Seats Bill was through. This was the final decision."

There is a very interesting glimpse of Gladstone at this very painful moment of his career which is well worth transferring to my pages. It is a note left by Mr. Bright of a meeting with him at this time—

"*March* 2, 1885. Dined with Mrs. Gladstone. After dinner, sat for half an hour or more with Mr. Gladstone, who is ill with cold and hoarseness. Long talk on Egypt. He said he had suffered torment during the continuance of the difficulty in that country. The sending Gordon out was a great mistake—a man totally unsuited for the work he undertook. Mr. Gladstone never saw Gordon. He was appointed by Ministers in town, and Gladstone concurred, but had never seen him."

It was at this critical moment that the Penjdeh imbroglio intervened, but that was satisfactorily dealt with.

Franchise Bill introduced, February 29, 1884

And now, finally, came two other tremendous problems, which at once threatened to ruin the Cabinet and to end the Ministry. The first of these was the question of extending Household Suffrage to the agricultural labourers. This problem went through various phases. At first there were strong declarations by some of the Tory leaders; but this irreconcilable position had ultimately to be given up. I remember hearing Lord Randolph Churchill, half self-pitying and half satirical of his friends, describe how, when at a meeting in Edinburgh, he announced his irreconcilable hostility to the new reform of the franchise, he was immediately thrown over by Mr. Balfour. Another point on which there was fierce difference of opinion was whether Ireland should be included or excluded from the new Reform Bill. Even the blindest and most obstinate anti-Home Rule Members of the House began at last to realize the coming domination of Parnell in Ireland, and to a certain extent, therefore, in the House of Commons, by the enormous accession of strength which would come to him by the admission of the new voters; but the Liberals, with the few exceptions of Tories like Goschen posing as Liberals, and all the Members of the Government, stood quite firm upon this question. Gladstone announced that the franchise was to be uniform, meaning applicable to Ireland as well as to England, "and from that position", he added, "nothing would induce us to depart".

In the interval between this proposal of the Franchise Bill and its resumption, there came the exciting "Dirty Trick Debate", which I have already recorded; but by May 1, when the debate was resumed, it was seen that opposition to the Franchise Bill was hopeless. So overwhelmingly had the feeling by this time developed among the friends of the Bill, and the division among its enemies, that its success was plainly assured. Even Mr. Goschen, who had voted against the second reading of the Bill, because no pledge against Ireland had been given, remained silent. He was not even to be seen in his usual seat, but skulked, shadow-like and ashamed, about the House. "Goschen, Goschen", cried the Irish Members, to bring out the cowed silence and the ugly shirking of their baffled and sea-green foe into bolder relief; but the Member for Ripon, growing greener, affected not to hear. At last, a few minutes after eleven, the question was put that the Speaker leave the chair, which is the last step before the arrival of Committee. There was a storm of "Ayes", and Alderman Fowler, who was something of a chatterer and a noodle, murmured the solitary "No" from the great Conservative Party, and the Bill had got into Committee. The Liberals and the Irish Members cheered long and loud at the Conservative surrender, and loud and long were the cheers again when Sir Arthur Otway took the chair and opened the epoch of Committee.

The third reading passed off with comparative triumph. Sir Stafford Northcote rebuked Gladstone for the challenge which his speech sent to the House of Lords; but when Sir Stafford announced that he did not intend to go to a division, a few of the professional obstructors like Mr. Warton, and some of the die-hards, muttered a few final objections.

Franchise Bill passed, December 5, 1884

Then a strange and dramatic scene took place. The Conservatives had quietly dropped out of the House, man by man, and when the moment came for putting to the House the third reading of the Bill, there was scarcely a single one in his place. Vast, gaping, dismal, stretched the void abyss. There was accordingly not a single "No" in response to the thunderclap of "Ayes" from the Liberal benches. Then there was an outburst of cheers that lasted for several minutes, and seemed destined to go on for ever. But Mr. Gladstone was observed to lift his hands, and it was perceived that he requested silence. Then, rising, he asked the Speaker if he would declare that the Bill had been passed *nemine contradicente*. The Speaker rose, put the question again, and there not being a single "No", did declare that the Bill had passed *nemine contradicente*. Then there was another and almost wilder shout of triumph from the Liberals. It was twenty minutes past eight.

I pause for a moment to recount one of those comic scenes with which the seriousness of the House of Commons is very often interrupted. There were a couple of Irish Bills dealing with the conditions of fishing in that country. Mr. Forster, for some reason or other, occupied his usual corner seat all through these debates. His appearance was somewhat unusual. His hair was more dishevelled than usual, his walk up the floor was painfully uncertain; he lolled about his seat in a semi-comatose stupor; but strangest of all was the look of his face during the brief intervals when he was not in stertorous slumber. All the fierceness and savagery had gone out of it, and it was clothed in a smile—vacuous, infantile, and universally affectionate. There had been a rumour that, perhaps owing to the perils of the position, perhaps to the dominating influences of Irish hospitality, Mr. Forster had developed a taste for good liquor, and that on this occasion he was under the influence of a too copious dinner. The Irish members, always delighted at having an opportunity of girding at their deadly enemy, began, in one form or another, to demand his intervention in the debate, affecting a grave anxiety to know what the opinion was of so experienced a judge of Irish conditions. The joke became universal, and there rose cries for "Forster, Forster", while the ex-Chief Secretary looked across with his great smile slightly dashed with a ray of cunning and caution.

He was not to be caught, remained in his seat, and left the problem a perplexity to all future historians—whether or not he was able on that particular evening to speak with consecutive sense and unbroken articulation. Shortly after he rose from his place. There was an awful pause as he descended the gangway to the floor, and men held their breath. The ex-Chief Secretary broke the short journey by whispering something to a friend who was painfully concealing his anxiety; then he reached the floor, gave one heavy lurch, but recovered himself quickly, and, spreading flat on the ground a foot whose proportions even a Chicago girl might envy, got himself out into the lobby; while the House, deprived of that great smile that had shone on it as conspicuously as the electric light in the Clock Tower, was sepulchred in darkness visible.

Redistribution Bill Debates, May-June 1885

For some weeks after this the struggle over the Franchise Bill took another form. Lord Salisbury succeeded in having it temporarily suspended, and the Government had to have an autumn session to carry it through. There were many signs of excitement before this question was disposed of, while the leaders of both sides were delivering violent speeches, and there were sometimes severe personal encounters, in which even Mr. Gladstone's usual composure was disturbed, and he made vehement personal attacks on the Tories who were gibing at him.

In spite of all these outward seemings, there were secret negotiations going on all the time. For such negotiations a man of the secretive mind of Dilke was eminently qualified. I do not profess to know the inner history of what happened, but I have an idea that the hands of the Tory leaders were deliberately forced, and their action at the same time facilitated by the publication in the *Standard* (a then strongly Tory paper) of the proposals on redistribution the Government were prepared to make.

Of course, there was a profession of great scandal in this unauthorized publication of a secret Government document, but everybody was delighted, because it meant that the quarrel was over. There was not even a violent outburst when Mr. Gladstone, in spite of the continuous protests of Mr. Goschen and Mr. Forster, and, of course, of the Irish Orange party, announced that Ireland was to retain the same number of members. Even that portentous announcement was received in silence; the Irish members were too delighted to express their feelings. And so redistribution, the reduction of the franchise, and thereby the omnipotence of Parnell over the future representation of Ireland, passed almost without a word of protest.

Mr. Gladstone in 1885, *aet.* 76

The Irish feelings of anger and ruthless hostility to the Gladstone Ministry remained unchanged. The Party had now the full confidence of their coming victory when the appeal to the country would come, and they eagerly looked for the opportunity of carrying the disruption of the Government. At last they saw their opportunity on the Budget. The Budget is always a difficult bridge for Governments to cross, and every Budget is bound to antagonize certain sections of the community and to embarrass certain trades. But there was no very strong indication that the debate on the Budget, which began on June 8, was fraught with any peril. Mr. Gladstone, through these closing days in which, as has been seen, he had to confront so many difficulties both inside and outside his Cabinet, had many weary and depressed hours. As early as March of 1885 it was observed that he was not in his place; after a while he entered rather pale, and he carried a stick on which he leaned, even when he rose to speak.

It was the first time I ever saw anything about him that brought home to the mind the undeniable but usually forgotten fact that he was a very old man. When he entered, the cheer was not very keen; but when, towards the close of question time, he did rise—still with the ominous stick supporting him—there was a really strong and sympathetic cheer. The old man could not conceal his delight; he paused for several minutes, gave a profound bow after the manner of a *prima donna*, and paused again until the applause had died away. A few days afterwards he looked his old self, with a ready and radiant smile, and he fell back on a habit which, to a certain extent he had given up, of carrying on constant and apparently playful conversation with his colleagues on the bench. The reason of it was soon revealed, when he was able to announce an improvement in the Russian situation over the Penjdeh incident; but, after all, it was premature. He had to make his demand for a war vote of eleven millions, and he did so in a speech of such consummate ability, and with such an appeal to the patriotism of all the parties in the House, that all the parties cheered, and he left the House amid this universal tribute to his oratory and policy.

Sir Henry Campbell-Bannerman, 1836–1908

After the resignation of Sir George Trevelyan, who left Ireland a prematurely broken and grizzled man, and at the very moment when things looked as black as they could be, Sir Henry Campbell-Bannerman became Chief Secretary. He was the son of one of those hardy and daring Scots provincials who, early in the nineteenth century, migrated to Glasgow in some dim anticipation of the gigantic size and wealth to which the city was by and by to attain. When his son Henry came down from Cambridge, he went into his father's drapery business, in which he remained during ten years.

The curious thing was that Campbell-Bannerman found his way to Liberalism on his own initiative, while his father remained a Tory. In his first election address, he said, "I am the son of a staunch Tory. I would have you believe that possibly the staunchness may run in the blood, that I may inherit his tenacity without his principles, and that, as my father, through a long public life, through good report and evil report, in fair weather and in foul, has stuck to his party and his principles, so his son in like manner will stick to his."

Elected for Stirling Burghs in 1868, he remained its member until 1908. He inherited a fortune from his father, and two other fortunes from uncles, and it was after one of these uncles that he adopted the name of Bannerman.

Considering his love of ease, his geniality of temper, his hatred of violent measures, Campbell-Bannerman showed great public spirit in taking up the thankless office of

Chief Secretary. One afternoon one of the Irish Party, Edward Dwyer Gray, formed a group of three men who were discussing the new Chief Secretary. "At any rate", said Gray, "everybody seems agreed that he is a sufficiently dull man." The unknown member of the three smiled—the smile broke across the shrewd broad face, and lit up the light-blue steady eyes—it was the "dull man" himself.

Following his appointment, I said the Government reminded me of a beleaguered capital; first they tried stone fortifications, then they tried guns, finally they resorted at the last extremity to a sandbag. For a while the nickname stuck, and Campbell-Bannerman was known as the "sandbag" Chief Secretary.

But we found we had met with a tough antagonist. Confronting Forster, we found that we could make even that rough and rude giant writhe as we denounced his regime. Trevelyan's face would shrivel up almost with visible pain—he himself said that he would sooner face a battery than these furious and eloquent Irish benches—and it was expected that Campbell-Bannerman, much less known, with a much smaller reputation, would prove a far easier prey. But he had unfathomable, unreachable depths of imperturbability. It might have been self-confidence, it was probably indifference, but there was no human being so impervious to attack. He laughed at vituperation, was jaunty under a cyclone of attack.

He did not remain Chief Secretary long. Gladstone's Government was defeated, and Campbell-Bannerman and the Irish met as allies. He was one of the very first to give his adhesion to Gladstone's Home Rule, and it was he who used the phrase that he had "found salvation".

CHAPTER XVIII

The secret of Parnell's power—Relations with his followers—Was he good-hearted?—His modest side—Incident on an Irish road—Liberal dissensions on Home Rule—Divided Cabinet—The final scene—Excitement in the House—The defeat—Mr. Gladstone's self-possession.

Parnell in 1885, *aet.* 39

NOW was coming the last great struggle which, after five exciting years, was to divide Mr. Gladstone's Government and ultimately to lead to the great smash. It would seem, during the years I have been chronicling, that more than once the Irish cause, and the leadership, and perhaps even the life of Parnell, were about to be destroyed past all resurrection. The Phoenix Park assassinations (neither the first nor the last blow that was almost to overwhelm us by the revolutionary section of the Irish in America), the terrific indictment by Forster, the two Coercion Acts—all seemed to mark us down for disaster, and yet in the end we seemed to have been always winning, always making some advance to our goal.

I have been often asked what was the secret of Parnell's power. Lord Rosebery was almost impatient with me one day after Parnell's death when, in answer to this question, all I could say was, "Personality"; and then, appealing to a subject with which he was so well acquainted, I asked him how could he explain the domination of Napoleon except by personality? He went on then to an explanation of Napoleon's leadership, beginning with his tremendous success as a general. But I can only repeat that the secret of Parnell's power was personality.

I repeat here that this personality was not exercised in the way that has been popularly described by writers since his death. He was never haughty; he was never overbearing. I remember being struck, one evening, when he, O'Connor Power, and I were dining together in a restaurant, by the difference between the two men. O'Connor Power (who, as I have said, was a man of irritable temper) snarled at the waiter, who possibly was inefficient; Parnell never said a word.

I have already shown how false to Parnell's character was that story of his pulling up one of his followers and saying: "*Mr*. Parnell, if you please". Parnell, I repeat, not only never said that, but he was incapable of saying it. At the same time, he had a tremendous dignity, and a pride as of Lucifer; he would have immediately checked any undue familiarity. I never heard him say anything harsh to anybody, but in those strange red-flint eyes of his there were terrible lights, and on a few occasions—not many—I have seen him direct those eyes upon someone who was saying something disagreeable to him, and their effect was immediate, overpowering. It was a look like this that he occasionally directed to Mr. Healy, when the latent hostility that burst into such fierce flame afterwards was already lying in both their souls; and Mr. Healy, with all his courage and self-confidence, was immediately subdued.

Parnell's Relations with his Colleagues

Was Parnell good-hearted? It would have appeared to many people a ridiculous question, so plain seemed the answer in the coldness of Parnell's expression and manner and speech. I remember hearing quite a distinguished Englishman once speak of Parnell as a fish-blooded man. Justin M'Carthy, who was not only a good but a benignant judge of human character, often said to me that he never knew Parnell to say a kind word of his colleagues, that there was always underneath an inner sneer. James O'Kelly, who was one of the most loyal of his followers when the quarrel came, and who was a man of dauntless bravery, covered with a curious rational caution as of a soldier discussing plans and chances of battle, went out to find the Mahdi, among other expeditions. When Justin spoke of O'Kelly's perils, Parnell replied—so Justin reported to me—that O'Kelly might be trusted to take care of his life.

When power ultimately reached Parnell, how could he avoid, being in the position of omnipotence which he occupied both in English as well as Irish politics—and really he became not merely the uncrowned King, but, if he liked, imperialist dictator of the political faiths of both countries—how could he avoid some degree of intoxication? Not, by the way, that he ever showed this. One of the things which William O'Brien—who ultimately found himself compelled, like myself, to go against Parnell in the great final struggle—used to point out as proof of Parnell's real greatness and real modesty, was that when he came in to take his seat at a sitting of the House of Commons, at the very moment when Gladstone was proposing Home Rule for Ireland, and when he knew how much lay behind this extraordinary advance on the part of the greatest of British statesmen, Parnell almost deliberately chose the obscurest seat on the bench where his colleagues sat. Usually his place was the second seat on the third bench below the gangway, a fairly conspicuous position; but while the Home Rule Bill was in preparation he sat on nearly the last seat on the third bench below the gangway—a seat which really concealed rather than exposed him.

I saw one or two instances of a readiness of sympathy which possibly I might not have expected from him. One dark night he and I and some colleagues were driving on an outside car from one Irish town to another. Suddenly we saw a cart standing in the road; Parnell was the first to jump off. He went to the front of the car, and there found the drunken driver with his head right under one of the wheels of his cart. A move of the cart meant his death. Parnell was the most active and the most willing in rescuing the poor driver, and his eagerness to help was noted by his companions. He himself used to say that one of the most shameful parts of the disorder and crimes committed in Ireland was that of cruelty to animals; that in his youth he had himself prosecuted a man for cruelty to a donkey.

Sometimes one is disposed to think that the intensity and concentration of the passion for a woman, which ruined and killed him, was partly due to his freedom from warm affection for others; but here once again one must remember things to the contrary. John Parnell, his brother, and he were once the victims of a railway accident when they were travelling in America, and John Parnell used always to declare that, of all the nurses he had ever had in his life, his brother was the kindest and the best. There I must leave this side of him.

The now palpable advance of Parnell to be in command of Parliament after the election had compelled some at least of the Liberal leaders to face the problems which would then be presented to them, and especially the problem of the attitude they would take to the demand, which Parnell and his party would immediately make, for bestowal of self-government on Ireland.

When party conflict became violent, sarcastic references used to be made to the suddenness of Gladstone's conversion to Home Rule; and this would be explained by his desire to get the support of the big Irish Party which came into existence after the election of 1885. The statement can be proved historically incorrect. Again and again, cautiously and in not too definite language, Gladstone revealed his readiness to consider the claim of Ireland for some form of self-government. These views he afterwards communicated to his Cabinet, and here he found himself confronted by very opposing counsels. A man like Lord Hartington, then as always, was opposed to any concession whatever. The hostility of the Forsters and Goschens outside the Cabinet might also be confidently expected, and, indeed, the Liberal Party elected in 1880 could not be relied on to give united support to anything like Home Rule.

Cabinet decide to renew Coercion, June 5, 1885

And here there entered another complexity into the already complex situation. The provisions of the Coercion Act, which had been carried and of which Lord Spencer had made such effective use, came to an end with the August of 1885, and Lord Spencer and those who supported him were for a renewal of at least some of the provisions of this Act. Lord Spencer by this time had risen, through his courage and through what was supposed to be his success, to a dominating position in the affections and admiration of his associates. Mr. Chamberlain and Sir Charles Dilke had never been enthusiasts for Coercion; Mr. Chamberlain especially had been known, as has been seen in my previous narrative, to be in secret hostility to Mr. Forster, which ultimately brought down that gentleman and his policy. I fancy Dilke went then, as for so many years, with Chamberlain. A decision had to be made, however, and in the end Mr. Gladstone agreed to give notice of a proposal to renew some provisions of the dying Coercion Act. This notice sealed his doom with the Irish members, who were bound to vote against such a proposal, and against any Government that made it.

But meantime another complexity was found to create similar divisions of the Cabinet, and that was the particular form and the particular extent of the self-government which was to be given to Ireland. They all seemed to be in favour of some sort of delegation, to take the form, according to the more moderate section, of the creation of County Boards with certain limited powers, and the whole charge of justice, police, and prisons. There was, in addition, the proposal to have an elected Central Board. A committee of the Cabinet had been appointed to consider this proposition. "Some", says Morley, "remained stubbornly opposed; as the discussions went on, some changed their minds, and, having resisted, at last inclined to acquiesce." It was hinted that if such a proposal were made, Parnell would approve, and would even agree to consent to a very limited Crimes Bill. But the proposal was turned down by the majority of the Cabinet. "All the Peers", says Morley, "except Lord Granville were against it. All the Commoners, except Lord Hartington, were for it"; there was a majority against it. Then Gladstone made a portentous prophecy. "As the Cabinet broke up", says Morley (May 9), "the Prime Minister said to one colleague, 'Ah, they will rue this day'; and to another, 'Within six years, if it please God to spare their lives, they will be repenting in sackcloth and ashes'."

And then there came, strangely enough, another difficulty, and that was the suggestion of a gigantic Land Purchase Bill. I cannot understand how any fair-minded man, whatever his party, could object to such a proposal.

The landlords of Ireland, if Home Rule were passed, would be placed at the mercy of an assembly in which possibly not a single member of their class would be a member. This meant a danger of confiscation. Let it be distinctly understood that at no time was confiscation a proposal of the Irish Party; but still, hard terms would naturally and inevitably have been proposed to the landlords, because of the natural desire of their tenantry to get the best terms possible, intensified by the accumulated hatred of the centuries in which the landlords had oppressed them. It is characteristic of Gladstone that, when the Whitsuntide recess came in the middle of these difficulties, and when he returned to Hawarden, he "dived into Lechler's *Wycliffe*, Walpole's *George III.*, Conrad on German Union, Cooper on the Atonement".

Then, when he returned to London prepared to take up again the attempt to reconcile his Ministers on the question of Ireland, suddenly there came up an unexpected and, as it turned out, an even more immediate and more disastrous difficulty.

The Budget Resolution, June 8, 1885

Now I come to the final scene, I remember it all very well, but I think I had better not make any attempt to give a new description of it. At seven o'clock in the morning after the fateful division, I was called up by Mr. Stead, then editor of the *Pall Mall Gazette*, to write an account of the great scene of the previous night. I do not think I have ever refused to write an article on the ground either of fatigue or hurry, and so I sat down there and then, and this is what I wrote:

The wild, mad, strange scene, which ended the sitting of the House between one and two o'clock in the

and, looking at Lord Randolph, he pointed at him with outstretched finger and spoke of an Opposition "which calls itself sometimes Conservative and sometimes the Tory Democracy". Lord Randolph took off his hat and bowed in ironical acknowledgment of the allusion.

To sum up, Mr. Gladstone thoroughly enjoyed himself, and the House thoroughly enjoyed Mr. Gladstone, and when he sat down, Mr. Childers was to be seen complimenting him highly; while the delighted face of Mr. Chamberlain, as he looked at his old chief luxuriantly sweeping away the arguments of the Tories, was even a stronger indication of the effect of the great orator.

Defeat of the Government, June 8, 1885

Still, there was no excitement in the House, and the numbers were not watched with that crowding at the doors which usually takes place when the result is uncertain. The different sides streamed quietly and a little wearily into the lobby, the Parnellites, as usual, joining the Conservative Opposition. Nor in the Conservative division lobby was there any excitement while the division was proceeding. There was no expectation anywhere of a Government defeat. It was only as the division was approaching its end that some suspicion of the truth began to dawn upon the Tories.

At once a state of unusual and fierce excitement supervened. Lord Randolph Churchill was particularly vehement. It was seen that the stream from the Government lobby was getting thinner and thinner, while that from the Opposition was still flowing in full tide; and each successive Tory, as he got into the House, was almost torn to pieces as he was asked what was his number. There were hoarse whispers and eager demands, and a slight and tremulous cheer. But it was too soon as yet to give way to a joy that might be premature.

At last certainty began to come in thickening signs. Lord Kensington walked to the table from the Government lobby, and stated the numbers to the clerk. That was almost decisive, as it showed the exhaustion of the numbers of the Government; and here were the Conservatives still coming in. The number of the Government was now known to be 252, and the great question was whether the Conservatives had beaten this. It was soon known that 252 had been beaten, and then the flood-gates were opened. Lord Randolph Churchill was the leader of the uproar; and Gavroche celebrating a victory at the barricades, or an Eton boy triumphing over success at cricket, could not have been more juvenile in the extravagance of his joy. He took off his hat and began to wave it madly, and soon he had actually got up and was standing on his seat, and from this point of vantage kept waving his hat. Some younger Tories sitting beside him imitated this mad example and waved their hats.

The Parnellites, meantime, kept silence, having delivered so many blows that had just stopped short. But when the paper was handed to Mr. Winn (the Chief Tory Whip), the Parnellites felt secure, and burst out into a deep, wild note of triumph. "Coercion!" "Buckshot!" "Spencer!" and, in one solitary instance, "Miles Joyce!" rose from their thick and excited ranks. Their self-controlled leader did not join in the cries, but his pale face was a trifle paler, and there was a happy smile upon it. Throughout all this mad tumult, Mr. Gladstone remained outwardly untroubled, unheeding, even unhearing. He sat in his usual seat with his despatch to the Queen on the portfolio on his knees, writing apparently with undisturbed swiftness the account of his own defeat. He never once looked up.

At last the numbers were told; then more wild cheering; and then the dull, heavy, and inarticulate voice of Sir Erskine May recalling the House from its passionate heights of tragedy to the Orders of the Day. But the descent was too sudden, and would not be allowed. There were loud and deafening shouts of interruption and protest; and at last it was evident that the Government would not be allowed to escape without giving some evidence and confession of its defeat. Mr. Gladstone rose. His face was quiet and just a trifle sad and meek. There was a burst of enthusiastic cheers from his followers. It was answered by the loud shouts of triumph from the other side, and the storm went on for minutes, cheer answering cheer and exclamations answering exclamations.

Mr. Gladstone stood calm amid it all. He looked at his despatch, and, when the tumult grew loudest, even affected to cross its t's and dot its i's. At one time it seemed as if he would have to sit down without a word. But at last he was allowed to move the adjournment of the House. Then there were more cheers, and the House began slowly to empty. And then it was that the most touching event of the night occurred.

The House had half emptied. Mr. Gladstone and Lord Richard Grosvenor were standing up talking to each other. Lord Richard, as senior Liberal Whip, had the main responsibility for the disaster of the night. Between him and Mr. Gladstone there was a strong and deep attachment. The Prime Minister shook his faithful friend and follower by the hand. Everybody who saw the incident noted and was touched by it, and interpreted its plain meaning: "I forgive, and—farewell".

I was swept away by the enthusiasm around me, and

spoke enthusiastically of the future of our movement. Parnell, who had remained calm, said with a dry smile, "We shall see". Did he already forecast the coming of the dark tragedy which was to ruin and kill him, and for years to ruin his Party?

APPENDIX I

THE STORY OF THE GREAT FAMINE, 1845–1849

THAT the reader may better understand the economic conditions which led to the rise of the Parnell movement, I propose to append here an account of the Irish Famine, which may be said to be the key event in modern Irish history. It set going the Irish emigrations on a vast scale and the clearances and evictions, which had always been going on, assumed a new rigour, so that the millions of Irish people who settled in the United States told a harrowing story that has scarcely yet passed out of the memories of their descendants.

John Stuart Mill wrote of the Irish landlords: "Returning nothing to the soil, they consume its whole produce minus the potatoes strictly necessary to keep the inhabitants from dying of famine". Thus, the potato had a tragic importance in the economy of Irish life. All the wheat and oats which were grown on the land and all the stock went to the payment of the rent, while the tenant kept for himself only enough of the potato crop to save his family from absolute starvation. The potato suited the soil and the climate; alone among vegetables, it would support life without anything else; it was the thin partition between famine and the millions of the Irish people.

The plant that had so dread a responsibility had its bad points as well as its good; it was fickle, perishable, liable to wholesale destruction, and more than once already had given proof of its terrible uncertainty. There was, however, no anticipation of disaster in 1845. The fields everywhere waved green and flowery, and there was the promise of an abundant harvest. There had been whispers of the appearance of disease in other countries that then seemed remote —in Belgium, in Germany, or Canada. In the autumn of

1845 the disease was detected in the Isle of Wight, and in the first week of September most of the potatoes in the London market were found to be unfit for human food.

In Ireland the autumnal weather was suggestive of some calamity. For weeks the air was electrical and disturbed; there was much lightning unaccompanied by thunder. Then a dark green spot—such as would come from a drop of acid—was found in the green leaves. The canker spread rapidly, and in time there was nothing in many of the potato fields but bleached and withered leaves emitting a putrid stench.

Side by side with the blighted fields were fields of abundant oats. While wholesale starvation was impending over the nation, every port was carrying out its wheat, oats, and cattle to feed other lands. O'Connell and the Dublin Corporation pleaded that the export of provisions to other countries should be immediately prohibited, and that at the same time the Corn Laws should be suspended, and the Irish ports opened to receive provisions from all countries. But the land system rendered necessary all these vast exports amidst the stress and horrors of famine. It was one of the necessary consequences of the Legislative Union that Ireland was inextricably involved in the struggles of English parties. Peel had put forward the Irish Famine as the last event that broke down his faith in protection and altered his view on the Corn Laws. And now all the Protectionist Party in Parliament, all the organs of the landlords in Ireland, united in the statement that the reports of distress were unreal and exaggerated. "The potato crop of this year", wrote the *Dublin Evening Mail* in 1845, "far exceeded an average one; the apprehensions of a famine are unfounded, and are merely made the pretence for withholding the payment of rent." "The potato famine in Ireland", exclaimed Lord George Bentinck, "was a gross delusion—a more gross delusion had never been practised upon any country by any Government." "Famine in Ireland", said Lord Stanley, "was a vision—a baseless vision."

At this very moment, when the peasantry were confronted with universal hunger, a passion seized many of the landlords for wholesale clearances. Thus, a Mr. and Mrs. Gerard had turned out in one morning the entire population of a village in the County of Galway—270 persons in number. The roofs had been taken off the sixty houses, and when the villagers took refuge under the skeleton walls they were driven thence, and the walls were uprooted from the foundations. After huddling together before fires in the ditches for some nights, they were again driven forth, the fires were quenched, and these vagabonds disappeared from the vision of man.

This was the moment chosen, too, to introduce a Coercion Bill which threatened transportation for seven years as the penalty for anybody being found on the highway at night; and this at a time when the roads of all Ireland were crowded with wanderers, houseless, homeless, starving and dying. By an alliance of the Whigs, the Protectionists, and the O'Connellites, the Bill was defeated on the second reading, and Peel resigned. The change of administration was dearly bought by Ireland, even by the defeat of a Coercion Bill, for the new Prime Minister, Lord John Russell, was much less competent than Peel to deal with the terrible crisis that had now come upon Ireland. The Famine of 1846 was at hand.

The people still stuck to the potato, which was their only hope. In preparing the new crop they worked with an energy that was frantic, with a hopefulness that was tragic—they must not and should not fail. Everywhere they begged, borrowed, pawned, and appealed for credit to find the means whereby to crop the land again. The signs of the seasons were watched with anxiety. The spring was unpromising enough; snow, hail and sleet fell in March. But there was a June of tropical heat; vegetation sprang up with something of tropical rapidity, and everybody anticipated a splendid harvest. In July there was the alternation of tropical heat and thunderstorm, of parching dryness and excessive rain. St. Swithin's Day was looked forward to with great eagerness. There was a continuous downpour of rain; and on the following day a terrible thunderstorm burst over Dublin. Still the crop went on splendidly; and all over the country once again wide fields of waving green and flowery stalks promised exuberant abundance.

In the early days of August an awful portent, seen simultaneously in several parts of Ireland, suggested the ghastly truth. A fog—which some describe as extremely white and others as yellow—was seen to rise from the ground; the fog was dry and emitted a disagreeable odour. Justin M'Carthy told me that he had seen it come up from the land about Bantry Bay, and that the companion who was with him exclaimed at once that the blight was coming. He was right; the fog of that night bore the blight within its accursed bosom. In a single night, throughout the whole country, the entire crop was destroyed, almost to the last potato. Father Mathew, the apostle of temperance, described how he passed from Cork to Dublin at the end of July and the whole country-side bloomed green with the luxuriance of an abundant harvest. Returning a week later, "I beheld with sorrow one wide waste of putrefying vegetation".

Towards the end of August the symptoms of famine were everywhere to be seen. Some of the people rushed into the towns; others wandered listlessly along the high-roads, in the vague and vain hope that food would somehow or other come into their hands. They grasped at everything on the chance of sustenance; they plucked turnips from the fields; in some cases they ate the carcases of horses, asses, and dogs. The dead were discovered with grass in their mouths. Nettle-tops, seaweed, diseased cattle were eaten, and there were inquests in many places on people who had died from eating diseased potatoes.

The workhouse was an object of dread and loathing; it was associated with the rustic victims of vice and the outcasts of the towns. Thus it came that fathers and mothers died, and allowed their children to die along with them in their own hovels, rather than seek a refuge within those hated walls. But the time came when hunger and disease swept away these prejudices; only for hope again to be cheated—for the accommodation of the workhouses was far below the requirements of emergency. At Westport three thousand people sought relief in a single day. It was this town that Mr. Forster described as showing "a strange and fearful sight like what we read of in beleaguered cities: its streets crowded with gaunt wanderers sauntering to and fro with hopeless air and hunger-struck look". Driven away from the workhouses, the people began to die on the roadside, or, alone in their despair, within their own cabins. Corpses lay strewn by the sides of once-frequented roads, and on the doorsteps in the towns. "During that period", wrote Mr. Tuke, the Quaker philanthropist, "roads in many places became as charnel-houses, and several car and coach drivers have assured me that they rarely drove anywhere without seeing dead bodies strewn along the roadside, and that in the dark they had even gone over them. A gentleman told me that in the neighbourhood of Clifden one inspector of roads had caused no less than 140 bodies to be buried which he found along the highways." In the body of this book I have related the story told to me by a native of County Kerry: how, as a boy, he saw along the road to Tralee the corpses of a whole family, first of the youngest children, then of the elder children, and finally of the father and mother.

In the stricken cabins dead and dying lay side by side, sharing the same pallet of rotting straw and covered by the same rags. When the inmates found that death was inevitable, they made no further struggle, sought the assistance neither of the Government nor of their neighbours; and occasionally, as was related by Mr. Tuke, the last survivor of a whole family "earthed up the door of his miserable cabin to prevent the ingress of pigs and dogs, and then laid himself down to die in this fearful family vault".

Men could be seen carrying the corpses of their dear ones in a few deal boards patched together, without mourner or ceremony, without wailing or lamentation. A curate in Galway told the story of meeting a man with a cart drawn by an ass, on which there were three coffins, containing the bodies of his wife and two children. When he reached the churchyard he was too weak to dig a grave, and was only able to put a little covering of clay on the coffins. The next day the priest found ravenous dogs devouring the corpses. In another part of the country a woman with her own hands dug the grave of her son.

Lord John Russell suddenly closed the relief works which had been set on foot by Peel. At the time when this decree went forth there were 98,000 persons employed on the relief works; and the effect of adding this vast army of unemployed to the population whose condition has just been described may easily be imagined. He approached the task of relief weighed down with economic theory. The first important statement was that the Government did not propose to interfere with the trade in Indian corn and grain, which were now being rushed to Ireland in quantities. "They would take care", he said, "not to interfere with the regular operations of merchants for the supply to the country, or with the retail trade." The price of grain at once went up, and speculators were driven to frenzy by the prospect of fabulous gains. Strange and almost incredible results followed. Wheat that had been exported by starving tenants was afterwards reimported from England to Ireland; sometimes before it was finally sold it had crossed the Irish Sea four times—delirious speculation offering new bids and rushing in insane eagerness from the Irish to the English and from the English to the Irish market. Stories used to be told in Ireland with grim satisfaction of greedy speculators who overreached themselves. More than one Shylock kept his corn obstinately in store while the people around him were dying like flies, and, when he at last opened the doors, found not his longed-for treasure-house, but an accumulation of rotten corn that had to be emptied into the river. But, in Cork alone, one firm was reported to have cleared £40,000 and another £80,000 by corn speculation. The people died with money in their hands, knocking at the doors of the Government stores and vainly begging for food.

The inflated price of corn and the difficulty of obtaining it at any price, high or low, co-operated with Lord John Russell's Labour Rate Act enormously to increase the sum of suffering and the total of deaths. Under the Labour Rate Act relief works were to be set on foot by the Board of Works when they had previously been presented at Presentment Sessions. For these works the Government were to advance money at the rate of 3½ per cent, repayable in ten years. In the poorer districts the Government were to make grants to the extent of £50,000. Again economic theory was to be respected; the works must not compete with private enterprise, and the money was all to be devoted to exclusively "unproductive works", by which were excluded railways, reclamation, and the like. Roads were made leading to nowhere; hills were dug away and then filled up again; the Knight of Glin complained that on the Glin Road some people were filling up the original cutting of a hill with the stuff they had taken out of it.

Even this useless work was not allowed to be done without the maddening preliminaries of official delays. One firm reported that it had sent to Ireland "ten thousand books, besides fourteen tons of paper". Bewildered Barony Sessions strove to comply with the innumerable schedules and specifications, and to satisfy the officials, of which there were ten thousand sent to administer the Act. These officials insisted on making the Act still more cruel by the regulations under which it was to be worked. "Those who choose to labour may earn good wages", Colonel Jones, the head of the Board of Works, wrote to Mr. Trevelyan at the Board of Trade; and so it was ordained that the work done should be task-work. The feebler a man was, the less help he was entitled to receive. The works attracted nearly all the farmers of the country from their own fields. The prospect of immediate wages proved more enticing than the uncertainty of a remote and fickle harvest. The labourers followed their masters, and the fields were left without hands to prepare them for the harvest: so that the means that were taken to meet the famine of 1846 proved the precursors and preparers of the famine of 1847.

Meantime, another calamity was added to those from which the people were already suffering. Pestilence always hovers on the flank of famine, and, as well as wholesale starvation, there were other circumstances that rendered a plague inevitable—the crowding together at the public works and in the workhouses, the vast number of corpses that lay unburied, and the consumption of unaccustomed food. The plague which now fell upon Ireland was of a peculiarly virulent kind. It produced at once extreme prostration, and everyone struck by it was subject to frequent relapses. The people called this new affliction "the road fever". Attacking as it did people already weakened by hunger, it was a scourge of merciless severity. The panic which the plague created everywhere intensified the miseries of those whom it attacked. It was a common custom of the period to have food left at the doors or handed in on shovels or sticks to the people inside the cabins; but often the wretched inmates were entirely deserted, their passage to the grave uncheered by one act of help, by one word of sympathy. The fever-stricken wretches who had energy enough to crawl from their own homes and seek a refuge became the heralds of disease wherever they went, and often suffered tortures more prolonged and darker than those who had lain down and died by their own hearthstones.

"In cases succeeding exhaustion from famine", said a writer, "the appearances were very peculiar—the fever assuming a low gastric type, indicated by a dry tongue, shrunk to half its size and brown in the centre; lips thin and bloodless, coated with sordes; skin discoloured and sodden; general appearance squalid in the extreme, and hunger-stricken. These symptoms, and a loathsome, putrid smell emanating from their persons, as if the decomposition of the vital organs had anticipated death, rendered these unhappy cases too often hopeless. They used to creep about the city while their strength allowed, and then would sink exhausted in some shed or doorway, and often be found dead."

The workhouses and the hospitals were besieged more than ever. "Before accommodation for patients", wrote the Census Commissioners, "approached anything like the necessity of the time, most mournful and piteous scenes were presented in the vicinity of fever hospitals and workhouses in Dublin, Cork, Waterford, Galway, and other large towns. There, day after day, numbers of people wasted by famine and consumed by fever, could be seen lying on the footpaths and roads, waiting for the chance of admission; and when they were fortunate enough to be received, their places were soon filled by other victims of suffering and disease.

"At the gate leading to the temporary fever hospital erected near Kilmainham were men, women and children lying along the pathway and in the gutter, awaiting their turn to be admitted. Some were stretched at full length, with their faces exposed to the full glare of the sun, their mouths open, and their black and parched tongues and encrusted teeth visible even from a distance. Some women had children at the breast, who lay beside them in silence and apparent exhaustion—the fountain of their life being dried up; whilst in the centre of the road stood a cart containing a whole family who had been smitten down together by the terrible typhus, and had been brought there by the charity of a neighbour."

The crowding in the institutions rendered it impossible to separate the sick and the healthy, sometimes to separate even the dead and the dying—there were not beds for a tenth of the applicants; and thus the epidemic was spread and intensified, instead of being alleviated and diminished. The general effect was summed up in the report of the Poor Law Commissioners for 1846: "In the present state of things nearly every person admitted is a patient; separation of the sick, by reason of their number, becomes impossible; disease spreads, and by rapid transition the workhouse is changed into one large hospital".

In this extremity, even the prison came to be regarded as a refuge. Only smaller offences were at first committed, but as the pressure of distress began to be greater and the hope of ultimate salvation less, graver crimes became prevalent. Thus sheep-stealing became a common offence, and a prisoner's good fortune was supposed to be complete if he were sentenced to the once dreaded and loathed punishment of transportation beyond the seas. The Irishman was made happy by the fate which took him anywhere away from the land of doom; and Botany Bay was transformed in peasant imagination from

sheds of Skibbereen". "Crowded and filthy, carrying double the legal number of passengers, who were ill-fed and imperfectly clothed, and having no doctor on board, the holds", said an eye-witness, "were like the Black Hole of Calcutta, and deaths in myriads." Of the dreadful statistics of the "coffin-ships", as they were called, I will only repeat here the story which I have included in the body of this work: how I heard an Irish-American tell in a speech at one of my meetings in Grand Rapids, Michigan, that his father and mother and three sisters sailed on a boat with four hundred Irish on board. "By the time the boat reached New York", he said, "three hundred out of the four hundred had died."

All this time evictions went on ruthlessly. Whatever became of the people, the landlord must be paid and protected. It will scarcely be believed that after all the ravages of hunger, the decimation through fever, the terrible emigration, it was deemed that the remedy for Ireland was more emigration. Indeed, the unfitness of Ireland for the Irish and of the Irish for Ireland was a dogma preached with something like the fine frenzy of a new revelation in those days. "Remove Irishmen", wrote *The Times* (February 22, 1847), "to the banks of the Ganges or the Indus, to Delhi, Benares, or Trincomalee, and they would be far more in their element there than in a country to which an inexorable fate had confined them." The idea was gravely discussed of transferring the Irish population piecemeal to various parts of the British Empire. A body calling itself the Irish Committee drew out an elaborate scheme under which a million and a half of the people were to be sent to Canada, at a cost of £9,000,000, which was to be levied in the shape of an Income Tax.

Apart from the Government, blundering in the throes of its economic theory, the British people worked hard to alleviate the sufferings of the Irish. Relief societies were formed almost everywhere. "The British Association for the Relief of Extreme Distress in Ireland and the Highlands and Islands of Scotland" collected £263,251. A Queen's letter was raised with the same object, and a sum of £171,533 was collected. Among those who went to Ireland on a mission of relief were Mr. W. E. Forster, afterwards Chief Secretary, and his father. I have myself heard an Englishman say that he remembered the Famine because, being a child at the time, he was not permitted to take butter with his bread, in order that some money might be saved for the starving poor of Ireland. But it is easy to understand how the Irish should have been embittered to frenzy when they saw the dominant nation, that claimed and had carried its superior right to govern, so performing its functions of government that roads throughout Ireland were strewn with the gaunt forms of the starving and the starved, and that every ship was freighted with thousands fleeing from their homes. In America I have met with men who were evicted from Ireland in the great clearances of the Famine time; there was a strange glitter in their eyes and a savage coldness in their voices as they spoke of these things, and it was easy to see the effect that would be produced upon their American-born children when told by their parents that tragic story of hunger, eviction, and expatriation. It was the tradition of these clearances, the famine, and the plague that nourished the frenzy of the irreconcilable element among the descendants of the Irish in American life—an element that has only been weakened by the sanity of British liberalizing statesmanship, but kept up an intense warfare against every Irishman who tried to work towards his country's liberation by constitutional methods. So intense was that feeling that my colleagues and I used to meet with considerable opposition when we went to plead the cause of our movement among our countrymen in the United States; all sorts of stories were circulated about us, and no doubt believed by some of fanatical credulity, such as that I was in receipt of £80,000 a year from the British Government. On my recent visit to the United States an attempt was even made to revive some of these legends, and I received an anonymous communication threatening my life.

The population of Ireland by March 30, 1851, at the same ratio of increase as held in England and Wales, would have been 9,018,799—actually it was 6,552,385. It was the calculation of the Census Commissioners that the deficit, independently of the emigration, represented by the mortality in the five Famine years was 985,336—nearly a million of the people. The emigration for the same period was 1,180,409. It was calculated that 200,668 persons died on the way or soon after landing.

APPENDIX II

THE PARNELL FUND, MARCH 17, 1883

ONE of the most curious stories in the strangely chequered career of Parnell is that which tells how he was saved from bankruptcy by a Papal Rescript which was designed to turn the Catholic people of Ireland against him and leave him stranded, politically and financially.

It was in the early part of 1883. Parnell was in pecuniary difficulties. He had no sure source of income. His estate, Avondale, was heavily mortgaged. While he stayed there, all the necessities in the way of food and drink were supplied from the hotel at Rathdrum—the railway station for Avondale—and there was a bill owing to them of several hundred pounds. He gave a dinner to his colleagues of the Irish Party at the Café Royal, London. The account, I believe, was never paid. As was disclosed years later in the Divorce Court, Parnell had at this particular time entered into relations with Mrs. O'Shea, and was maintaining, or helping to maintain, her household.

This was the position when, early in March 1883, I got a letter from Dwyer Gray, proprietor and editor of the *Freeman's Journal*, as to the advisability of starting a public fund to present a testimonial to Parnell. He wanted me to ascertain what Parnell thought about it. Knowing what a proud and sensitive man Parnell was, I decided that he must not be approached on the subject. So I wrote to Dwyer Gray to go ahead. We agreed that £20,000 must be our aim, and that anything less than £10,000 would mean failure.

The fund was started by the *Freeman* on St. Patrick's Day; it was called a "National Tribute to Mr. Parnell in recognition of his great personal worth and splendid public services". It was represented that he had been the subject of vile slanders in the House of Commons, and had made great personal sacrifices, even in a pecuniary sense, for Ireland.

The Tribute had a good send-off in a letter from Dr. Croke, Archbishop of Cashel—the leading Nationalist prelate of the time—enclosing a subscription of £50, and declaring that it was essential for the Irish people to evince in an unmistakable manner at that juncture of affairs their determination to uphold the Nationalist policy, of which Parnell was the embodiment.

Three or four other Bishops followed the example thus set by Dr. Croke, and accompanied their subscriptions with eulogies of Parnell, than whom, they said, no one was more worthy of the nation's gratitude. Still the Tribute hung fire. As ill-luck would have it, the hideous memories of the Phoenix Park murders were acutely revived at this time by the trials, convictions, and hangings of the Invincibles. The people seemed to have fallen into a numb state in mind and action; so the responses to the appeal were slow. A few subscriptions came dropping in daily to the *Freeman*, but there was nothing like a spontaneous expression of public feeling.

The Papal Rescript, May 10, 1883

Then a wholly unexpected thing happened. A Papal Rescript was addressed by the Holy See to the Irish Bishops. It was signed by Cardinal Simeoni, Prefect, and Monsignor Jacobini, Secretary of the Sacred Congregation of the Propaganda Fide. "The Parnell Testimonial Fund", it declared, "cannot be approved by the Sacred Congregation, and consequently it cannot be tolerated that any ecclesiastic, much less a Bishop, can take any part whatever in recommending or promoting it." The Sacred Congregation were moved to take this step, they said, because of the intimidation and other criminal acts associated with the Nationalist movement. "It was lawful for the Irish to seek redress for their grievances", the

Rescript continued, "and to strive for their rights, but always remembering that it is wicked to further any cause, no matter how just, by illegal means."

The country was somewhat puzzled by the Rescript. What did it mean? But the general feeling was one of indignation. What call had the Holy See to take such a step? The answer of the country was swift and decisive. On May 11, the date of the Rescript, the Parnell Tribute amounted only to £7000; a few days later it was £10,000; within a month it was £20,000. Some wild things were said. I think it was Joe Biggar who went the length of suggesting that "Peter's Pence" (the yearly collection for the support of the Pope) should be boycotted as a retaliatory measure. But such talk was discountenanced and rebuked by the Party.

Tom Mayne, another Irish member, said: "The Pope is the head of the Catholic Church, Mr. Parnell is the head of Ireland. They move in wholly different orbits and have no relation whatever one with the other."

The attachment of the Irish people to the faith of their fathers and their devotion to the Holy See were unaffected by the Papal Rescript. It was felt that the issue of the Rescript was not within the legitimate function of the Holy See, and a blow struck at the Nationalist movement from the outside was not the less intolerable that it came from Rome. Religion from Rome, yes; but not politics.

But, it will be asked, how was the Sacred Congregation induced to do such a thing? It was the outcome of intrigue, British and Irish, in Rome. The moving spirit was George Errington, an Irish member of Parliament, a Catholic and a Whig—the last of the Irish Whigs, in fact. He went to Rome in the first instance as the agent of the Irish anti-Nationalist prelates and laity, who bitterly resented the active and influential part taken in politics on the popular side by certain of the Bishops and most of the priests of Ireland. In time Errington came to be regarded at the Vatican as a British envoy.

He was not officially recognized in Downing Street. To have done so would have aroused the evangelical Protestants to fury. But it was admitted by the Liberal Government of the time in the House of Commons, when the question of Errington's status in Rome was raised by the Nationalist members, that Lord Granville—Secretary of State for Foreign Affairs—had given Errington a letter of recommendation which he had authority to show to the Secretaries of State of the Holy See; and it was admitted further that Errington's letters from Rome were deposited, like those of British Ambassadors and Ministers, in the archives of the Foreign Office.

Such was the origin of the Papal Rescript. It made the Parnell Tribute a splendid success. The total amount received was £38,000. It consolidated Parnell's following and strengthened his authority. On the other hand, it left unshaken the ecclesiastical jurisdiction of the Pope in Ireland. The attendance at Mass on Sundays did not fall off by a single worshipper. What was established was that Rome's pronouncements in politics would be received in Ireland, not with submission but with angry defiance.

Parnell Tribute presented

The excitement in Dublin over the presentation of the Tribute to Parnell was tremendous. It took place at a banquet that was held in the Round Room of the historic Rotunda—the scene of many a stirring political demonstration, even before the Union as well as since. There were a thousand persons present (including between three or four hundred ladies who sat in the surrounding galleries) though the ticket of admission was priced 25s., a very large sum at that time. In its representative character the assemblage was also imposing. The Lord Mayor of Dublin presided in his scarlet robes and gold chain of office. At his right hand sat Parnell. Both occupied a slightly raised platform, so that they could be seen by everyone in the immense company. Most of the members of the Irish Party were present, I myself being among them.

It was an unforgettable spectacle—the crowd, the glamour, the atmosphere, the personality of Parnell and the intense devotion he aroused. Before the proceedings opened, a curious thing happened. Suddenly restlessness and agitation were noticed among a section of the ladies in the galleries. It soon became apparent that it was caused by the appearance in the room of Joe Biggar. In fact some of the ladies were objecting to his presence. Shortly before this, Biggar had been the defendant in a breach of promise action that was tried in London. The plaintiff was Miss Fanny Hyland, the daughter of a Kilkenny solicitor who lived with her widowed mother in Paris, where she met Biggar when the suppression of the Land League, of which he was treasurer, compelled him to take refuge there with the funds of the organization. The case was tried by Lord Chief Justice Coleridge. The two most eminent counsel of the day were engaged—Edward Clarke for the plaintiff and Charles Russell for the defendant. The court was packed to see the lover—misshapen, with a twisted face and a croak like a raven.

Biggar in the witness box admitted having frequently kissed Miss Hyland, but asserted that he had always made it clear to her that he could not marry her owing to an obstacle. This obstacle, he explained, were two natural children. "As to the children, is the mother living?" asked Edward Clarke in cross-examination; and there was loud laughter at Biggar's blunt reply—"Both the mothers are living".

Miss Hyland asked for £5000 damages. The jury awarded her £400. The case had a remarkable sequel. Biggar wrote to his counsel, Charles Russell, complaining that his conduct of the case was "thoroughly inefficient". "I have heard", he continued, "the late James Whiteside and Abraham Brewster cross-examining witnesses, and I must say that compared with them you are a very dull man." "I admit it", was Russell's laconic and modest reply.

It was on account of this case that some of the ladies of the Parnell League objected to Biggar's presence. A few of them carried their protest to the extent of leaving the room. They thought there was an end to the application of Tom Moore's couplet:

On our side is virtue and Erin,
On theirs is the Saxon and guilt.

But the outstanding incident of the banquet was Parnell's speech. It was much talked about for a long time afterwards. It was remarkable not so much for what it said, but for what it left unsaid. The Lord Mayor read an address to Parnell which recalled that he had stepped out of the ranks of a selfish aristocracy, and flung youth and fortune into the service of the Irish cause with an energy and resource that had borne down every obstacle—all very true; and then presented Parnell with a cheque for £38,000. Parnell, amid the wild cheers that greeted his uprising, was seen to fold up the cheque and put it into his waistcoat pocket. He then spoke for almost half an hour, mainly a bitter attack on the Liberal Government of the day, but made not the slightest reference to the cheque!

Was this ignoring of the Tribute a deliberate thing? If it had been, it would have been characteristic of Parnell. The cheque was overshadowed by the cause. One sentence of the speech expressed the man. He said the proposed extension of the franchise to all householders would enable the Irish voters in Great Britain and Ireland to decide at the General Election which would follow whether the new Government was to be Tory or Liberal. "If they will not permit us to rule ourselves," he added, "we shall see that they are governed as we choose."

APPENDIX III

THE TREACHERY OF WILLIAM KEOGH

I PROMISED towards the end of Chapter IV. to give a sketch of the conditions to which Irish representation had been reduced in Parliament before the rise of the Home Rule Movement.

The classic example of this political knavery was the demagogue who afterwards became Judge Keogh. When I saw this perfidious double-dealer first presiding at an assize court I was shaken with laughter; for such a promotion savoured more of Bedlam than of a sane world. It was for my native town of Athlone that William Keogh stood. He was then a barrister without clients and without law. I remember him as a small man, with a muscular and powerful frame, a chest of enormous depth. His face recalled that of Napoleon, and even when it had grown flabby, it still wore an appearance of dignity and strength. He had pugnacity and tenacity. Though almost illiterate, he had an untiring flow of verbosity; he was in fact the apotheosis of the "eloquent Dempsey". But these words —described by the *Nation* as "a jumble of bog Latin and flatulent English"—set off by a sonorous voice, vivid gesture and his commanding face, made him the idol of mobs. All through his life he was a heavy drinker and loved the pleasures of the table. He embarked upon politics as on a desperate chance that would lead on to fortune or ruin. In one of the most exciting moments in his career the bailiffs were in his house, and even when he was fighting one of his elections the House of Commons was wading through sheaves of his unpaid bills, in order to find whether he had the necessary qualification of £300 a year.

William Keogh's Political Progress

A judicial office was then the haven in which the hard-pressed Irish lawyer discovered wealth, ease, and dignity. From the first moment he embarked on a political career, a judgeship was Keogh's single purpose. For this end he was ready to don the livery of every political party in turn; to pass through sloughs of deception, lying, and broken oaths, and to betray the mob as quickly and shamelessly as he had pandered to its worst passions.

Keogh had plenty of bovine courage. He would march through the streets of our town while stones were hurled at him and his supporters. When he was delivering a speech to a violent crowd, a bottle came flying at his head. "That's a mighty bad shot, ——," said Keogh, mentioning the name of the person, a well-known local politician, who had thrown the bottle. Equally are there stories of his desperate straits—how he raised money in several cases by the trick of borrowing five pounds on each half of a five-pound note. One night he was expecting some money in aid of his candidature from one of the London political clubs. A near relative was to be the bearer of the treasure; and when he arrived he had to announce that the mission was a failure. Keogh fell to the floor, grovelled there with the contortions and groans of one demented, and finally, when the agony had passed, rose up, went out into the town, and harangued the mobs with a self-confidence as great, a wit as ready, a hopefulness as inflexible, as if his highest expectations had been realized.

My native town was neither better nor worse than most of the Irish and English constituencies of the time. Its distinction was that the number of voters was small and that, therefore, the amount of the bribe was high. The bribe averaged £30 or £40 the vote; and there were tales of a vote having run up to £100 in one of Keogh's elections. With many of the people the periodic bribe entered into the whole economy of their squalid and weary lives. Men continued to live in houses who had better have lived in lodgings because the house gave a vote. The very whisper of a dissolution sent a visible thrill through the town.

Keogh's first election was financed by John Sadleir, the founder of the Tipperary Joint-Stock Bank, who was building up a party that would be bound to him by ties of blood and of financial aid. Sadleir was a solicitor until, seized with the idea of making a large fortune rapidly, he became a financier. The deposits which, as he established his political prominence, he obtained from the grimy pockets of Irish farmers, he invested in English speculations, and in time became chairman of the London and County Joint-Stock Bank. In Keogh he purchased a powerful political ally, and his party consisted besides of two cousins, a nephew, two brothers named O'Flaherty, a Dr. Maurice Power, and a Mr. Monsell, who afterwards became Lord Emly. They were all self-seekers, and as such they were the sworn foes of the contemporary Tenant Right movement, whose object was to obtain security of tenure for the farmers of Ireland, and as such pledged its members to independence of English parties. The policy of the Tenant Righters was the very opposite of that of the Sadleirites; the one wanted Tenant Right, and did not care for Ministries; and the other wanted office, and did not care for Tenant Right.

Had there been a straight issue between the parties, Tenant Right must have won.

"The Pope's Brass Band"

But the outbreak of religious hostility in Great Britain to the Pope's action in setting up the English hierarchy in 1850 caused a counter-storm of popular passion in Ireland. Sadleir and Keogh were not slow to see the use to which Lord John Russell's Ecclesiastical Titles Bill could be turned. These self-seekers knew the passionate attachment of the Irish people to their religion, and shrewdly calculated that any politician who was able to pose as a defender of that religion would establish a claim to their confidence. And it was an issue that would not endanger the champion's "advancement", for already the early violence of "No Popery" had spent itself, and the Bill was not a favourite with any English party. Accordingly, Keogh and Sadleir made a very showy opposition in the House. Many of the Irish people, looking on at this manœuvre, were easily led to believe that the struggle of the "Irish Brigade", as they styled themselves, was heroic. By the English the party was known by the less flattering title of "The Pope's Brass Band".

Monster meetings were organized by Sadleir and addressed by Keogh. The bishops of the Catholic Church attended, and Keogh excelled everybody else in the fulsomeness of the eulogies which he poured upon their heads. A "Catholic Defence Association" was formed at a great meeting in the Dublin Rotunda. Sadleir was one of the secretaries, and Keogh was the chief orator. To Archbishop (afterwards Cardinal) Cullen, who was in the chair, Keogh was laboriously complimentary. "I now," he said, "as one of Her Majesty's Counsel, whether learned or unlearned in the law, holding the Act of Parliament in my hand, unhesitatingly give his proper title to the Lord Archbishop of Armagh." At a meeting in Athlone he paid court to Archbishop MacHale. "I see here the venerated prelates of my Church, first among them, 'the observed of all observers', the illustrious Archbishop of Tuam, who like that lofty tower which rises upon the banks of the yellow Tiber, the pride and protection of the city, is at once the glory and the guardian, the *decus et tutamen* of the Catholic religion."

Keogh and Sadleir were constantly taunted by the Tenant Righters, who drove them at last to give the desired pledges that they would not take office. Once he had taken the plunge, Keogh was loudest of all others in forswearing office. "I will fight for my religion and my country," he declared, "scorning and defying calumny, meeting boldly honourable foes, seeking out treacherous friends; and so long as I have the confidence of the people, I declare in the most solemn manner, before this august assembly, I shall not regard any party. I know that the road I take does not lead to preferment. I do not belong to the Whigs; I never will belong to the Whigs. I do not belong to the Tories; I never will have anything to do with them."

Keogh's "So-Help-Me-God" Speech

These pledges were renewed, always with great pictorial emphasis, at meeting after meeting, until the climax was reached at a meeting in Cork. It was to choose a candidate for the city in place of one of the "Irish Brigade", Dr. Power, who had accepted office as Governor of St. Lucia. Sadleir put forward one of his nephews for the vacancy, but at the meeting a prominent Tenant Righter openly expressed his doubts of the honesty of Keogh and Sadleir and the "Irish Brigade".

It was a critical moment in the fortunes of the adventurers. An adverse vote that day might have been the beginning of the end. But Keogh was never more Napoleonic, as he sprang to his feet and with flowing eye and dramatic fire exclaimed:

"Great God! in this assemblage of Irishmen have you found that those who have been most ready to take every pledge have been the most sincere in perseverance to the end? or have you not rather seen that they who, like myself, went into Parliament perfectly unpledged, not supported by the popular voice, but in the face of popular acclaim, when the time for trial comes are not found wanting? I declare myself, in the presence of the bishops of Ireland and of my colleagues in Parliament, that let the Minister of the day be whom he may—let him be the Earl of Derby, let him be Sir James Graham, or Lord John Russell—it is all the same to us; and, so help me God, no matter who the Minister may be, no matter who the party in power may be, I will neither support that Minister nor that party, unless he comes into power prepared to carry the measures which universal popular Ireland demands. I have abandoned my own profession to join in cementing and forming an Irish Parliamentary Party. That has been my ambition. It may be a base one. I think it is an honourable one. I have seconded the proposition of Mr. Sharman Crawfurd (on Tenant Right) in the House of Commons. I have met the Minister upon it to the utmost extent of my limited abilities, at a moment when disunion was not expected. So help me God! upon that and every other question to which I have given my adhesion I will be—and I know I may say that every one of my friends is as determined as myself—an unflinching, undeviating, unalterable supporter of it."

Keogh had won the day. No man could do more than swear fidelity before God to his principles. During the election of 1852 his tongue was at the service of the "Catholic Defenders" everywhere. His speeches were remarkable for their vituperation, the brutality and criminality of his appeals to the mob. In Westmeath, where the Ribbonmen were particularly strong, he used these words: "Boys, we are in the midst of a delightful summer, when the days are long and the nights are short; next comes autumn, when the days and nights are of equal length; but next comes dreary winter, when the days are short and the nights long: and woe be to those, during those long nights, who vote for Sir Richard Levinge at the present election."

The "Catholic Defenders" came back unshaken in numbers, but the Tenant Righters were the chief victors; they had compelled the Defenders to swallow the Tenant Right pledge. The pledge against taking office, except from a Government that made the settlement of the relations between landlord and tenant a Cabinet question, was forced from every candidate for a popular constituency. When accordingly a Tenant Right conference was held in Dublin, all the Irish members returned on popular principles were compelled to attend. A resolution was submitted which put into definite form the pledge already taken at the hustings:

"Resolved: That in the opinion of the conference it is essential to the proper management of this cause that the Members of Parliament who have been returned on Tenant Right principles should hold themselves perfectly independent of, and in opposition to, all Governments which do not make it part of their policy, and a Cabinet question, to give to the tenantry of Ireland a measure embodying the principles of Mr. Sharman Crawfurd's Bill."

This resolution was proposed by Keogh himself and subscribed to by all the "Irish Brigade".

The Great Betrayal, 1852

The position of parties in the House of Commons rendered it perfectly possible to carry this policy to a successful issue. Those Irish members held the balance of power. In December 1852 Mr. Disraeli's Budget was rejected by a combination of different parties and the Ministry resigned. Now was the moment when those Irish members held the fate of a Liberal Ministry in their hands. But the only price the "Catholic Defenders" demanded from Lord Aberdeen was their own personal advancement. Not Tenant Right but treason! Broken faith and perjured oaths! Sadleir was Lord of the Treasury, Keogh was Irish Solicitor-General, Edmund O'Flaherty was Commissioner of Income Tax! People thought ruefully of Keogh's "so-help-me-God" speech, and half expected the fate of Ananias to overtake him.

Such was the degradation of his constituency that Athlone re-elected him. The desperately needy voters saw in a Government official a man the better able to bribe themselves and to obtain situations for their sons. These were the days before open competition, and nomination to a Civil Service job was the appanage of the Parliamentary representative, and one of his chief means of advancing his interests with his constituents. Keogh used his power of nomination in the most lavish manner; it was a saying in his day that every young fellow who could or could not write his name had obtained a place in the Customs or some other of the public departments.

The bishop of the diocese continued to support Keogh. His name was Dr. Browne, and he had a reputation beyond that of any other bishop of the period for gentleness and piety. O'Connell had called him the "Dove of Elphin", and by this name he was familiar and dear to the people. In his speech on the hustings, Keogh in his best "eloquent Dempsey" manner made the following allusion to the attitude of the bishop: "Since I came into town, no matter where I went, no matter by whom I was accompanied, whether in the town or around the town, upon the hill-side or the ditch-side, on the public road or the narrow by-way, or in any other imaginable place, I have been received as the man of the people. How many hundred women have said this morning 'May God bless you!' How many hundred pretty girls have wished me success!" (A female voice: "You have the bishop's blessing, which is better than all!") "Yes; and I am authorized to announce to you, and he does not shrink from the announcement—you all know it; you all saw it — that I have the support, the kind wishes, the anxious, throbbing expectations for my success of my revered friend the Roman Catholic Bishop of this diocese."

The influence of the bishop, the sums of money Keogh had at his disposal, with the prosperous turn in his fortunes and a system of organized mob violence carried him to victory. My own father, an exemplary Catholic, was assaulted by the unfortunate women of that garrison town in their pathetic but furious sally because, supporting Keogh's opponent, he was supposed to be an enemy of religion and holy things.

For a while things seemed to go well with the "Irish Brigade". Sadleir, defeated in Carlow, bought his way to victory in Sligo. There was a petition, the bribery was clearly proved, but it was the men whose votes he had bought who were prosecuted. When Keogh was appointed Attorney-General he had to seek election once more, but so broken was the spirit of the country that no attempt was made to defeat him; and to add to the tragic completeness of the situation the "Dove of Elphin" came to the hustings and proposed Keogh as a "fit and proper person" to represent the constituency. Gavan Duffy, one of the chief figures of the Tenant Rights Act, sailed for Australia, and some time afterwards said there was "no more hope for Ireland than for a corpse on the dissecting-table".

The Fall of John Sadleir, February 1856

It was at the moment of their complete triumph that Nemesis began to fall on the "Irish Brigade". Sadleir was the first to be shaken. Dowling, an elector for Carlow, took an action for false imprisonment; intending to vote against Sadleir, he had been arrested on the morning of the election. Dirty work was proved, and Sadleir had to go into the witness-box. He swore boldly and unflinchingly, and the jury had to brand either him or Dowling a perjurer. The jury gave the verdict for Dowling, and Sadleir had to resign his office as a Lord of the Treasury. Shortly afterwards his friend Edmund O'Flaherty, the Commissioner of Income Tax, disappeared, leaving behind bills amounting to £15,000 in circulation, some of them bearing names—Keogh's among the rest—which were stated to be forged. Meantime Sadleir approached the abyss. There was a whisper that, instead of being a millionaire, he was in financial difficulties. The rumours were true. The vast schemes on which he had embarked proved in many cases disastrous, and then he took to all kinds of expedients for raising money; finally he resorted to the forgery of title-deeds, conveyances and bills. In February 1856 the crash came. Glyn's dishonoured some of the bills of the Tipperary Bank. The news spread; a run took place on some of the branches. Sadleir made a last desperate effort to "raise the wind" in the City, and failed. On Saturday night he agreed with his solicitor that the Tipperary Bank must on Monday stop payment. At half-past ten his friend left. Sadleir spent some time in writing letters. He then got up to go out. As he passed through the hall he met his butler, told him not to stay up for him, and then put on his hat and went out. As he left it was striking twelve; it was Sunday morning. When day broke, on a mound on Hampstead Heath the passers-by observed a gentleman lying as if asleep. A silver tankard smelling of prussic acid was at his side. It was the body of John Sadleir—dead by his own hand.

O'Flaherty fled; Sadleir, whose frauds amounted to a million and a quarter, dead; how was it with Keogh? His name had been coupled with Sadleir and with O'Flaherty in the most intimate political association for six years. Was he also going to be exposed, and to choose flight or death in preference to shame or exposure? There was no such fate in store for him. The very papers that were laden with reports of court proceedings arising out of his friend's swindles announced that William Keogh had been made a judge.

The *Nation*, which had pointed out that Keogh had a worse public character than either Sadleir or O'Flaherty, wrote—

"The administration of justice in Ireland has sustained a most grievous disgrace—a disgrace which would not be tolerated by the bench, by the bar, or the people of any other country on the face of the earth. . . . Fancy the effect of Mr. William Keogh going judge of assize to try the Westmeath Ribbonmen whom he incited to midnight violence—trying perjury in Athlone or Cork, before whole communities who heard him swear the oath of whose breach his presence on the bench before them is the startling evidence! It is an example sufficient to disgust or to demoralize the whole profession, and shake faith in justice."

END OF VOLUME I

Printed in Great Britain by R. & R. CLARK, LIMITED, *Edinburgh.*